Tarkentos

from

Rowland Bourton-Moller

1966

FITFUL REBEL

SOPHIE DE MARBOIS, DUCHESSE DE PLAISANCE
By Lefèvre
Ethnological Museum Athens

FLORENCE CODMAN

FITFUL REBEL

Sophie de Marbois
Duchesse de Plaisance

ARTS ET MÉTIERS GRAPHIQUES

DÉPOT LÉGAL 4ᵉ TRIM. 1965, Nᵒ 121

IMPRIMEUR, Nᵒ 3846

© BY ARTS ET MÉTIERS GRAPHIQUES 1965

PRINTED IN FRANCE

CONTENTS

ACKNOWLEDGMENTS

In the United States I am grateful to Mr. Wayne Andrews and to Mr. George Dangerfield for the information they gave me concerning the unpublished letters of Barbé de Marbois and the Duchesse de Plaisance in the Robert L. Livingston and the Albert Gallatin Collections in the New York Historical Society, and to the late Mrs. George Stuart Patterson for answering questions about the Duchess, her distant relation. To Miss Agnes Sims, and to Mrs. Deborah H. Calkins, I owe photographs of Rhododaphne.

In France, the hospitality of Madame La Princesse Ella de la Tour d'Auvergne at the Château de Grosbois allowed me to dispel the confusion of the Belgiojoso affair to which Madame La Princesse Hélène de Brancovan gave me the first clue. La Comtesse Henry de Gontaut-Biron, whose parents were the fifth and last Duc et Duchesse de Plaisance, graciously lent me her family's papers. La Comtesse Jacqueline de Léon went far beyond the limits of friendship with her patient co-operation. La Comtesse Plater Syberg and Monsieur Jean-Michel Jasienko were tireless in their efforts to confirm references. Miss Monica Stirling shared with me her great knowledge of Napoleonic bibliography. The Chief Rabbi of the city of Metz gave me information concerning the benefactions of the Duchesse de Plaisance to his community; and the Mesdemoiselles Lieutaud and Jeanmaire of Metz lent me out-of-print histories of that city and kindly took photographs of Buchy for me. Monsieur Philippe Erlanger obtained official permission for me to have copied the letters of the Duchesse de Plaisance which have been in the French Consulate in Beirut since 1836. Monsieur Blaise Alan secured my first knowledge of the Léopold Robert incident.

Madame Dorette Berthoud of Neuchâtel, whose *Lettres de Léopold Robert, d'Aurèle Robert et de leurs Parents* was out of print at the time of writing this book, generously allowed me to consult her copy.

In Athens, I owe to the devoted friendship of Mrs. John Calamari, the granddaughter and namesake of Rosa Botzari, introductions and a knowledge of Greece I could never otherwise have obtained. Mr. Dimitrios Skouzès and the Misses Elena and Marietta Gripari, the grandchildren of Elena Kapsali, searched through family papers and taxed their memories in my behalf. Mrs. John Serpieri opened the Othonian Collection at La Tour Reine to mé, and Mr. Dimitrios-Note Botzaris opened the collection of relics of the Greek War of Independence in the Ethnological Museum to me. Mr. A. Baltazzi, who is responsible for the admirable reconstruction of Rhododaphne, permitted me to use letters and documents in his possession. Professor Hadzidaki allowed me to see parts of the Byzantine Museum which are not open to the public. Mr. and Mrs. Philip Dragoumis offered me books and family lore through an introduction given me by Dr. Stefan Xydis. From the beginning of my work Miss Eurydice Demeteracopoulou of the Gennadios Library has been of steadfast help. Mr. Philip Sherrard of the British School of Archeological Studies made it possible for me to consult the Finlay Papers in the School's Library. Without the translations from the modern Greek and the unwavering interest of Mrs. Alexandra Placotari the Greek section of this biography could not have been written.

To all of these and to Le Baron et La Baronne d'Uxküll-Gyllenband, La Baronne A. d'Uxküll-Gyllenband, Lady FitzHerbert, Miss Eva Freeman, Mr. and Mrs. William P. Leonard, Mr. Gordon Sager, and Mr. Donald P. Gurney I owe more than this formal acknowledgment can express.

F. C.

FOREWORD

A figure of gossip and mirth during her life, which she did everything to embellish and nothing to correct, Sophie de Marbois, Duchesse de Plaisance, became after her death in Athens in 1854, the subject of fiction for several novelists and would-be biographers — Greek, French, German, and English. So insubstantial was her early legend that a foreign traveller to Athens two years after her death gained the impression that she had been an Italian. As recently as 1960 the latest Guide Bleu *to Athens twice refers to her as the Princesse de Plaisance. Except for three men, Edmond About who knew the Duchess and attempted to give a fair description of her in* La Grèce Contemporaine, *D. G. Cambouroglou, the Athenian scholar, who wrote in 1926 of her years in Greece, and Louis Hastier who wrote a sketch of her life in 1959 in* Piquantes Aventures de Grandes Dames, *writers have enjoyed skipping accuracy in order to exploit her myth. Her participation in the Greek War of Independence, her hold-up by brigands, her excessive attachment to her daughter's corpse, her inclinations toward Judaism, her elusive love affairs, the originality of her dress, and the perversity of her behavior, are natural temptations of literary imaginations. My intention, however, has been to trace as far as possible the Duchess' whole life, to make the distinction between fact and fabrication in order to detach the woman from her shadow, the better to know her entire originality.*

Unfortunately lacunae remain : there are too few documents relating to the Duchess' years in Metz to clarify the effects upon the formative years of her childhood of the Terror of the French Revolution and the mischief of her father's banishment from France under the Directory. Fewer records exist of the decade of her life after Waterloo. Yet, while all deductions, unless otherwise noted, are my own, no fact I state is without substantiation in letters, legal documents, and memoires.

F. C.

NOTES

Professeur Theodore Besterman has estimated that in the Eighteenth Century a franc was the equivalent of one dollar and that in the Nineteenth Century 100,000 francs (livres) represented about $ 20,000 or 4,000 English pounds.

Edmond About stated that in Athens in the 1850's. 1 drachma equalled 90 centimes; 5 francs equalled 5 drachmas 58 leptas.

The name Lebrun was spelt at times Le Brun, but the Duchess' husband's family preferred the first form.

During her marriage the Duchess signed her name S. Marbois-Lebrun. After her separation she wrote her signature, Sophie de Marbois.

For Greek names that have long been familiar in English by their Latin spelling, I have used the latter forms. Others, less known, are given in transliteration from the original Greek.

All dates, unless otherwise noted, are given in New Style.

I

RED SKY AT MORNING

Red sky at morning
Sailors take warning...

PHILADELPHIA   1779-1785.

On June 17, 1784, there took place in Philadelphia, the capital of the United States, the first important international marriage after the close of the American Revolution.   In the nearly two centuries since then, the example has been followed many times.   Within a decade Sally Kean, daughter of the Governor of Pennsylvania, married Don Carlos Yrujo.   In 1828 Louisa Caton married the Seventh Duke of Leeds; and later still more familiar American names added to the fashion, among them, Jennie Jerome, Consuelo Vanderbilt, Anna Gould, Ava Willing, Grace Kelly.   But this earliest marriage between a daughter of well-known Americans and prominent foreigners was the first to result, for better or for worse, in an American woman becoming a Duchess.

The bridegroom was François Barbé de Marbois, Secretary of the French Legation to the new Republic.   His bride was Elizabeth Moore, whose family had produced civic and financial leaders since the earliest Colonial days.   Because Barbé was a Roman Catholic, a nuptial mass was performed in the morning of the wedding day in the chapel of the Legation.   Since Elizabeth was an Episcopalian and not a convert to the groom's church, a Protestant marriage service was read in the afternoon of the same day at the home of her parents.

The witnesses to these ceremonies also confirmed the couple's circumstances.   For the bride, besides her two brothers, Thomas Lloyd and Robert Kearney Moore, they were John Dickinson, President of the Supreme Council of the Republic of Pennsylvania, and Charles Thompson, Secretary of the United States Congress.   Pierre François Barbé, French Consul to Rhode Island, acted for his brother, the Secretary, as did the Chevalier de Luzerne, French Minister to the United States, Thomas Mifflin, President of the Congress of the United States, Van Berkel, Minister from the Low Countries to the new nation, and the Chevalier d'Amours, French Consul to Maryland and Virginia.   Not a witness, but giving the loftiest American endorsement to the union, was General George Washington.   In explaining by letter to Barbé why he and Mrs. Washington were unable to attend the wedding, the General wrote that of the many proofs of the French Secretary's predilection and attachment to the United States « yet this may be considered not only as a great and tender one but as the most pleasing and lasting. »

Barbé had met Washington, as he had the Moore family and other important Americans, through his official position.   Named with Luzerne in the spring of 1779 to the second Legation France sent to Britain's rebellious Colonies, he and the Chevalier sailed to America in June of that year on the French frigate, *Sensible*.   It was a long and uneasy voyage against the Prevailing Westerlies.   To the usual threat of attack from Freebooters, the American Revolution, still forging toward its climax, added the menace of British Men-of-War. Cramped quarters and attacks of sea-sickness increased the discomfort. For Barbé, apart from his reading, the pleasantest compensation for these disadvantages was the company of two American passengers. The elder was John Adams, returning home for consultation from his post as American Minister to Holland.   The younger was Adams' son, John Quincy. Adams and Barbé had met before in France and had learned to respect each other's abilities. Now, John Quincy, a lively lad, endeared himself to Barbé by his intelligence and enthusiastic willingness to tutor Barbé in English.   And he was sufficiently successful by the time the *Sensible* docked at Boston for the Secretary to speak English well with a sound Bostonian accent.

From Boston the two Frenchmen set out overland by coach and horseback to Philadelphia. They crossed Massachusetts, went as far south in Connecticut as Hartford and, skirting the British lines, reached Fishkill on the Hudson in New York. Here, out of respect for their official mission, General George Washington met them and conducted them to his camp at West Point. It was during this visit to West Point that Barbé made his first sympathetic impression upon the American Commander-in-Chief. His opportunity to know William Moore and his family in Philadelphia was the natural consequence of his being a foreign diplomat in the small capital of a small nation in which citizens of authority were few. (Philadelphia numbered about forty thousand inhabitants and only some three million others populated the Thirteen States.) In Barbé's case, as a representative of America's first and most important ally, the opportunity was inevitable. William Moore, whose forbears had immigrated from the Isle of Man, was a successful merchant and one of the American Revolution's fervent partisans. In 1776 he served on Philadelphia's Committee of Safety, a group whose counterpart was formed in all the Colonial cities to carry on functions of government during the war. Three years after Barbé's arrival in Philadelphia, William Moore was President of the Supreme Executive Council of Pennsylvania, the governing body of the Commonwealth whose purpose was to implement and support with money, arms, and troops the Revolution. In 1783 he became judge of the Court of Errors and Appeals, and a year later, when his daughter married Barbé, he had become a member of the State Assembly, a director of the Bank of Philadelphia, and a trustee of the University of Pennsylvania founded by his friend, Benjamin Franklin. Obviously a man of parts. His wife, born Sarah Lloyd, was the daughter of Welsh Quaker settlers. Her marriage to William Moore, an Anglican, and her adoption of her husband's religion upset the usual equanimity of Quaker tolerance. Hers was an act of courage, for while there was no religious persecution in the City of Brotherly Love, the Quakers resented the defection and publicly read Sarah out of the Society of Friends.

What is known of Elizabeth, the daughter of William and Sarah,

is vague, the few known facts of her youth were dimmed by the
suppositions about her later life.   No portrait of her has been found,
yet she was said to have been a lithe little woman, possessing the
self-assertion and independence of her mother, and the initiative and
capabilities of her father.   John Quincy Adams, who met her a year
after her marriage, wrote she was « a spruce, pretty, little woman
who spoke French very well, and had none of the rigid principles
of the Quakers, among whom she was born. »

Almost everything is known about Barbé from portraits, his own
diaries and letters, memoirs of others, and recorded history.   He was a
thin, angular man with a clean shaven face of high forehead and cheek
bones, a long, delicate nose, and straight, firm mouth.   At the time
of his marriage he was thirty-nine years old and an experienced
diplomat.

Born in Metz, in the Moselle, in 1745, he was the son of a family
that traced its origins there back to the Thirteenth Century.   His father
was a merchant and the Director of the Royal Mint in the city.   There
was a family legend that, after Barbé had completed his education
with the Jesuits of Metz, a friend of his family encouraged him to go
to Paris to study law and, at the same time, cautioned him that no
provincial bearing a name as plain as Barbé could advance far in the
capital of Louis XV.   True or false as the story may be, Barbé arrived
in Paris in 1765 with a particule, calling himself Barbé de Marbois,
an addition said to be of his own fabrication.

Soon thereafter he was engaged as tutor to the children of the
Maréchal de Castries, and through this employment he secured the
post of Secretary to the French Legation at Ratisbon.   Between 1771-
1778 he served also with this rank at Dresden and Munich.   When the
French Minister in Munich, the Chevalier de Luzerne, contracted small-
pox, Barbé represented France in the negotiations between Prussia and
Austria over the future of Austria.   Because Barbé favored the Prussian
claims, he aroused the animosity of Marie-Antoinette, and returning
to Paris, discreetly resigned from office.   However, eight months later,
in May, 1779, when Luzerne was named Minister to the American
Colonies, Barbé was sent as Secretary of the Legation.

Having served together in Germany, the two men understood each other. Luzerne, a dour man, disliked entertaining and thought Barbé, who enjoyed dancing and playing the violin, was frivolous. Genial by nature, Barbé was glad to take over the lighter functions of diplomacy and during his years in Philadelphia, he made the Legation the social center of the capital. Every week he gave a large dinner party and every two weeks a ball. Between the festivities he entertained with smaller parties and musicales. Following the victory of the American and French forces at Yorktown in October, 1781, Philadelphia became crowded with American officials and French officers, some with their wives, and all ready for lighthearted relaxation. In the following June, as a climax to the gay season, Barbé arranged a fête to celebrate the birth of the Dauphin. In the grounds of the Legation, a spacious pavilion, bright with colored paints and streamers, and designed by the architect L'Enfant, was built for dancing while flares were set up to illuminate the garden. Invitations went out to seven hundred people for seven in the evening. Long before that hour thousands of uninvited sensation-seekers clogged the adjacent streets to goggle at the spectacle. Dancing started at eight-thirty, fireworks were set off an hour later; and at midnight supper was served in three large tents. Dr. Benjamin Rush, eminent physician and a signer of the Declaration of Independence, found the guests to be very mixed including « men who were never moved by beauty, harmony, or by rhyme or reason ». Notwithstanding, the affair was the most ostentatious and successful Philadelphians had ever seen.

Yet its success represented only one of the French Secretary's talents, for by the time Barbé reached America, he had cultivated an unusual variety of personal interests and had developed the soundest qualifications for a public servant. Already under two monarchs, Louis XV and Louis XVI, he had demonstrated his loyalty and ability not so much by assiduously fulfilling orders as by the principles and forthrightness with which he acted. For his published article denouncing the flagellations of the Holy Week processions in Ratisbon he had been reproved by his Foreign Minister for indiscretion and received a second reproof at the time he displeased Marie-Antoi-

nette.   Neither stopped him, four years before he was sent to America,
from calling his government's attention to the decline in trade between
the British Colonies and France in favor of Saxon goods.   Later when
he was Secretary in Philadelphia he officially opposed American claims
to Newfoundland fisheries on the grounds the new nation should not
yet extend its conquests beyond its original boundaries.   For this opinion he was rewarded with violent public disfavor in Philadelphia from
which only his genial manner and the Delphin fête rescued him.
More curiously forgotten has been Barbé's responsibility for one of
the most famous documents in American history.   In reply to a ques-
tionnaire he addressed to the heads of the first thirteen states concerning those states' inhabitants and resources, the answer he received
from Virginia has since become known as Thomas Jefferson's *Notes
on Virginia.*

John Adams said Barbé was the best informed and most reflecting
man he met in France, and Barbé was not long in America before a
notable confirmation of Adams' appraisal was given him.   Within six
months of his arrival in Philadelphia, Barbé was made a member of
the American Philosophical Society, the Society, then as now, the
American equivalent of the English Royal Society and the French
Institut de France.   Nor did the honor recognize only Barbé's diplomatic attainments.   A Greek and Latin scholar, Barbé also knew
German as well as English, and at the time of the first partition of
Poland, he had learned Polish in order to report fully upon the matter
to his government.   An habitual reader, he once said literature was
his « vice ».   His liveliest interests were ornithology and horticulture.
In his letters from America he described birds which did not exist
in France, such as the mocking and humming birds.   He wrote of the
flycatcher plant by quoting from Tibullus, Propertius, Quinault, and
Chanlieu.   He had shipped to France for planting seeds of magnolias,
red cedars, certain kinds of oaks, persimons, and catalpas.

Wherever Barbé went and in whatever he did, he acted with
informed and opened eyes slanted by an understandably European
scale of measure.   Little in the American scene escaped his comment.
In his letters he remarked upon the absence of beggars in the United

States, the odd custom of bundling, the humane treatment of slaves in Philadelphia, the custom of saying Grace before meals, the presence on the table of all the courses for a meal, women evangelists, and the startling number of inebriates. He deplored, as he deplored slavery, the submissiveness of wives to husbands. He ventured a geological deduction, from the study of its strata, that the site of Philadelphia had once been under the sea. « Architectural marvels, or elegance, taste, and the conventions of arrangements are not to be found », he wrote home. To his European eyes, the simple Eighteenth Century comeliness of Independence Hall in Philadelphia was a poor thing. There were no palaces, he recorded, in the land, no Titians, Raphaels, Corregios, nor Poussins, no Gluck nor Sacchini, no castles nor saints. The only martyrs he found were those to liberty. Then he added, while there was no Greuze, there was no salt tax nor obligatory permits to leave a town.

Underlying his perspicacity and sophistication was also, as the mouth in the portraits suggest, a different trait of a sterner sort. Barbé could be strict, and when money was in question, he could be parsimonious. In one of his letters he admitted to a profound change in his character. In his youth he had had a deep scorn for money and had often spent more than he had, but at the age of twenty-five he had reformed, paid his debts, and begun to save. Now he found the habit of self-denial had made him rich and had even corrupted him. Recently in Philadelphia a destitute woman had begged him for assistance and instead of helping her, he had arranged for a usurer to lend her money.

Happily, this pettiness never affected his wife whom he loved with a steadfast devotion and generosity. Not long after their marriage, Barbé took Elizabeth on a wedding trip which was in all the comfort, convenience, and pleasure the Northern States could then offer. They left Philadelphia in a carriage followed by two other vehicles holding servants, luggage, and food, and drove through the Jerseys — now the state of New Jersey — to the Hudson. There on a sloop Barbé had chartered, they sailed north to Albany, passed the razored Palisades, the tree-hooded heights of West Point and Storm King which, five

years before, Barbé had first seen as George Washington's guest, and
so on through the broad upper reaches of a river whose steeps, promontories, and bowered shores make it one of the loveliest of
America's waterways.

Three months later, in early 1785, the capital of the United States
was transferred from Philadelphia to New York. Shortly before this
change, the Chevalier de Luzerne was recalled to Paris and Barbé was
named Chargé d'Affaires for France in America. One of the responsibilities of the office required him to follow the American Government
and move the French Legation to the new capital. Because Elizabeth
expected her first child soon, Barbé considerately left her with her
parents and went alone to New York to establish his headquarters.
At the same time he rented a house on Long Island in which he
and his family could spend the summer away from urban heat and
its annual threat of Yellow Fever.

Having completed these arrangements, Barbé returned to Philadelphia. There, on April 2, Elizabeth gave birth to a daughter. Christened in the Roman Catholic Church, Marie-Anne-Sophie, she was always
known simply as Sophie.

Sophie's sojourn in her native city was too brief at her age for
her ever to remember it. At the age of eighteen days her parents took
her to Long Island. Nor was her stay there of any significant length
since in early August word came from France that Barbé had been
offered the governorship of Saint-Domingue, Santo Domingo in the
Caribbean. The offer posed a serious question. For nearly twenty years
Barbé had served the French Ministry of Foreign Affairs. Besides
having been named Chargé, he had also been made Consul General
for the United States, indications that he might naturally expect further
advancements in his career. Santo Domingo, while it was then
France's richest colony, was under the jurisdiction of the Ministry of
the Navy, and to accept its governorship meant severing all ties with
the Foreign Office and risking the uncertainties of a new career.
However, the attainment of the highest diplomatic ranks was dependent upon the favor of men in the highest places of government,
and when Barbé decided to take the risk, he was influenced by the

fact his former employer, the Maréchal de Castries, had become the Naval Minister. On September 25, 1785, he sailed with his wife and daughter from the United States to Le Cap Français.

SAINT-DOMINGUE 1785-1790.

The family reached Le Cap on October 22, and eight days later moved on to take up residence in the island's capital, Port-au-Prince. The colony supplied two-thirds of France's overseas trade and most of the coffee, sugar, dyestuffs, and tropical wood for Europe, yet it was suffused with corruption. Graft and cheating were taken for granted; and the benefits which might have accrued to it from large profits were non-existent owing to the transference of the profits to absentee landowners living in Paris and from the hoarding of money by residents whose dream it was to save enough to go to live in Paris. Within two years of his arrival, by insisting upon economies and strict accounting, Barbé established fiscal order. Typically, he also encouraged the improvement of sugar-cane and sought to diversify produce by the importation of more than eighty varieties of fruits, spices, and flowers, and by the cultivation of chincona and bread-fruit trees.

Nothing is known of the impression, if any, the island made upon Sophie. The boredom of the planters' lives, the endless meals, the cards and gambling, the mulatto mistresses, the wholesale duels between as many as twenty men at a time were hardly of her baby world. All that was novel or exotic to adults could only be looked upon as normal to the eyes of a growing child who was too young to remember anything different. Wild orchids, gaily turbaned, dancing negroes, the sound of the banza, the sickening heat of summer and the hot rains of winter were as natural as the sight, the sounds, and the touch of her parents. The Duchess' question forty years later about her American relations suggests how dim or uncertain were her earliest impressions. She might have been too young to recall, when she was two and a half, the birth of her sister, Elizabeth-Laure, at Port-au-Prince.   Evidently she retained nothing from a trip she made during the next summer to Philadelphia where her grandfather, William Moore, a man of striking appearance and bearing, was still alive.   Her uncle, Thomas Moore, had married and had a daughter of his own.   On August 9, her grandmother Moore, the apostate, died. Whatever distinct pictures these experiences may have made could easily have been erased by harsher ones which followed after her return to Saint-Domingue.

Barbé's fiscal probity had aroused resentment against him among the Islanders.   After Luzerne's recall to Paris to take Castries' place, Barbé and the new governor disagreed over the opening of the poorest ports of the island to foreign trade.   The law limited all trade to France and Barbé upheld the law. Although his position was approved by the government in Paris, the resident planters refused to recognize the ruling.   Barbé asked to be relieved of his post.   While waiting for a reply, his agreement, without instruction, to allow the election of deputies from the Island to the Estates General, added nothing to his credit.   The absentee landowners denounced him as pro-black. Even when he, like other officials in Saint-Domingue wore the cockade after the fall of the Bastille, his enemies were not appeased. On October 19, 1789, a sans culotte group in Le Cap declared him guilty of prohibiting the import of flour for the poor and voted to hang him, burn his body, and cast his ashes to the wind.   Barbé was unmoved.   His letter of recall arrived and he refused to have his departure hastened by threats.   He calmly put his accounts in order and wrote a long memorandum for his successor.   On October 26, word reached him of a mob of five hundred advancing on Port-au-Prince to seize him.   Only at the Governor's urging did he consent to escape. A French ship, the *Ariel* was lying in the harbor.   That night at nine o'clock he and Madame de Marbois, each carrying one of their daughters, walked to the shore and stepped into the ship's longboat. Later in the darkness, the *Ariel* weighed anchor and headed for Cadiz. None of the Marbois family saw North America again.

METZ 1790-1800.

From Cadiz they drove North and arrived in Paris on December 3. The city displayed all the signs of revolutionary ardor and unrest. While Mirabeau and the newly installed National Assembly attempted to purge the country of old wrongs and to reorganize its government, church, laws, and finances, the capital suffered from lack of food, money, and unruly mobs. The audiences at André Chénier's *Charles IX* applauded its contrast of patriotism and constitutional order to tyranny, treachery, and fanaticism, but General Lafayette, as military commander of the city, had no success in stopping lynchings. Unintimidated, as always, Barbé kept his family with him in Paris while he informed his superiors of the reasons for his actions in Saint-Domingue. Save as these testified to his personal integrity, their importance was diminished politically when the Saint-Domingue Assembly decreed that henceforth it would govern the island and represent it in matters relating to France. Early in April Barbé retired with his family to his country estate, Buchy.

Barbé had purchased Buchy before going to the United States and although it was sold during his life-time, it has changed little under other owners in two hundred years. Twelve miles south of Metz, it lies along a crossroad leading to Pont-à-Mousson. Its little church, its peasants' houses, barns, stables, and cow-sheds still stand. Across a wide courtyard, the long, narrow gray stone house faces large graineries. Befitting a country gentleman, it is an unpretentious dwelling whose symmetry and proportions, balanced between a double entrance stairway, suggest ease and comfort. Around it the land rolls open and fertile in fields and pastures. In 1790 there were also woods and a garden, lovely places for children to play.

Buchy was a contrast for Sophie. There were four seasons, and the air was always cool. The grains that were green in Spring turned yellow in Summer and, when cut, left brown autumnal stubble. In Winter earth and sky were often the same soft color of gray. During the first year at Buchy Barbé wrote a book on the cultivation of clover, alfafa, and sainfoin, and Sophie learned of what grew in the fields. At Buchy she also learned to ride a horse and to read and write precariously in French, English, Latin, and Greek. There, and on visits to Metz, she met her father's family. She made the acquaintance of a grandmother and two aunts. One of the latter was Aunt Marguerite who was married to a lawyer named, Sauvage; the other, Aunt Anne-Marie, was married to an army officer named Kellermann. Aunt Marguerite had no children. Aunt Anne-Marie had a son and a daughter who were fifteen years older than Sophie, and the son, Etienne, was already an Army officer serving in the United States with the Ambassador Ternan.

Idyllic as these personal surroundings appeared to be, they could not shield a child from her country's predicament. France was rapidly becoming an armed nation. In July of 1790, the first units of the National Guard absorbed men from Metz and the nearby villages. The city had long been a garrison town, and the regular troops then in it were disgruntled by unfulfilled promises of a rise in pay. They lived by requisitions which took grain and horses from the estates and farms of the countryside, and before new methods of supply were instituted their needs shortened all supplies and aggravated tensions. From the public distemper and his own inactivity, Barbé grew restless. He bought a house in Metz in the Rue de l'Esplanade, and consented to serve as secretary to the Messenian Electorial Assembly. In late May of 1791 he travelled to Switzerland to visit the Maréchal de Castries who now lived in retirement at Ouchy. The summer and autumn he spent with his family at Buchy, and there, little Elizabeth-Laure, fell ill and on November 2, died in Barbé's arms.

For the next nine years the family's lot became part of the exorbitance of Revolution, a prolongation of the escape from Saint-Domingue. These years were Sophie's early youth, and like many children accustomed only to the anxiety and distress of their elders, she seems to have fared better than they. In January of 1792 Barbé was named Minister to the Diet of Ratisbon and Special Envoy to Vienna. His mission was quickly interrupted by the new Girondin Foreign Minister, Dumouriez, who found Barbé to be not sufficiently Royalist. In protest

Barbé resigned and returned to Metz to take up residence with his wife and child in the Rue de l'Esplanade.   In the early summer word came of William Moore's failing health, and Madame de Marbois made plans to go to the United States.   Although she made her way to Holland with the intention of sailing from there, she was unable to secure passage and returned to Metz.

By the time of her return in August, Metz had become a reinforced stronghold.   On April 20, pressed by fear of a hostile England and the possibility of a belligerent coalition on the Continent, the French Government, in order to protect its revolutionary gains, had declared war on the king of Prussia.   The first engagements of the war were disastrous to the French.   The Austrians crossed into France over the Brabant border.   On August 5, Thionville, less than twenty miles from Metz, was bombarded by the Prussians.   Sophie's uncle, General Kellermann, was ordered to proceed from Wisenburg, where he had been stationed, to Metz to act as General of the Army of the Center. On September 1, Verdun, forty-five miles to the East, fell to the Germans. Thereupon, Kellermann led his regulars from Metz to a plain a little to the northeast of Ste. Menehould where, on the great rolling plateau of Champagne, he met a volunteer army under Dumouriez and prepared to oppose the Prussians encamped across the plain.   Kellermann spread his men along the top of a rounded hillock on which stood the mill of Valmy.   Atop this rise on the morning of the 20th, he sat his charger and waited for the Duke of Brunswick with the finest soldiers of Prussia to attack.   When the Germans attempted to storm the hill, Kellermann, with a half-trained force, routed them and by routing them, as Gœthe said, « changed the history of the world ». Two days later the French Republic was proclaimed.   Not for twenty-one years was the soil of France again so menaced.   The victory of Valmy had assured the course of the French Revolution with all its consequences to the future.

Yet within its safeguards, France was racked by treachery, weakness, and irresolution.   Prisoners awaiting trial were massacred in Paris and in Versailles; eight thousand peasants marched in the Vendée shouting, « Vive le roi »; royalists were put to death by the method Dr. Louis

Guillotin recommended as the least painful.   Danton, Marat, Robespierre...   Whatever pride and patriotism surged among the Marbois
family after the Battle of Valmy were soon tortured by the craft of
Revolution.   In Metz, on October 6, Barbé's brother-in-law, Jean-Louis
Sauvage, was listed as an émigré.   On November 9, the name of
Anne-Marie Kellermann described as « the wife of the citizen, general
of the Armies of the Republic » was added to the same list.   Confiscation and public sale of property, imprisonment, even death were
the penalties for this crime against the State.   Sauvage was put in jail.
His crime was to have gone to Buchy by order of the Commandant
of Metz.   His name was not removed from the list for two years.
Madame la Générale and her daughter had gone to Schwalback in
the Spring of 1792 to be near the General at his request and had
returned to Metz before the law against the émigrés was promulgated.
It took the General seven months to have his wife's name crossed
off the list.   In January of the following year Madame de Marbois
was listed as an émigrée for having gone to Holland.   She went into
hiding while Barbé instituted means to save her.   His efforts were
interrupted when, early in March, he, too, was accused, arrested, and
thrown into prison for two days.   Upon his release, he took up his
wife's defence by appealing for her as an American, to Gouverneur
Morris, the United States' Minister in Paris, and, as the wife of a
Frenchman, to Lebrun, the Foreign Minister.   He also wrote and published a statement of her innocence.   But, although, she never suffered
punishment, Elizabeth Moore Barbé de Marbois' name was never struck
from the list of émigrés.
     The macabre and ruthless process grew worse.   Metz had a popu-
lation of forty-thousand excluding the garrison whose numbers, varied
by circumstances, were at least twenty thousand.   Beginning with the
Roman Gate, much of its long history was visible.   St. Pierre-aux-
Nonnes, built in the Seventh Century, was the oldest church in France.
The Templars' Chapel dated from the Twelfth Century, the German
Gate from the Thirteenth.   The Basilica of St. Vincent and the Gothic
Cathedral of St. Etienne marked the centuries when the city had been
the capital of the Three Bishoprics, Toul, Metz and Verdun.   There

were the Romanesque Hôtel Saint-Livier, Renaissance facades, and
the early Eighteenth Century City Hall and Law Court.   The Rue
Jurne took its name from the first Jews who lived in it seven hundred
years before.   Now the Jews lived in and around the rue de l'Arsenal,
a squalid quarter so overcrowded that extra floors had had to be
added to their houses to shelter them.   South of the Cathedral were
the smaller houses of merchants and shopkeepers.   The broad Esplanade went to the Moselle and over its Pont Moyen was the Place de la
Comédie with a large theatre which had been built a few decades
before the Revolution.   The taste of ages was in the city's architecture
and to it was added on November 7, 1792, directly before the theatre's
entrance, La Louise, the guillotine.   In her honor the Square's name
was changed to, Place de l'Egalité.

The executions were held between five and five-thirty in the afternoon and were attended, as elsewhere, by an audience of sensation
seekers.   That Sophie ever attended one of these spectacles is unlikely
owing to her parents discretion and because the Place was beyond
the center of the city at a distance from the rue de l'Esplanade.
Other Revolutionary diversions were unavoidably nearer.   Metz had too
many churches for anyone to remain unaware of their sack and the
sale of their altars, benches, floors, organs, and plate.   Once desecrated,
the new inscription across their portals, Temple of Reason, protruded
in fresh paint.   Nor could the sounds from those other circuses of
sops and propaganda, the Fêtes, be ignored.   There was a Fête within
a week of Valmy to celebrate that victory at which, in Paris Louis XVI
sang the *Marseillaise*. Between then and 1800 in every village and
city, there was a succession of Fêtes replete with parades, dancing,
Hymns to Reason, and interminable oratory extolling everything from
liberty to husbands.   At the same time the undercurrent of coercion
threatened everyone.   A national decree, requiring the registration of
all citizens, posed to those who had reason to remain obscure, the
choice between foregoing all civic rights, including ration cards, and
the risk of calling attention to themselves.   Barbé took the risk by a
compromise.   He gave his occupation as agriculturalist, a designation
which, if safety demanded, could conveniently be defined as farmer;

and in signing his name he dropped the particule and wrote simply, Barbé. A certificate of residence was also issued to one, Marie-Anne-Sophie Barbé-Marbois, aged eight, but it was signed in a bold, childish hand, Barbé de Marbois. It is the only clue to herself which Sophie gave during the Revolution, yet it bespeaks pride in what she had been taught and self-possession.

Nothing, however, was of avail before the connivance and opportunism of the demagogues. A few months after his niece's display of courage, General Kellermann was released from his command and ordered to appear in Paris before the Convention. When asked what he had done in behalf of the Revolution, the old soldier retorted, « At Valmy, I saved it. » For this he was rewarded by being thrown into the prison of the Abbey of St. Germain-des-Prés. At the beginning of 1794, the subjects for prescription having grown few, the arrest of all former Intendants was ordered, and Barbé was placed under house arrest at Buchy.

With Robespierre's head went, in August of that year, enough tensions to free Kellermann and allow him to regain his army rank. Barbé, too, was liberated and named Mayor of Metz. Two months later he was elected a deputy from the Moselle to the National Assembly in which, after the lower branch of the Council of Five Hundred had credited his loyalty, he became a member of the upper or, the Conseil des Anciens. Moderation now seemingly permissible, he took his seat under the name, Barbé-Marbois, and became an associate of other moderates among whom were Dupont de Nemours, Portalis, Laffon, and Charles-François Lebrun.

The elections in the Spring of 1797 strengthened their position, and Barbé was elected President of the Conseil. But the point of view of Barbé and his friends aroused emnity among the five members of the Directory, who had taken the place of the Revolutionary Government, and on September 4, troops of the executive branch of the government occupied the legislative chambers. Unable to convene, Barbé and his friends, with thirty others members of the Conseil des Anciens assembled at Laffon's house. At four in the afternoon they were all arrested there and taken to the Temple Prison. The next

day a rump session of their opponents of both Councils ordered
eighteen of them deported to Guiana, the future site of Devil's Island.
Barbé and Laffon were two of the condemned. Without accusation
or trial, they and sixteen others were immediately started on their
way to the coast to take ship to their place of banishment.

When word of her husband's arrest and sentence reached Madame de Marbois in Metz, she made haste to reach the déportés.
At Blois she overtook them and was allowed fifteen minutes with her
husband in the presence of a magistrate. She implored to be allowed
to go into exile with him, but Barbé himself forbade her on the
grounds that she could do more for him by remaining in France.
« You will not follow me, » he told her, « you will remain to demand
my return and my trial. » After bidding his wife to care for his
widowed mother and Sophie, he was led away to be herded with the
other prisoners into iron cages to continue the journey to the port
of Rochefort. Barbé's only reaction to this treatment was to complain
of a headache!

Within a year, of the eighteen men sent to Guiana with Barbé,
he and Laffon were the only ones left. Eight had escaped and eight
had died of fever. Determined to survive and be acquitted, Barbé
refused to escape. « Indeed, » he wrote in his diary, « my courage
has never broken. The sun burns me, rain and wind sweep into
my cell, poisonous insects torment me during the day and as I sleep.
In the midst of so many adversities, hope has never abandoned me
for a single instant. At four thousand and five hundred miles from my
native land, my wife and child recur constantly in my thoughts; they
are present when I wake; I never breakfast without telling myself
that I shall not always be alone; and that we must be three. I shall
see you again; yes, certainly I shall see you again. » A year later
in 1798, he wrote, « next year will be my last; the summer is fatal
here ».

He and Laffon had been sent to Sinnamary, a settlement of a
hundred people amid stinking swamps. After other déportés arrived;
dysentery took over. Fever and the fetid monotony of existence drove
many of the exiles out of their minds. The dying who fell to the

ground were left to be eaten by worms.   The dead who were buried
were trampled upon and their legs broken in order to fit their corpses
into makeshift graves.   Every death produced a moral depression
and illness that caused other deaths among the survivors.   It was, Barbé
noted, like the Terror.

He, himself, lay ill for six months with fever and recovered,
perhaps, by an immunity he had built up in Saint-Domingue.   He also
had the good fortune to be cared for by a French woman, Madame
Trion, who lived near his quarters.   She made herb teas for him and
brought him tame birds to divert him.   He kept his sanity by will-
power and self-discipline.   In convalesence he made an Aeolian harp
which he hung by the half-open window of his cell for the wind
to play.   When he was well enough he constructed a wheelbarrow to
show to Indians and white children who had never seen one.   He and
Laffon spent hours together discussing history, liberty, slavery, banishment.   He reminded himself that Diogenes, Thucydides, and Xenophon
had written in exile.   True to his old habits, he undertook the study
of the Indians of Guiana.

Thoughts of his wife, whom he always called, Elise, prompted
him to write a stanza :

Tonight, as if among a happy family
Elise appeared to me in a pleasant dream,
And while I celebrated her birthday, believed I saw my daughter
Sitting on her knee holding baskets of flowers.

In his waking hours Barbé dreamed of an end to exile and wrote
long statements in his self-defence.   Madame Trion bolstered his hopes
by giving him a parakeet she told him was for Sophie.   In reply to,
« Who is there ? », the bird was trained to say, « A déporté without
trial ».

Since most of his letters to France were intercepted, his family
knew little of his ordeal.   Enough information, however reached
Metz to cause Madame de Marbois to send some porcelain to Madame

Trion. With the gift was a note saying, « Madame de Marbois begs Madame Trion to accept this token of her gratitude. » Barbé knew even less of events in France. During the second year of his banishment, he received no letters from anyone. He knew nothing of the end of the Directory and the formation of the Consulate, and remained ignorant of any efforts in his behalf.

In July, 1779, he and Laffon presented an official appeal for a change in their place of exile. They moved to Cayenne and there Barbé discovered an old copy of a Philadelphia newspaper, *The Advertiser*, in which there was an account of an audience which Fouché, the Minister of Police in Paris, had granted Madame de Marbois. She had been one of a group of women with various pleas whom the Minister had received, and to her tearful defense of her husband Fouché had offered hope of his return.

Orders finally came through for Barbé and Laffon to go to Ile d'Oléron and remain there in custody. Late in January, 1800, after twenty-six months in Guiana, they sailed for France, but it was not until they arrived at Brest that they learned how recent events in Paris had altered their sentence. The Government now consisted of three Consuls, Napoleon, Cambacérès and Charles-François Lebrun. Lebrun, who had been surprised not to have been deported, had never forgotten his friends. After the Coup d'Etat of 1799, he had had their sentences annulled so that they stepped back upon French soil as free men.

It was then that Barbé learned of the death of his mother in the previous October. A year before his personal possessions had been seized and sold at auction for 8,269 livres. The purchasers were his wife who had paid 7,500 livres and two friends who paid the difference. Moreover, Madame de Marbois had done everything in her power to vindicate him and had gone from Metz to Paris not once but several times to plead for his release.

Four days after his return, on February 22, 1800, Barbé was called to Malmaison by Napoleon. Bonaparte as First Consul was already beginning to develop his idea which Carlyle recalled as « La carrière ouverte aux talents, the tools to him who can handle them. » Napoleon had heard of Barbé from Lebrun and wished to assess Barbé's ability for himself. Five months later Napoleon named Barbé to the Council of State, an advisory body on legislation to the First Consul. The appointment seemed a fair augur of the future. The Terror was a bad memory; the hell of Guiana best forgot; the family, as Barbé had hoped, was again three. And yet... The exact date is not known, but within two years of Barbé's return, Madame de Marbois' mind failed. Nor is it known the precise form the malady took — only that for the remaining thirty odd years of her life she required an attendant and lived sequestered. There was no balm in Revolution's end.

II

VESTED REMAINDERS

*Mon dégoût des grandeurs ne touche en
rien la fortune.*

La Duchesse de Plaisance.

*Vested remainders... are where the estate is
invariably fixed, to remain to a determinate
person, after the particular estate is spent.*

Blackstone.

Six weeks after her father's return from Guiana, Sophie had
her fifteenth birthday. She was short and slight like her American
mother, with an oval face, brown hair, and very blue eyes. She had
her French father's long, fine nose as well as his determined mouth
and chin. They were features which together suggested resilience and
obstinacy, a charm of contrary characteristics which, whatever they
may not have done to protect her childhood in Metz from the worst
of the Revolution, were convenient qualities with which to face her
new life in Paris. Within a year Barbé was named by the First Consul
Director, and soon after, Minister of the Public Treasury. He
brought his family to Paris, and by reason of past distinctions and
current office he, with his daughter, became a part of the bur-
geonning Napoleonic hierarchy.

While this group was not then so clearly disposed as it became
during the Empire, its degrees began to be distinct in the last years
of the Consulat. The victory at Marengo (where the decisive counter-
charge was led by Etienne, the son of the hero of Valmy) had

brought peace to France for the first time in eight years. Napoleon
returned to Paris determined to secure the peace and to re-establish
civil order.   Concordats and Codes were drawn up by the best available minds and all outstanding benefits to the country were recognized
by ranks in the order of the Legion of Honor.   Now marks of status
were to be the basis of a sound social system.   Napoleon wanted an
élite of brains and blood. « Marry », he ordered his officiers,
« Marry, keep open house.   Have a salon. »

Matchmaking was encouraged.   Napoleon's sister, Caroline, who
was married to General Murat, even attempted a match at long range
for her husband's chief of staff, General Charpentier. She first proposed
a niece of Admiral Decrès, and that failing, she suggested Sophie de
Marbois.   Neither effort succeeded because Charpentier, who was
stationed with Murat in Italy, could not obtain leave to go to Paris
to meet the young women.   That Sophie was ever a candidate for
this marriage, except in Caroline's mind, is unlikely since early in
the same year, 1802, another arrangement had been made for her.
On April 15, her engagement was announced to Anne-Charles Lebrun, the eldest son of Barbé's friend The Third Consul.

When Barbé formally apprised Napoleon of the engagement, the
First Consul acknowledged it in a note he dictated to his secretary :

Paris the 25 Germinal of the year 10 of the French Republic.

To the Citizen Barbé-Marbois.

*I learn, Citizen, with the keenest interest, of the marriage
you have announced to me of your daughter, with the
Citizen Lebrun, my aide-de-camp.   It's a fine young man
you are about to unite with your family; he will make your
daughter happy.   Have no doubt of the interest I take
in this and that I take in everything that concerns you.
I salute you.*

Added to the signature and also in the Consul's handwriting,
was the abbreviation, « Aff. » (Affectionately).

Seven months later the marriage contract was drawn up in the presence of the First Consul and his wife, Josephine, of Madame Louis Bonaparte (née Hortense de Beauharnais), of Cambacérès, the Second Consul, of General and Madame Kellermann, and General Chaussegros. On November 29, a civil marriage took place and on the next day the religious ceremony was held in the church of Saint-Eustache.

Sophie was seventeen and a half; her husband was ten years her senior. Anne-Charles Lebrun had been born in Paris in 1775 and had started his career at the age of twenty-one as a second lieutenant of the 5th Dragoons. Aide-de-Camp in 1800, he became distinguished at the battle of Marengo when he held the recent conqueror of Upper Egypt, General Desaix, in his arms while the General died from wounds. He was made a captain a year later, and at the time of his marriage, was a major. A sketch of his head, drawn at this time by Van Brée, shows an oval face with side-whiskers framing well spaced, heavy lidded eyes, a long nose, and a wide, straight mouth with a delicate bow over a full under lip. In the uniform of his regiment, white jacket with lemon colored braid, scarlet, fur trimmed dolman, and sky blue breeches, he was typical of the officers of the most élite corps in the army. All young, all good looking, all of good families, these men consciously fostered a spirit of recklessness and elegant swagger to which Charles was no exception. Brave in battle, he filled his leisure with hunting, dancing, and cards. The only interests he and Sophie had in common were horses. However, Charles was disciplined. Affable, and even tempered, he hid no nonsense behind his fashionable facade. And discipline was, no doubt, the attribute most needed by a young, spirited, and, so to speak, motherless wife.

The rupture of the Peace of Amiens, however, drastically limited Charles' opportunities to influence Sophie directly. Within a few months of his marriage, after having served as Aide in Paris, he was posted to his regiment at Montreuil. From then on, until after Waterloo, he spent his life with the army. During these twelve years, he saw his wife only on brief leaves usually spaced, as during the Russian

campaign, by several months.   He remains for lack of personal records
more an official figure than a husband.   Yet, from the thirty-eight
letters left of those which Sophie wrote to him during the Napoleonic
wars — and she wrote to him at least twice a week — many aspects
of their relations are clear.   Despite the prolonged separation from
one another, in keeping with custom, they both took their marriage
for granted, and each did all he could, in the circumstances, to make
it successful.   While the letters reveal more of Sophie's character than
of his, they testify to years of mutual affection and to more interests
in common than horses.

The first one was sent to Montreuil and dated, « Paris 29 Germinal (April 19) in the evening 1804 », and begins without salutation,

> *Madame de P. (Sophie Lebrun, one of Charles' sisters)*
> *was presented yesterday at St. Cloud by your father with*
> *whom she went alone with her husband, since for me my*
> *dear one, although I have not seen Madame B. (Joséphine*
> *Bonaparte) for almost five weeks, I dare not risk taking*
> *such a long ride by carriage.   Perhaps there would be no*
> *danger, but in order to know that I should see a midwife*
> *and I have decided to do nothing about this before your*
> *return.   Come back therefore since the length of your ab-*
> *sence grieves me more than I can say it puts me in a*
> *black mood and that falls on you.*
>
> *You can perceive my bad moods from the letters I*
> *write you but I beg you to forgive me once and for all.*
> *Likewise about any fears you have concerning the effect*
> *which my absence may have produced at St. Cloud you*
> *may be reassured about them, for your father has hinted*
> *to Mad. B. that he thought I was pregnant although*
> *I might not wish to admit it.   So she knows the motive*
> *which keeps me from going to see her and I do not*
> *doubt that she excuses me with her usual kindness.*
>
> *Besides, I do not go out at all in Paris, I walk as much*
> *as I can and when I am forced to take a carriage I am*

driven in the park. To go back to Sophie I can tell you that she wore all her diamonds that Charbonnier had given her a coiffure to harmonize with her rouged face, a muslin dress from her trousseau trimmed in silver and in fact better than I have ever seen her. Mad. B. received her with her customary graciousness and she was placed near her but her husband never said a word to her.

You see that this marks a mixture of minor misfortunes and pleasures and we ought to count ourselves happy in life when anything thus has its compensations. As for me who have withdrawn from the vanities of this world I wish for nothing more than to have lovely children beginning now with a fine boy, a pleasing companion to whom I can say of myself :

Content with his pleasures, wandering
through the woods. He watches at his
feet the favorites of Kings.

Nevertheless I could certainly use now the two or three hundred thousand livres if he who has promised them wishes to give them for I admit that my distaste for grandeur in no way applies to money.

Till this last of the year's four happy events arrives or not I kiss you and love you with all my soul my beloved Charles.

S. Marbois-Lebrun.

30 Germinal

Yesterday your father brought a letter from you, my dear one. I agree with all your reasons and no matter the pleasure I should have in seeing you I would not wish you in hurrying it to do anything contrary to your duty or detrimental to your advancement. I shall speak no more of your return I am resigned.

It is a spontaneous letter, intimate, disjointed, lively, and un-punctuated, and it gives an almost complete self-portrait. Its texture is already that of the colorful filament Sophie was to spin out of the threads of her life. Eventually her child became the center of her existence. The romantic dream of a bucolic life furnished the source of other ideas. At sixty-nine she still was apt to quote the mediocre verse and sententious maxims she had learned when young. Charm of manner she turned on and off as she wished, and in others it always beguiled her. The affected sigh at the letter's end cloaked courage and a firm self-reliance. Always gregarious, always ambitious for others, she was too intelligent to be impressed or fooled by pomp and circumstance. And money, as befitted her father's daughter, was ever a serious matter.

A month after the letter was written, Napoleon was crowned Emperor. On October 31, Sophie gave birth to a daughter who was christened, Caroline-Eliza. Both events immediately effected her life. The birth of a child added the bond of parenthood and the promise of a family to her marriage; the Empire became the historical stratum in which she and Charles were embedded. The aristocracy, carefully set up when he was First Consul, the Emperor now solidified by increasing its status. Like figures in a vast quadrille, its members all took a stately step forward. They were given titles. Charles' father was made a Prince and Archtreasurer. Uncle Kellemann was presented with the baton of a Maréchal and named Duc de Valmy. Barbé was made a Count and a Grand Officer of the Legion of Honor.

This was the second award which Napoleon had granted Barbé. In 1803, when the First Consul decided to sell the Territory of Louisiana to the United States, he chose Barbé to conduct the sale as the Frenchman who best knew America and the Americans. In a classic transaction of bargaining, Barbé acted from his knowledge of the United States' desire to secure free navigation of the Mississippi and obtained 30,000,000 francs more than the price set by Napoleon. In return for this profit, Napoleon gave Barbé a bonus of 192,000 francs.

Thereupon Barbé and Sophie entered into an equal partnership and together bought the Château de Noyers. Barbé still owned Buchy but Buchy, except for its yearly revenue of 9,600 francs, was too far from Paris to be otherwise desirable. Noyers in the Vexin, seven miles south of Gisors, was only fifty miles from the capital, a day's journey by horseback and carriage. It stood and still stands (although enlarged) amid broad and fertile fields like those about Buchy, but, as befitted it owners' new rank, it was far more sumptuous than Buchy, being a small château which had been designed by Mansard and having gardens and fountains that were miniature reproductions of those at Versailles — besides, Noyers yielded an annual revenue of 12,000 francs, half of which, of course, was Sophie's.

Within a year of this, her first business enterprise, Sophie also took charge of Charles' finances, keeping his accounts, attending to notes, loans, and the purchase of property. No one of the Napoleonic nobility was poor unless he was a wastrel, since official pay was high — Barbé's salary as Minister was 80,000 francs — and the Emperor bestowed generous gifts of money and valuable land as extra rewards for services. Land, consisting of arable soil and woods, was the safest of all investments and all the extra money Charles and Sophie had went into parcels of it. Although her father-in-law and father were the highest finance officials of the realm, Sophie at the age of twenty, investigated possible purchases and sent Charles her personal estimate of them. She told their agent which portion of Charles' pay to set aside for investment and which to hold in reserve for her use and her husband's. She regulated Charles' debts and saw to it that sums as small as 35 or 40 louis owed to Charles by his brothers Alexandre and Auguste were promptly paid. Sabers were rattled by soldiers but at least one soldier's wife insured the future, as Napoleon wished, by marriage, progeny, and sound money.

Yet neither a first child nor business responsibilities were sufficient to compensate Sophie for Charles' absence. Her patience was short and her obstinacy showed signs of high development. In August, 1805, after Napoleon gave up the idea of invading England and Charles had had no leave for four months, she threatened to leave

Paris and join her husband.   She could resign herself to a separation
caused by military action, but she refused to put on a brave front for
less.   She wrote to Charles that if he did not return to Paris when
the Emperor came, she would come to him and added, « if you
tell me to do no such thing I shall not listen to you ».   Only troop
movements deterred her.   Charles went East with Napoleon and Sophie did not see him until early in December when he rode to Paris
without stop from the battlefield to bring the first word of the victory
at Austerlitz.

Three weeks later Charles was sent South to join the assault on
Naples.   An unexpected opportunity gave promise to Sophie of a means
to shorten any further separation.   In response to an appeal to Napoleon by the Genoese to become again a part of France, the Emperor
named Charles' father, Governor of Genoa.   It was possible, Sophie
thought, because of this that the Emperor might grant another favor
to the family and give Charles a leave of three or four months, in
which case she would go to Genoa in the Spring and Charles could
join her there.   She conceded that a decision was up to Charles and
once again admitted that she would do nothing to hinder his chance
of promotion.

The latter was a matter of discouragement to Charles and of
indignation to Sophie.   In the latest promotions all the Lebrun brothers
had been passed over although Auguste, the youngest, had fought
with distinction; Alexandre, three years a lieutenant, had been wounded at Austerlitz; and Charles, having served as Aide-de-Camp, had
been sent to Italy without having been made a General.   On both
subjects Sophie made her opinions clear to Charles : if neither leave
nor promotion was forthcoming, he should ask to be returned to
Paris.   Naples, she argued, had been taken; in returning to Paris
Charles would fulfill the intentions of Napoleon who had sent him to
Italy only to be at the side of Prince Joseph during the hostilities
and not to remain in exile there.   Moreover, Sophie wrote to her
husband, she would present herself at the Emperor's door and if Napoleon deigned to receive her, she would tell him about Charles' return.
She would also, she said, speak to the Empress.   Eventually the matters

were arranged without her expertise : her father-in-law's mission accomplished, Lebrun returned from Genoa to Paris in the Spring; and although Charles stayed on in Italy, he was made a General.

While Charles' promotion gratified Sophie's sense of justice and her pride, it did not relieve her frustration. She wrote from Paris on April 21, 1806, « ... it is truly sad to be separated in this way without knowing when it will end; I could have patience if I was assured the Emperor had the intention to recompense us for so much tediousness, moreover I am afraid of one thing for which even this hope would not console me which is that you are looking for some Neopolitan woman to distract you. But let us be done with this thought ». There was also little at home to encourage her. She reported that Eliza was well and had fourteen teeth. But both her father and mother increased her unhappiness.

In the preceeding January, Barbé had been dismissed from office. The action was the climax of several disagreements between himself and Napoleon over methods of raising money as well as a series of devious financial manœuvres by the Chief of Army Supplies, and the fact that the national Treasury was almost empty. Barbé had not eased the situation by his reduction of advances to private bankers upon whom the nation's credit largely depended, nor by the advancement of funds to the Chief of Supplies without security or authority. The reduction precipitated a financial crisis in which a number of bankruptcies occurred including that of the Récamier firm. The loan, because it was done without his knowledge and which he only learned of on the night after Austerlitz, angered Napoleon. During the evening of January 26, following his return to Paris from the battle, the Emperor met Barbé and flying into a rage, dismissed him. In farewell, Barbé said, « I should like to hope that Your Majesty will not accuse me of being a thief »; to which Napoleon retorted, « I should a hundred times prefer that; at least knavery has limits; stupidity has none. »

Barbé accepted the end of his career by characteristically spending the next nine days in drafting reports for the use of his successor. Then with Sophie, Eliza, and his sister, Madame Sauvage, he departed for Noyers where, despite a heavy cold, he immediately started to oversee the planting of shrubs and trees and the erection of new farm buildings.

During the following months business took Sophie back and forth to Paris, offering her respites from life at Noyers which she found uncomfortable and depressing. She and her father, since his return from Guiana, had been unable to develop any mutual sympathy or affection, and Sophie felt ill at ease in his presence. The effects of his banishment and the strain of his wife's illness had destroyed Barbé's earlier spontaneity and charm of manner and had made him withdrawn and austere, traits which his summary dismissal at the age of sixty aggravated. At Noyers now, he kept to himself, only to appear for meals which he ate without speaking, or to ask his sister to stop her knitting and play tric-trac with him. Sophie, when she was at Noyers, rose at seven-thirty in the morning, played with Eliza or sewed until nine when she took the baby to see her grandfather. After breakfast at nine-thirty, she again played with her daughter, and between dinner at three in the afternoon and supper, she walked with her aunt and read her parts of a poem she had composed. She was bored to the verge of melancholy, and even in the rare moments when her father's reserve thawed a little, she shuddered in fear lest her aunt return to Paris and leave her alone with him. « I shall try », she wrote in desperation to Charles, « to keep her here as long as I can and to see our neighbors, for I have no desire to become like Maman. »

Upon Sophie fell the burden of arranging for her mother's future. The Comtesse de Marbois was under the care of the ablest psychiatrist in Paris — and the first humane one in the world — Dr. Pinel. Since the beginning of her illness the Comtesse had occupied, with her maid, the second floor of Barbé's house in Paris, but when her condition gave no hope of improvement, it was decided that she should live elsewhere. In February, 1806, Sophie inspected a house owned by some nuns near the river at Les Andelys where her mother would be the only boarder, and while Sophie was pleased by the house and the variety of fish, fowl, vegetables, and fruit available for the table, she doubted if her mother's maid would consent to move to the country. However, it was the Comtesse who did not wish to leave Paris, and to take her away against her will, would have requir- ed a police order and a guard. Even to get her into a carriage would have necessitated making her believe she was merely moving to another residence in Paris. Once she went beyond the city limits and saw she had been deceived, her affliction, Sophie feared, might worsen.

This is one of the only two clues to the nature of the Com- tesse's illness. In 1803 Barbé had written to Philadelphia to his brother-in-law, Colonel Thomas Moore, who had expressed the desire of his wife and himself to come to Paris, that there was nothing their presence could do to lessen his wife's crisis, but he urged them to come and to be his guests since « whether or not your presence should have the desired effect, I shall at least have the consolation that every possible thing will have been done to heal her mind ». This, with Sophie's report to Charles, suggests a form of schizophrenia.

The current situation was made more difficult by the Comtesse's maid who not only refused to budge but who spread rumors that her mistress was sane and it was her family who wished it to be believed that she was mad. In the end, late in April, the Comtesse entered a clinic run by a pupil of Dr. Pinel. The expenses, Sophie wrote to Charles were double the charge asked by the nuns, and it was possible that the Comtesse could only be accommodated for a month. However, Sophie felt, « in the circumstances one should not consider the difference in cost ».

Unlike her mother, Sophie was well, young, resilient, and in love. Only boredom and inactivity enduced moments of intolerable loneliness and these, as her letters to Charles showed at the time, could be relieved by writing him scrambles of mood and gossip, sense and banter. The one dated March 16-17 included an account of her father's dismissal, her intention to speak to the Empress about Charles' return from Italy, several bits of gossip, and ended, « I shall finish my collections of anecdotes with this one, « M. de Tarente of the Tri- mouille family wishing to secure authorization to form a regiment which he would support, addressed the Emperor and received an audience. After having conversed about his business he said he had the honor of being related to the prince his son through the Princess of Bavaria and to prove it he presented a genealogy. The next day the M. de Tarente received a note from the Emperor addressed to The Prince de Tarente in care of The Prince Louis de Trimouille. Following the contents of the letter, he returned to see the Emperor and was received with lavish ceremony, now everybody calls him Prince de Tarente and does whatever he asks so there he is highly pleased with himself and all those who have pretentions of being foreigners are in a flutter among others the Rohans (who were boastful of their connections with the royal houses of Scotland and Navarre) and with this my Colonel son of a Prince I love you and kiss you in the most proper bourgeois manner. »

In another letter she described with zest the appearance of her brother-in-law, Alexandre, dancing in the Princesse Louis' quadrille, got up as a Spaniard in white plumes, lace, green and black velvet suit, with a white scarf fringed and braided in silver. If such festivities continued, she thought the costumes would, as in former days, have to be given to the dancers and later passed on to the Opera. After which she remembered to write that her mother had entered the clinic.

But no matter the frivolous sequence of her thoughts she always took time and space to deal with business and awards with gravity.

The Emperor had begun to create and bestow kingdoms upon relations, principalities and duchies upon officials. His brother, Joseph, was given the Kingdom of Naples, Louis that of Holland, his sisters, Pauline and Eliza, received the Duchies of Guastalla and Massa Carara. Of the Maréchaux, Murat became Duc de Clèves, and Berthier, Prince de Neuchâtel — all with hereditary rights. Nothing was granted Charles. Early in April Sophie learned that the Emperor still retained certain fiefs in Italy and she decided the moment had come for Charles' fate to be settled. She wrote to her husband her evaluation and preference of the unassigned fiefs. First of all there was the district of Plaisance (Piacenza) provided it formed a whole. Dalmatia, she thought, would produce the highest revenue, a fact not to be disdained because as she said, « money adds a great deal to the respect that titles give and besides it is more elegant to be the Duke of a country than of a city ». Istria had the same advantage, and it was not so chopped up as Dalmatia, but the climate was unhealthy. As for the fiefs of Naples, any advantages they had were cancelled by the fact their owners would be dependent upon the sovereign of another Empire which, she remarked, « is the almost infallible way to displease the King of that country and if someday it happened that that King should have a little of the genius of the Great Napoleon, I think the Duchy might well be crunched ».

Late in 1806, Charles' father was made Duc de Plaisance, but, as he had done when he accepted the title of Prince, he accepted no hereditary rights with it, and Charles continued to be a mere General. Sophie had to find what solace she could for this in the fact that Charles left Naples in October for active duty on which he led a heroic charge against the Saxon infantry at Iéna, presenting after the battle a clutch of captured standards to Napoleon. In February of the next year he again distinguished himself at Eylau and for this he was given the command of a brigade. At Friedland he was wounded and at last sent home on leave. It was the longest leave he had had, over two months, and after he returned to the troops in September Sophie had the two extra compensations of his again being made an Aide-de-Camp, and of the beneficial effect his presence at home had had upon their daughter. « Eliza », she wrote to him, « has been as sweet as an angel since your departure. »

The end of the year brought another unforeseen relief when, in an about face, Napoleon recalled Barbé to be President of the newly organized Cour des Comptes. The decision may well have been owing to the influence of Charles' father since the Archtreasurer had recently set up the Court to serve as an administrative tribunal to pass upon the audit of all government expenditures and receipts, and it needed a man with the ability and experience of his old friend to head it. In any case, Barbé returned from Noyers to Paris in triumph. Seven carriages, surrounded by a detachment of cavalry conducted him to the former Augustinian Monastery which was to house the Court. The Archtreasurer paid tribute to him in a speech in which he gave all credit to the Emperor for the appointment. « He recognized in you », Lebrun declared in adressing Barbé, « deep feeling beneath an austere exterior, an absolute devotion to his glory, an inviolate fidelity to your duty... and suddenly without your daring to ask a favor, without friendship even pronouncing your name... His Majesty recalls you to functions linked with the greatest interests of the Empire. » Sophie reported to Charles that both their fathers had tears in their eyes caused by an emotion shared by all who heard the speech, making a very touching scene.

A year later, like many other Parisians, Sophie had grown tired of war. The alliance formed at Tilsit had not proved to be permanent, and the débâcle in Spain brought to light a defection among Napoleon's own ministers; the perfidy of Talleyrand and Fouché. Aware of the general unrest, the Emperor let it be known that he saw no reason to presume there was danger ahead. But Charles remained on active duty, and Sophie, for the first time, expressed her distaste for war. Soldiers, she wrote to him, knew from experience what glory meant; women knowing it only by reputation hardly knew enough to talk well about it. « We are left », she said, « only the happiness (and) mine consists of seeing you again, and the news of your return is the only one which can satisfy your Sophie. »

Although she filled her days as best she could with business, with excursions, with reading, she fretted. To her vexation, Barbé committed another blunder. On a required list of his staff which he presented to Napoleon, he added some unsolicited comments about its members. The Emperor left the paper on his desk where someone read it and repeated the comments to the people concerned. Barbé defended himself by explaining that he had followed an old custom. Old custom or not, Sophie said, in his place she would have waited to be asked for an opinion.

She went with Madame de Rumfort, the widow of the great chemist, Lavoisier, and an old family friend, to visit the new château at St. Gratien near St. Denis which was being built by the Comte de Luçay, Master of the Imperial Household. The park contained three hundred acres of water and the same amount of land. Sophie found the water and the views of beautiful trees were embellishments, but the columned exterior of the house was only rather pretty and the interior was decidely mean. She received more pleasure from the recently published letters of Mademoiselle de Lespinasse to Guibert. In fact, she had never read any book which so demonstrated what she called, « the empire of style ». While she was grieved by Mademoiselle's infidelity to her old lover, Mora, she found a certain charm in the writing which made it impossible to tear herself away from the book.

Her ethical standards were more deeply offended when, after some one set fire to a building on Charles' estate at Vaucresson, she learned, to her horror that their agent, Laflotte, believed the punishment for arson was death. She believed it to be the galleys, and in this belief she intended to neglect nothing in order to find the culprits. « But », she wrote to Charles, « I have always thought the sentence of death should be limited to murderers and I should not wish to cause anyone to lose his life for some bits of charred wood. I strongly hope you think the same for it is a terrible thing before God to be covered with a man's blood. If unfortunately you are not of the same opinion as I, you can correspond with Laflotte for I am no longer going to involve myself in the matter. »

Her daughter, as she grew older, offered momentary diversions for she was a clever and mischievous child. One day she disappeared and after neither her maid nor her nurse could find her, Sophie went through the house in anguish calling her name in vain. At length Eliza darted from behind a door, which her mother had already passed several times, and pertly enquired, « I was well hidden, wasn't I ? » She always urged her mother to tell her father that she was good, but she resented the time Sophie spent at her desk and once interrupted her writing by asking, « Maman, if you please, would you like me to torment you ? ». Sophie admitted that she succumbed to such blandishments. Yet Eliza remained an only child, and to Sophie the lack of more children was another misfortune that dogged her marriage. In her letters to her husband she recorded the births of sons to friends, and in 1809, after seven years of marriage, she told Charles, « I really have the right to say you are unlucky to the point of having chosen a wife who only knows how to give you a daughter. »

It was far from easy to be a virtuous and a lonely woman and at the same time to be a vigorous one, and to ease her tensions, Sophie started to ride horseback again. She rode in the afternoons after dinner, and when she was in Paris she rode from Ivry where Charles kept a stable. She was delighted, after Charles sent orders to sell a certain mare, to be able to tell him that the groom said there were many horses for sale and no buyers. Of course, she wrote, she would sell the mare if she found the right price for her, but she let it be understood that the mare was the only horse she could ride. Yet it was one more reason to be sullen, and after the defeat at Essling, she went so far as to upbraid Charles for not finding time to write her news which she had had to learn from his father : Alexandre had had a horse shot from under him, and Auguste had been given the Legion of Honor.

Late in June she went to Noyers with her father and father-in-law, and there word reached them of the victory at Wagram. A few days later the Archtreasurer informed Sophie that Charles had been made Duc de Plaisance. But even this unusual transference of a title to an eldest son during a father's lifetime did not give the new Duchess, who was also the first American born duchess, immediate satisfaction. She and Charles were indebted to the Emperor for the special decree which transferred the title, but the Archtreasurer had seen to it that the decree permitted him to retain the revenues of the Duchy! (Napoleon had divided the income from the fiefs of Parma and Piacenza between Cambacérès and Lebrun, the latter's share being 150,000 francs before maintenance charges were deducted.) The new Duchess was enraged, but helpless. She consulted the Journal of the Empire only to read that while the eldest sons of Princes did become Dukes, Charles' case was an unique exception. The next day, July 20, in her letter to Charles she made no mention of the title; her spirits were high only because there was talk of peace. Her interest was to know how soon after peace was declared would Charles arrive home.

Although England and Russia saw to it that there was no peace, an attachment the young Duchess now made stiffened her morale. A growing knowledge and admiration of her father-in-law inspired a friendship which gave her what Charles had no opportunity to give, a companion and a mentor. Charles-François Lebrun was a savant as well as a statesman. Born in 1739 into an ancient family of Norman landowners near Coutances, he travelled as a young man through Belgium, Holland and England studying those countries' arts and governments. He already knew Greek, Latin, Italian, Spanish, and English and had written poetry in each of them. Before he was thirty-five he translated the *Iliad* and Tasso's *Gerusalemme Liberata*. « Literature », he once said, « is the sweetest and noblest of diversions, but one must cultivate the humanities not for the brilliance they bestow but for themselves; because they elevate the soul and enlarge the domain of thought. » After studying law in Paris, he entered the government of Louis XV as an assistant to Maupeou. He became a friend of Benjamin Franklin when Franklin represented the American Colonies at the court of Louis XVI. He sat in the National Assembly and was imprisoned in 1793. At the time Barbé was sent to Guiana he escaped deportation because the Directory believed him to be in league with Napoleon. As Third Consul he was given charge of national finances, public law, and economy.

Over sixty when the Duchess first knew him, Lebrun was a tall, large, white haired man, distinguished by the delicate clarity of his mind and a simple, kindly manner. In a milieu of ambitious climbers politically and socially, his modesty was phenomenal. He kept no journal; published no memoires. « I have taken great pains to hide my life », he said, « and if my name is cited in history, it will be in spite of me. » It was this modesty, as well as a belief in the futility of titles which also caused him to state, « Call me Highness, Prince, Duke, Monseigneur, Sir or Citizen, it's all the same to me. » To his daughter-in-law he offered a warmth of feeling and sympathy which she never received from Barbé, and his erudition and intelligence remained, unlike her father's, lively attractions to her as long as he lived. Like the Duchess he was gregarious and affable. While Barbé was strict in his conduct and so punctilious his neighbors in the rue de Grenelle set their clocks by his habit of setting out from his apartment there on the dot of nine every morning for the Court, the Archtreasurer accomplished his work with equal devotion and less obduracy. A widower since 1800, Lebrun did not remarry — although he was closely acquainted with the widow of General Lacoste. The Duchess took up her residence with him in the former hôtel de Noailles in the rue St. Honoré and acted as his hostess. She had found her most congenial and sympathetic friend.

After Louis Bonaparte abdicated the throne of Holland in the summer of 1810, the Prince Lebrun was named Governor of Holland and the Duchess began to spend much of her time in Amsterdam acting there, too, as his hostess. On October 1, 1811, Napoleon and Marie-Louise arrived there for a visit of twenty days of continuous fêtes. The following June, for the first anniversary of the baptism of the Roi de Rome, Lebrun gave a dinner for sixty people and further entertained his guests with horse racing, water-tilting, and fireworks. Charles, temporarily in Paris, received this information in a letter from his wife mixed with word of an affair his brother, Auguste, was enjoying with a woman whose husband was a complacent gull, with the Duchess' instructions where to send her new gray shoes, how often the mattresses should be aired at home (once a week), and the expression of her pleasure should her husband wish to sleep in her bed.

A month later, the Duchess, who was still in Holland, wrote to her husband, who had joined the Emperor in Poland, about a new governess who had been proposed for Eliza. The Duchess said she preferred a woman not too much older than herself. The woman, who was recommended, while a good piano teacher, and with virtues that would grace a convent, was no more equipped to teach than she was. Her great fault was her lack of English, and the Duchess wrote, « You know what stress I place upon English. Balance all this and decide », she instructed a soldier who was struggling with the Grande Armée toward Moscow.

Eliza required a firm hand and in lieu of an English speaking

governess, the Duchess saw that she had it.   At eight the child was
as spirited and as wilfull as her mother.   She liked to romp and in
doing so once cut her forehead severely enough to suggest she would
retain a scar.   She played tricks on her maid and when she refused
to apologize, the Duchess told her she would have only bread for lunch.
« I won't eat », Eliza replied, « I shall never eat again; I shall die
of hunger. »   Her mother's smile only increased the tantrum.
« You laugh now », the child retorted, « but you will weep when
you no longer have a child... you laugh but not gladly... When I am
dead you will have to write to Papa and he will no longer want
you for his wife. »   Eliza ate her dry bread, but she spent the rest
of the day in tears.   She wished to go out with her mother, but
the Duchess said her table-manners were not those of a well brought
up person and she was too disagreeable with other children to be taken
where there were any.   That night, after dining out, the Duchess
returned home to find Eliza waiting in bed, crying for her.

In August, the Duchess was back in Paris, puffed up with pride.
During the offensive in Poland, Charles had received the Legion of
Honor for valiant conduct, and congratulations were offered the Duchess by their friends.   One of these, the Marquise de Souza-Bo-
thelho (the author of popular novels on the Eighteenth Century whose
son, Charles de Flahaut, became the father of Queen Hortense's
illegitimate son, the Duc de Morny) confessed that she was frightened
to death by the dangers she heard Charles had been through.   The
Duchess replied that once the peril was over she could find only
the glory and happiness in having distinguished one's self without
accident.   To Charles, she confided that she could not understand
why anyone as sensitive as the Marquise was frightened now.   Why
had she not become frightened the moment the Army set off and
remained scared until peace was declared ?

On September 1, the Duchess was named a Lady-in-Waiting to
the Empress, a position she held until Napoleon's abdication eighteen
months later.   It was not an occupation, entailing as it did endless
hours of perfunctory formality, of special interest to a woman who
preferred spontaneity and the company of savants, but the Duchess

carried her new honor as she did her title with grace and responsibility.   Talleyrand, who was present when she renewed her oath of
allegiance seven months later with other Ladies-in-Waiting, found her
the most polished.   His own niece, Madame Just de Noailles blushed,
got caught up in her train, made only one curtsy instead of three,
and laughed when she spoke the oath.   Madame de Marnier wore
the shortest dress of any woman ever to take the oath.   But the
Duchesse de Plaisance, he later told the Comtesse de Kielmannsegge,
« is naturally gracious and modest.   She read the text of the oath
extremely well, made her few steps and her curtsies in a very proper
manner ».

The Duchess shirked none of her duties, not even complaining
of the tedious hours she spent being fitted for court clothes by
Leroy who had created the Empire line in the gowns he made for
Josephine and become the most fashionable dressmaker of the Empire.
A list of some of the Duchess' wardrobe included redingotes in rose
velvet and sea-green Kashmir, capes in satin, dresses in rose moiré,
and blue percale, printed silks, hats trimmed in lace and marabout,
gloves, a mantilla...   Even Eliza had a dress from Leroy in striped
percale with long sleeves, and a bonnet edged in blonde lace.

The Duchess received 3,000 francs a month for her attendance
at court, a sum that was increased by the honorarium of the affection
the Empress stimulated in her.   Marie-Louise frequently suffered from
symptoms which physicians were unable to diagnose, but the Duchess
thought they might well be caused by the Empress' separation from
her husband.   Any reminders of occasions when she had been with
him affected her : she could not take part alone in any entertain-
ment or fête without tears in her eyes.   At the ball she gave for her
sisters in Prague in December, 1812, when a guest congratulated her
upon being once more with her family, she merely replied with large
tears, « The Emperor is not here. » « Certainly », the Duchess told
Charles, « she is incapable of affectation the more I see her the more
I am persuaded that no one unites in a higher degree, breeding and
dignity, goodness and simplicity. » Judgement of character, considering
Marie-Louise's behavior after the Empire with her swift alliance with

Neipperg and her desertion of the King of Rome, was not one of the Duchess's strong points.

In September, 1812, when the Duchess wrote of the Empress, she had had a longer experience of separation from a husband, and both women were under the duress of the Russian campaign. Letters from the front took at least a fortnight to be brought to Paris.   On October 9, word came of the burning of Moscow yet no hint was given that the Retreat had begun four days before. Having heard earlier that it was impossible, because of winter weather, for the army to progress after mid-October, the Duchess had hoped winter quarters would be set up and the Emperor would return for several months to Paris, bringing Charles with him.   Word of the conflagration ruined those dreams.   Where now, she asked, would the troups bivouac ?   If Charles foresaw an opportunity to come home, he must, she begged him, let her know.   She was very despondent; her sadness, she wrote, showed in her face and that was a bad thing to carry outside one's house and above all to Court.

By early December the worst was known : the bitter chill, the hunger, the dead, the rout.   Alexandre, Charles's youngest brother, was killed as he led his regiment in a charge to protect the remnant of the army.   Napoleon wrote in his own hand to inform the Arch-treasurer of his son's death.   On the third of the month, the Duchess sent with her letter to Charles a cross of the Legion of Honor in diamonds which his father had had made for him, but there was no joy in her heart.   The Austrians were said to be pillaging and committing horrors wherever they went.   Some idiots in Paris believed their approach meant good luck.   If only the French people were united, the Duchess was convinced they could repulse « those English our eternal enemies, those Germans, those Spaniards, those Russians who have so much vengeance to wreck; but », she said, « I tremble lest we see them in Paris. »   The Emperor announced that he would either be victorious or dead in three months.   The Duchess, who was never fooled about practical matters, thought there was more certainty in the fact that the enemy numbered 80,000 men on France's eastern frontier.   She was certain the enemy would do all the harm they could, « but is that », she wished to know, « going to make us submit like lambs to something which with energy we can stop » ?

There were no cracks in her courage and her loyalty to Napoleon never faltered.   Three years before, when the Emperor started to lead his armies for the second time to Vienna, she had written, « Eight days after quitting his capital the Emperor vanquished the Austrians! All the exclamations that could be made over a similar exploit would be well beneath its greatness : the Alexanders, the Caesars all the conquerors history presents, even those of fable cannot be compared to the Emperor. »   It was a true expression of her emotions.   To the end of her life she remained a Bonapartist, loyal to the man to whom she and her family, and France owed so much.

In the darkening days of 1813, she had no patience with faint hearts and deserters, and she repeated with satisfaction Napoleon's short-tempered reprimand to the Duchesse d'Alberg for her husband's timidity.

The Duc d'Alberg, the last offshoot of an ancient family who, as the Comtesse Potocka remarked, had always treated Napoleon as a tyrant and usurper, was engaged in spreading obstructive rumors. One evening, seeing his wife at a card-table the Emperor approached her and told her that her husband, whom he had pulled out of the dust and covered with favors, was spreading alarm.   When the Duchesse d'Alberg began to cry at this taunt, Napoleon assured her that he knew she had no part in the matter and added, « Your marriage is so disrupted it is easy to believe you know nothing of your husband's actions and feelings ».   For the Duchesse de Plaisance, the present test of faith was not a temptation to desert; it was an opportunity to remain steadfast.   Her example was her father-in-law who, when the people of Holland rose in rebellion, refused the offer of a safe-conduct and, leaving the Governor's Palace in broad daylight, proceeded without menace to the frontier.   The Duchess' letters began to reflect the strain of events : the increasing threat of the Coalition against France, the bickering of the Maréchaux, Ney's desertion. The effects of eleven years of war could not be denied and the tone of her letters grew temperate, but the modulation was not a symbol of defeat; it was a sign of maturity. She had grown wise enough to accept defeat as a possibility but not to allow it to subvert her character.

As usual, battles or no battles, victory or defeat, she kept a clear head about money. Recognizing the possible consequences of the general financial instability, she asked Charles, who after the Retreat had been appointed Military Governor of Antwerp, if he could reduce his official expenses. She tried always to keep direct control of their finances and to take neither risks nor poor returns. A sum of 60,000 francs, which by a misunderstanding, she allowed her father to invest for only 7 $^1/_2$ %, she retrieved as soon as possible. She could do better with it if she could find a good piece of land to buy. If she could not, she preferred to let Charles' father hold the sum since, unlike Barbé, the Archtreasurer allowed his son and daughter-in-law free access to what was theirs. Experience had taught the Duchess how to take care of money; common sense made her respect it. She was never a miser, her point-of-view being that idle capital was wasted and, like a good horse, deserved exercise and consideration in order to be of use and to endure.

The debts of her friend, the Duchesse de Dino, caused her grave concern since they added unecessary shame to what already was a disgraceful predicament. The Duc de Dino was Talleyrand's nephew and a licentious ne'er-do-well. When in, 1809, Talleyrand had wished to take political advantage of the Duchesse de Courland's friendship with the Emperor Alexander of Russia, he arranged a marriage between his nephew, Edmond and the Duchesse de Courland's fifteen and a half year old daughter, Dorothée. Timid, and a child whom Talleyrand described as « puny », Dorothée was soon mistreated by her husband and abandoned by his uncle. In June, 1813, when she was twenty, she was pregnant for the third time since her marriage and had developed an abscessed breast. Alarmed by her condition the Duchess took Dorothée with her to Noyers where she sought by kindness, distractions and ass's milk, to build up her strength. But no sooner did Dorothée show signs of improvement than word came of her husband's enormous gaming losses, and she had a relapse. The Duchess appealed to Charles. Charles, she thought, might be able to

have Edmond transferred to a post with less temptations and fewer
bad companions.   Charles might even appeal to Edmond's sympathies.
« Paint », she wrote, « the sad state of his wife but with the delicacy
of which you are capable...   I write with a full heart, with tears in my
eyes to see a person of such worth destroyed without the Prince
de Bénévent (Talleyrand) who took her from her native land and forced this senseless marriage on her, doing the least thing to ease her
situation, without her husband for whom she is too good, doing anything but add to her troubles. »   A week later the Duchess knowing
Edmond's tastes, asked Charles what sort of woman the Duc de Dino
now had with him, remarking that she was no doubt some pretty little
creature who did not cost him much.   « His wife », she added, « will
die of shame; for I do not see how they will get out of the abyss
where they are 1,400,000 in debt. »   Again the Duchess' sympathies led her to misjudge character for the young Duchesse de Dino left
her husband and went to the Congress of Vienna with Talleyrand, later
to become his mistress, and to outlive the Duchess by eight years.

During Dorothée's stay at Noyers, word came of the arrival of
Napoleon and Marie-Louise at Mayence.   Again there was talk of
peace, and the Duchess' spirits rose.   Again the expectancy was unfulfilled.   Charles was transferred to Mayence, and by November the
best the Duchess could hope for was that he would have leave.
« But », she told him, « I dare not complain at this moment when
after so many mortal worries, I know at least that you are safe.   It
seems to me an offense against God not to tolerate a disappointment
when so many other people have true sorrows to deplore. »   As the
year wore out, she held to this principle, never again mentioning
peace or leaves but, giving as she had always done, word of Eliza's
health, rumors of military and political events, noting vital statistics...
the death of Narbonne, the birth of the Duchesse de Rovigo's first
son.   On December 29, four months before Napoleon's abdication,
she wrote a short note in the evening :

> *The news of the day is that the Emperor, as soon as*
> *the Legislature votes on the Budget will gather all the*

money he can find and will leave taking with him the
Empress, the King of Rome, the chief officials, the Senate,
and everything he can possibly obtain in order to reassemble
the troops, and he will form a camp entrenched between
Metz and Namur.

Adieu. How are you?

Three days later the Prussians crossed the Rhine at Coblentz,
the Austrians at Bâle.   On January 23, in her role of Lady-in-Waiting,
the Duchess was at St. Cloud when Napoleon, in the presence of the
Empress, their son and other relatives, announced to the officers of
the National Guard of Paris that he was leaving for the front and
entrusted them with the defense of Paris and the protection of his
family.   In the evening, in writing to Charles, the Duchess repeated
from memory as much as she could recall of what Napoleon had said,

The Austrians are... the French Comte, but I shall leave
in a few days and I hope with the aid of God and the help
of the French... that in these same provinces they shall find
their graves; nevertheless I am leaving you the objects of
my dearest affections.   The Empress my wife, and my son
the King of Rome — here there were cries from all
sides we shall defend them.   I do not entrust them to
mercenaries, paid hands.   I put them among the French
in the heart of the capital.   If... some few detachments
should reach here... you will be given canon to defend
the gates... They will only arrive by passing over my dead
body... I entrust this infant the... the hope of the nation...
strong in... strong in my destiny.   I shall see them again
those days of triumph and of glory which are still not too
far from me.   This unprepared and unexpected speech
was extremely well received, producing a good effect.

Later in the same evening the Duchess was summoned to appear
in full court dress at the Tuileries to witness the Empress take her

5

oath as Regent, but upon this act of diplomacy on which Napoleon counted upon his wife's Austrian birth to lure Austria from the Coalition, the Duchess made no comment. She merely wrote, « Every sign points to a hasty departure. It is said the enemy has appeared at Ste. Menehould », and she went on to note that bank-notes had lost twenty percent of their value; the bank would change only a total of half a million francs worth; and she had on hand but two notes each of five hundred francs.

However, at this crucial moment, the Duchess' main concern was with human behavior. The closer the enemy came, the more she despised back-sliders, the more her own convictions strengthened. On the evening of the 25th she watched the crowd which appeared to see the Emperor leave, and observed that some came through duty, a few by expediency and others led by curiosity. Among the latter was Madame Just de Noailles who had been shirking her duties lately as a Lady-in-Waiting by saying she had trouble with her eyes. She showed up, the Duchess said, to see what was going on and added that her husband had behaved in the same way in the National Guard, neglecting his duties by pretending to be ill and putting in an appearance only to keep himself informed of what went on. « All these people », she wrote, « are feeling the lie of the land and, like the King of Wurtemberg, paying out rope ready to fall in on the side of the victor. »

The members of the Provisional Government she thought were different. For the most part they looked dejected and felt more dejected than they looked. Since it would have been ignoble of them to show concern over their loss of fortune or importance, they excused their anxiety on grounds of sentiment as if the objects of their affections had become endangered only since their favors were lost or in peril and as if this had not been true during the previous and indeed glorious military campaigns. For herself, she declared, « It seems to me that those who are guided only by sentiment ought now to have more courage than ever for since the enemy has crossed the Rhine our cause being more just we can once more hope that God will come to our aid if we do not forsake ourselves. »

The last clause is telling since she never forsook herself. A month before Paris fell, while the city awaited in depression and gloom the entrance of the enemy, the Duchess was not fooled by Napoleon's victories over Blücher and York. « ...but the Austrians », she commented to Charles who was in Antwerp, « are still intact and forty miles from us. » When the Comte de Chabrol, Prefect of the Seine and married to Charles' sister, Dorothée, turned against Napoleon after Paris fell, the Duchess told him « My brother, one can reasonably critize many things in other people, but you cannot be an ingrate. » What she thought of her father, who was one of the four commissioners to draw up the Decree of Dethronement is not known; but in view of what is known of her principles, it could scarcely have been flattering.   Of all her family, she remained the one die-hard.   Following Napoleon's abdication, the Maréchal Kellermann at the age of seventy-nine retired to his estate at Soisy-sous-Montmorency.   Her father-in-law, the Archtreasurer, while he refused to have anything to do with the Emperor's dethronement, worked on the new Constitution and Charter and signed the act to recall the Bourbons to the throne.   Her husband and her cousin, General Kellermann, remained in the army, Charles becoming Inspector General of Hussars, and François-Etienne, Inspector General of Cavalry at Lunéville and Metz.

The Armistice of April 23 and the Restoration offered them a little relief.   She was still the wife of an officer on active duty, but there was peace in Europe for the first time since 1802.   With no more official duties to fill, she could find relaxation farther from Paris than Noyers.   In July, she took Eliza for her health to spend a month at Spa, near Aix-la-Chapelle, to take the Waters.

On the way they spent two days at Baden-Baden arriving the same day as the Princess Stephanie, Josephine's cousin and Napoleon's adopted daughter, who had married the Grand Duke of Baden, but the good effects of the Waters.   The hotel served a wine for six francs spoken to her in her life, she thought she now could very properly dispense with an introduction.   « You know », she wrote to Charles, « that we seek out the beauties of nature, the masterpieces of Art and, as much as possible, people distinguished by their merits.   As for

Princesses they are all over the place and we are not made unhappily curious by them. » Her example, again, was her father-in-law.

She did not enjoy Spa. The countryside was not beautiful; the weather was deplorable, and she was afraid it would counteract the good effects of the Waters. The hotel served a wine for six francs a bottle called Château Margaux which did not compare with the Margaux Barbé owned. At six every morning Eliza walked to the spring at Geronstère, three quarters of an hour away. The spring was in a neat garden in the middle of an unkempt wood. The only bearable feature of the place was her apartment. It consisted of three bedrooms, Eliza's and the maid's on each side of hers which was on the front, in the middle of the hotel, with a balcony. From the balcony she could see everyone passing along the miserable promenade and farther off she could see the road to Aix.

This depression was a return of the mood which boredom always produced in the Duchess. Now it was worsened by enforced leisure and by the fact that she was no longer familiar with idleness. She returned to Paris with relief, but only to be assailed by an uneasiness of a different sort. Despite the Armistice, despite the Charter, despite Peace, it became evident throughout the autumn and winter that Louis XVIII was far from secure on his throne. Military and republican factions engaged in separate plots. Word of the unrest, reaching Elba, prompted Napoleon to action. On March 1, he landed at Cannes with a thousand men and marching North to the cries of « Down with the priests! Down with the nobles! Down with the Bourbons! », and the strains of the *Marseillaise*, he reached Paris on March 20.

That evening old soldiers and loyal citizens surged round him at the Tuileries while loyal officers, officials, and former Ladies-in-Waiting to the Empress waited to pay him homage. Among his first official acts was the reappointment of the Duchess' father-in-law to be Archtreasurer as well as Rector of the Sorbonne. Charles was made Commander of the 2nd Military Division and again Aide-de-Camp. But Napoleon had no patience with Barbé; he called him an ingrate and refused to see him. As buoyant as ever at seventy, Barbé went back to his trees and plants at Noyers where he began to write an essay on Benedict Arnold's treason.

In August, two months after Waterloo, the Napoleonic sunset was already fading. The standards with their eagles stood furled to gather dust. The Court regalia of Ladies-in-Waiting were laid away in boxes and portmanteaux. The dead, like Alexandre, rotted in foreign fields; the maimed and the blind wore their medals as sops or, like Balzac's Colonel Chabert, became forgotten men. The Arch-treasurer retired to his property of Sainte-Mesme near Dourdan. Charles was placed on the inactive list. Of the family only Barbé was recalled, first, as Minister of Justice, then as Keeper of the Seals and Privy Counsellor.

Yet old or young, busy of idle, Marbois, Kellermanns, Lebruns, survived defeat. They continued to be what the Emperor had judged them worthy of being — aristocrats. They kept their lands, their titles; they preserved their talents; they guarded their vested remainders. The Duchess had her heart's desire : her husband was home at last. Writing to him five years before, she had exclaimed, « The Emperor can conquer, he can prevail, ah Dear God may he wish for peace, then I should see once more all I love! » In more ways than one Napoleon had granted her her wishes.

III

SOME NAIAD AIRS

To the glory that was Greece,
And the grandeur that was Rome.

Edgar Allan Poe.

Three years after Waterloo, the Duchess sat for Lefèvre, one of the Bonapartists' favorite portrait painters. She was dressed in a cream colored gown of the Empire style and wore a tiara, pendant earrings and necklace of pearls. She was thirty-three and looked younger. Only the brief shadows under her large eyes suggested the strain of revolution and war. The set of her delicately shaped mouth and long chin were as firm as they had always been, and these, with her slender, quivering nose, give an impression of vivacity and of will-power. It is not a beautiful face, but it is a strong and an attractive one — the face of an intelligent woman, lacking introspection, who was spontaneous and emotional without having a jot of sentimentality in her nature.

Once, during the war years, the Duchess had had to break the news to some friends of the death of their son in battle. The father's stoicism and the mother's tears and desire to learn if her son had received the sacraments before he died, moved the duchess to exclaim, « God and death, those are what remain »; and she wrote to Charles begging him to send all the details he could offer « to their avid sorrow ». « When circumstances lead us to a sorrowing family », she added, « when by yet a more grievous concurrence, we are obliged to become the interpreter of the sorrow, it is impossible, alas, not to make some reflections upon one's self ». Her reflection had been the hope that the Emperor would wish to grant peace and to give her back what she loved.

Her resentment of injustice to individuals continued to assert itself. Bred as much by the strength of her own character as by experiences of childhood, her mother's proscription, her father's banishment, it became, as she grew older, an irresistible impulsion to action. After Napoleon's final exile to St. Helena, there followed another period of terror in France, The White Terror, brought about by recrimination, envy, and politics. Among those who were condemned to death was the Comte de Lavalette, the head of the Postal Service. At the time of Lavalette's sentence, Barbé was Minister of Justice and in December, 1815, the Duchess took Madame de Lavalette to see her father to make a personal plea for clemency. She took Barbé's hand in hers and pled with sufficient vehemence to cause Barbé to weep. But he wept silently and without reply, upholding, as usual, the law; and Lavalette was only saved by a ruse. Two days before the date set for his execution, his wife visited him in prison and, donning her cloak and scarf, he made his escape.

Early in 1816, Barbé was reappointed President of the Cour des Comptes. Shortly afterward he bought a house across from the Church of the Madeleine, 1 Rue du Rempart, which later was numbered 1 Place de la Madeleine, and is now 3 Boulevard Malesherbes. As its first address indicates, it once was far from the center of Paris, and at that time had been the country house of the composer, Jean-Baptiste Lully. In the early part of the Nineteenth Century it still had a spacious garden extending from its rear to the Rue Boissy d'Anglas and sufficiently rural for Charles' dog to point a quail in it for his master to shoot. The Duchess, Charles and Eliza had apartments in the house, the first and only home they ever shared as a family.

For the next nine years their lives alternated between the Place de la Madeleine and visits to Charles' properties at Vaucresson and Ivry, to Noyers, and to the old Archtreasurer at the Château de Sainte-Mesme. At Sainte-Mesme, Lebrun established a mill for the weaving of muslins and printed tissues which gave employment to sixty workers each of whom was also provided with a house and a garden. He built a school for their children, for education was one of the old gentleman's continuous interests; and at Sainte-Mesme he took personal pleasure in instructing his grandchildren in sciences and languages.

Each summer the Duchess spent some time at Noyers which had been increased, since its purchase, by Barbé's acquisition of nineteen more pieces of land. Among these, and across the road from the Château, was La Maison du Bois, a small manor house with a walled garden where the Countess de Marbois was installed with an attendant and servants. Some years later, in a letter to Richard Willing of Philadelphia who had married Madame de Marbois' niece, Barbé told him, « Madame de Marbois' infirmity has not ceased, however she is calmer; she lives in the country in a retreat which I have made as agreeable for her as is within my power. Every desire she expresses is immediately satisfied. » Vast stretches of grain fields surrounded the Château and the Maison, and there was also a model farm nearby for agricultural experiments one of which developed an apple still known in France as the Marbois. Like, Lebrun, Barbé was a responsible chatelain, who repaired the roads of his commune and re-roofed the houses of the poor at his own expense. Through his beneficence, the village school was rebuilt and two acres of fertile land were given it as an endowment. In gratitude, every September, the school master went to the Château with a small sheaf of wheat and examples of the best penmen in his classes. These he formally presented to the Duchess.

During the winter months the Duchess continued to spend her time among officials and intellectuals. Contrary to one of the first fabrications of her legend, she did not hold a salon. She met old friends and foreign visitors among the people who came at certain evening hours to see Barbé — the Duchesse de Dino, Madame de Souza, newer friends such as the poet and playwright, Casimir Delavigne, and George Cuvier, the scientist, Villemain, the literary critic and historian, Suard, the permanent Secretary of the French Academy, the

Duc de Broglie, the Comte de Daru, and Guizot whose first public post had been in the Ministry of Justice under Barbé. From time to time she went to Madame de Barante and Madame Saint-Aulaire, to Madame de Rumfort, Madame Suard, and Madame de Dino. During the seven years from 1816 to 1823 when he was the American Minister to France, she saw Albert Gallatin and his family for Barbé was always a host to Americans. In 1827 James Fenimore Cooper, on his first visit to Paris, made haste to call upon Barbé, hurrying after dinner to pay what he called « a visit of digestion », explaining that on account of his great age, Barbé retired so early one was obliged to be punctual or he would find the gate locked at nine. Despite his age, Barbé was surrounded that evening by thirty people including Charles, Madame de Souza, Cuvier, Daru, Villemain, and the current American Minister, to France, James Brown. Villèle's reactionary government had just fallen and Cooper was impressed by the conversation he heard, remarking in his *Gleanings in Europe,* « It is necessary to understand the general influence of political intrigue on certain *coteries* of Paris, to appreciate the effect of this intelligence on a drawing-room filled, like this, with men who had been actors in the principal events of France, for forty years. »

There were also relations whom the Duchess saw frequently : Kellermann cousins and second cousins, Charles' surviving brother, Auguste, his two sisters with their children, and Alexandre's orphaned son, Jules. Aunt Kellermann died in 1812 shortly before the word of Alexandre's death reached Paris. But the only sharp severance of family ties for twelve years came with the death of the Maréchal at the age of eighty-five on September 13, 1820. Two days later at the funeral service in the Church of Saint-Thomas d'Aquin in Paris, Barbé read a short Adieu which Kellermann had dictated to him shortly before his death in which the old hero requested that, instead of vain eulogies over his body, there should only be said that in fighting to maintain liberty and the defense of French soil, he had softened as far as he was able the horror of war. Then he, who had served every ruler of France since Louis XV, gave his loyalty to the new king and, with remarkable prescience, concluded, if the peace and loyalty

predicated by Louis XVIII were destroyed by factionalism, civil war
and all its accompanying calamities would be inevitable. A month
later, following his request, his son, the new Duc, took his heart
to Valmy and placed it in the little obelisk that marks the site of the
victory.

Besides their official and intellectual prominence these friends and
relations of the Duchess shared the bonds of fervent patriotism and
moderate politics. Like them the Duchess retained an earlier
Eighteenth Century balance between emotions and judgements. Fads
or what seemed to her at the time to be fads, had no appeal. The
resurgence of an interest in religion, which had been stimulated by
Napoleon's concordat and nourished by Chateaubriand's *Le Génie du
Christianisme* and which was carried to excess by idle ladies of
fashion, appeared ridiculous to her largely because her religious requirements were answered by the rites of the Church. The tracts
written by titled female authors on the Fall, Grace, and the Foundation
of Dogmas were too superficial to attract her interest.   No one coming
to her door was ever greeted, as at many other houses, by a lackey
who instead of saying, « Madame is not at home », announced,
« Madame is at vespers » or « Madame is attending the sermon of
Father So-and-So. »   She was not tempted by such avant-garde pieces
of French Romanticism as *Atala* and *René*, as *Paul et Virginie*,
or Madame de Staël's, *De l'Allemagne*.   She was not prepared for
those vertiginous perfumes, for that madness of lyricism and art which
Gautier said were the ingredients of Romanticism.   And the early
clamor over the Greek War of Independence remained for a long
time only a noise in her ears.

More intimate matters gave her an immunity from much that
was modish.   One day in the summer of 1823, without any immediate
provocation, she lost her temper with Charles.   She created a scene
in which she called him soulless, infamous, and a thief.   Charles
expressed surprise and, good natured man that he was, held his tongue,
willing to believe that his wife's anger was a momentary tantrum.
But it was not; and as the months passed, the Duchess' behavior
toward him, in private and in public, became more and more perverse.

In Paris, where she and Charles ate in Barbé's dining room and the Duchess served the food, she stopped putting any food on her husband's plate and forced him to help himself. One evening in Barbé's salon, while she was reading aloud from a newspaper, Charles moved closer to her the better to hear. At his approach, the Duchess dropped the journal and screamed, « The monster has sworn he will be the death of me! » and she fled from the room. She later repeated this performance in the presence of Germain and Casimir Delavigne, and of her cousin, the Duc de Valmy. She began to ignore Charles altogether, never speaking to him, and when he asked her a question, keeping an obstinate silence. Her behavior became so embarrasing to others, especially her growing habit of vilifying Charles' character to anyone who would listen that the Duc de Valmy and the Comte de Daru each attempted to reason with her. For their consideration she informed them that Charles was truly infamous and wished to steal part of her fortune. After that she refused to go to the dining room and ate in her own apartment. Kellermann was so vexed with her that for a long time he refused to see her.

Charles always maintained that he knew of no good cause for her conduct except that in 1814, a grave indiscretion which disclosed a matter of no importance, had led, despite his attempts to placate the Duchess, to a coldness between them which became permanent. It was a situation he said he endured both in the hope his wife would relent and because he did not wish to inflict sorrow upon Barbé. But ten years later the Duchess' malice had nothing to do with the old indiscretion. In July, 1824, Charles' father the old Archtreasurer, died. Having missed a chair a servant was holding for him to sit on, he fell, hitting his head upon a large porcelain stove. The internal injuries he suffered quickly killed him. Shortly after his death, Charles asked the Duchess to give him a marble bust she owned of his father. To this request the Duchess, who had lost in the old Prince her truest friend, snapped back, « The only thing I have from my father-in-law is this bust; he gave it to me; I shall not give it to his unworthy son; I am willing to refrain from dishonoring the Duc de Plaisance as I could do by publicizing his conduct,

but he will have to comply with my demands ».   Her demands were
her independence — a legal separation, and full control of her half
of their joint estate.   Her reprehensible conduct was a carefully
planned strategy to secure them.

She had little choice.   When Madame de Rumfort realized in
1809 that her second husband — Benjamin Thompson, an American physician from Woborn, Massachusetts, who had settled in France
and been made the Comte de Rumfort — was a cad and she would
be well rid of him, the Duchess wrote to Charles asking him to
speak to Napoleon about a separation for her friend. « The laws
concerning these matters », she observed, « seem above all to be
directed toward young women of bad character who are tied to husbands, and the men who made these laws have, doubtlessly, suppos-
ed them to be reasonable ».   It was a man's world in which women
without honorable husbands had few rights.   Charles, however, was
an honorable man without designs of any sort, least of all upon his
wife's money; and he was not a cad.   The Duchess was an honorable
woman, and her reasons for wishing to be independent were also
honorable, but there was no law that permitted a separation because
of them.

Even with an indifferent wife Charles was content.   He was
well occupied by the management of his affairs and his attendance
at the Chamber of Peers of which, following his father's death, he
was made a hereditary peer.   He had a warm respect for Barbé
and Barbé's friends and enjoyed their company.   He had his horses
and his hunting to amuse him.   The Duchesse de Broglie found him
the most amiable man in the world.   « He accepts and sees everything on the bright side », she wrote of him, « he is at peace
with all nature. This natural peace is a most remarkable gift ».
While this was true, it described only a part of Charles' character
because, for all his reasonableness, Charles was dull.   He had been a
brave and earnest soldier with a mind adaptable to military manœuvre
and leadership, but is was neither an original nor an elastic mind.
Upon one occasion after Eliza had made a penetrating remark, the
Duchess called the attention of Charles' father to the similarity of

the girl's intelligence to his. « Yes », the old Archtreasurer replied
with no paternal pride, « that is something which passed clean through
Charles ». Now, after ten years of daily contact with him since
Waterloo, the Duchess was bored with Charles. It was the most profound and menacing boredom she had ever experienced and it wracked
her patience. It dampened her spontaneity and threatened her well-
being.

When Charles returned to live at home after the collapse of
the Empire, she had had at last the opportunity to fulfil her dreams
of an idyllic marriage. There is nothing in her letters to Charles
during the blackest days before Waterloo to indicate she ever relin-
quished those dreams. Friends said her display of aversion to Charles
in 1823 was sudden and unexpected, but there is no reason to believe
she had not tried since his return to attain the happiness for which
she had waited so long. The one thing she had wanted in life
was to have her husband with her, to have Eliza know her father, and
for the three to love one another. Granted her obstinacy, her
acknowledgment of failure must have been bitter. That she had had
only one child must have added humiliation; but she was too wilful,
too proud, and at the age of thirty-eight still too great an idealist,
to be satisfied with a marriage held together by substitutes for congenial-
ity and respect. Her actions after her initial outburst suggest a
conscious plan, a means of exploiting her one chance of escape from
a situation which had become intolerable and desperate.

The way was not easy. No divorce was recognized by the Church,
and no separation could be obtained on the grounds of incompatibility.
The civil code recognized but three causes for a legal dissolution of a
marriage : infidelity, maltreatment, and defamation. Since Charles was
never unfaithful nor abusive, the latter was the Duchess' only
chance. In despair, and to emphasize her intention, the Duchess made
use of another stratagem, distance. Taking Eliza with her, she began
to travel in Italy.

In October 1825, she and her daughter sailed from Marseilles on
La Madone du Laurier for Naples. Two friends were also aboard
the ship, the brothers Casimir and Germain Delavigne. Seven years

before, Casimir had become famous by the publication of the first of
his series of poems called *Les Messéniennes*.   These were neo-classic
odes which in lamenting France's defeat at Waterloo and the subsequent
pillage by her foreign conquerors, had appealed to the nation's
patriotism.   A few months afterward he added another ode on Jeanne
d'Arc; and a year later his *Les Vêpres Siciliennes* made him as
famous as Lamartine. In 1823 Talma and Mademoiselle Mars appeared in his play, *L'Ecole des Vieillards*.   Four months before he sailed
for Naples, he had been admitted to the French Academy.

Seventy-five years later a gaudy embroidery on this voyage was
woven into the Duchess' legend which depicted it as a voyage d'amour.
Casimir, so the fabrication went, having fallen desperately in love
with the Duchess, beseeched her to leave France with him and, succeed-
ing, set sail with her for Genoa.   As the ship left the port of Marseilles, Casimir beguiled the Duchess by improvising verses and by
quoting some he had already written.   But his attentions were soon
diverted by a rising wind.   The Duchess responded to the might of
the gale by having herself lashed to a mast better to enjoy the storm.
Casimir became repugnantly seasick; and as soon as the boat docked
at Genoa, the Duchess, disgusted by his weak stomach, deserted him.

According to Germain Delavigne who was aboard the ship to
Naples with his brother and the Duchess, the true reason for Casimir's trip was to regain his health after overwork; a respite ordered
by Casimir's physician.   The two brothers spent a year travelling
through Italy where Casimir wrote more poems for *Les Messéniennes*, and where he met and fell in love with the reader and
companion of Queen Hortense, Mademoiselle Elisa de Courtin, whom
he later married.   However, part of the winter of 1825-1826 was spent
in the company of the Duchess and Eliza.   Lady Blessington met
the two women with the poet and his brother in Naples that
autumn, among a group of English, Germans, Austrians, and Russians,
at the house of the Archbishop of Taranto who, her ladyship observed, « still presided over a posse of cultured cosmopolitans ».   A
year later, when the Duchess was again in Italy, Casimir sent her from
Paris a copy of his new *Messéniennes* and in the letter he wrote to

go with it, he asked her to accept the book as proof of his and Germain's gratitude for the trouble she had taken to reveal to them the beauties of Naples and of Rome. Both men, he wrote, had been tormented by homesickness, and in retrospect, Casimir realized what it must have cost her to have been so helpful to them. That memory, he added, was associated in their hearts with the loveliest and noblest emotions they had felt in Italy. It was hardly the letter of a cast-off lover.

Meanwhile, after those few months in Italy in 1825, the Duchess and Eliza returned to Paris. Their absence had had no effect upon Charles, and the Duchess reopened her campaign of calumny against him. She repeated that he was untrustworthy and infamous, and had tried to water her share of their common property. Still Charles made no legal move, and again the Duchess and Eliza took off for Italy. The only member of her family who made excuses for these excursions was Barbé. Writing in September, 1826, to his old friend Albert Gallatin, who had recently been named the American Minister to the Court of St. James, Barbé told him, « my daughter and grand-daughter are visiting several places in Italy for the sake of their health which I hope will improve and remain cured ».

And, indeed, the Duchess was working herself into such a frenzy of discontent that there was some truth in what her father wrote. Charles' continued tolerance drove her, when she returned to Paris in February, 1827, to outrageous extremes of conduct. She composed a defamatory memorandum against him and had a number of copies of it made. She even drew up a list of people, friends and members of the Chamber of Peers, to which she threatened to send the document. The situation became so grave that the Comte de Daru attempted to reason with her and failing, urged her to leave Paris. The Duchess reacted to this advice by screaming every time she saw her husband, « Help, he wants to kill me! » In an effort to stop the spread of scandal, Charles did all he could to avoid meeting his wife. He went so far as to absent himself from Barbé's salon when she was there. On March 31, the Duchess wrote to Gallatin suggesting that the United States should name him its first minister to Rome. Her

argument was that it would give her the pleasure of seeing him during
the winters she spent there.   In a postscript to this letter, she added,
that her health had been very poor during the last few years and was
only restored « by a mild regime followed in the calm that I have
found by placing myself at a distance from the Duc de Plaisance ».

In the same letter she thanked Gallatin for having sent her his
own news and « that of interesting » people.   Other faces besides
Charles' were increasing her unrest.   She was even dissatisfied with
Paris, and in this she had the support of one distinguished foreigner.
The poet, Longfellow, on his first visit to the city the year before, found
it gloomy, « built of yellow stone, streaked and defaced with smoke
and dust; streets narrow and full of black mud, which comes up
through the pavements, on account of the soil on which the city is
built; no sidewalks; cabriolets, fiacres, and carriages of all kinds driving
close to the houses and spattering or running down whole ranks of
foot passengers; and noise and stench to drive a man mad ».   These
inconveniences were redeemed in part for the poet by the elegance of
the city's gardens and its boulevards.   Partial redemption came to the
Duchess when she finally developed symptoms of what was known as
the Greek Fever.

Following the outbreak of the Greek War of Independence in
1821, the Greek Fever had spread to epidemic proportions over two
continents.   That the Duchess was immune to it for five years was the
result of a quirk of character — her stubborn resistance to matters
outside her personal interests.   Of course, she was aware of the
malady and of its origin.   Living with two Bonapartists, her husband and her father, who were also members of the current government, she could not have been uninformed about European politics.
Whatever else made up Napoleon's legacy to Europe, one of its most
far-reaching effects was the determination of the peoples who rose
against him to continue, after his disappearance, to assert their independence.   The fear of this growing nationalism in Italy, in the
Low Countries, and in Northern Germany sparked the entente between
Prussia, Russia, and Austria — the Holy Alliance.   From its headquarters in Vienna, Metternich was attempting to dictate a policy of

repression against all manifestations of liberalism and nationalism...
with but temporary success. The contagion of freedom had also pierc-
ed through the lethargy of four hundred years of Ottoman rule to
quicken the spirits of the Greeks.

Had politics been of no interest to her, the Duchess, if willing,
could have responded earlier to the Greek cause by reason of her
classical education. Neo-Classicism, that post-Rennaissance revival
wnich began in the middle of the Eighteenth Century, had surrounded
her since childhood. As their writings and tastes reveal, both Barbé
and Lebrun were products of it; and one architectural evidence of it
was as close to the Duchess as the Square on which she lived — the
Greek Temple that was the Church of the Madeleine. Not far off
in the Place Vendôme, as a commemoration of the victories of La
Grande Armée, stood a copy of Trajan's column. Both the American and French Revolutionists indulged in an image of themselves
as the direct heirs of republican Greece and Rome. Although the
French Terrorists found Marie-Joseph Chénier's play about the Co-
rinthian liberator of Sicily, Timoleon, too heady and proscribed it, the
Americans encouraged performance after performance of Shakespeare's
play of the liberty loving Roman, Coriolanus. It was not by chance
that the symbolic cap of the French Revolution was inspired by the
ancient Greek domain of Phrygia, nor that the government, of the
new United States commissioned L'Enfant to lay out its capital city.
L'Enfant, who had served as a French volunteer in the American
Revolutionary Army, was convinced the epitome of art had been reached by the ancient Greeks.

Under various guises Neo-Hellenism was hardly to be avoided by
any educated person in Europe or the United States. Jacques-Louis
David, the leader of the school of Neo-Classic painting, worked for the
French Revolutionists and for Napoleon. The buildings of the great
spas of England owed much to the inspiration of Greece. Lord
Elgin sent home his marbles in 1802. A year later Schiller wrote,
in pure Attic form, his play, *Die Braut von Messina*. The marbles
of Aegina were purchased in 1812 by Prince Ludwig of Bavaria,
godson of Marie-Antoinette and protégé of Napoleon, who, later

6

when King, built a new Munich in the Greek style. In the United States the building for the Second Bank of the United States in Philadelphia was modeled after the Parthenon. Near the same city, Nicholas Biddle built his country house, Andalusia, as a lovely Doric temple. Returning to Boston after two years of Greek studies at Göttingen and a trip to Greece, Edward Everett was made at that stronghold of Puritan-Hebraic studies, the college of Harvard, its first professor of Greek.

However, when the Greek War of Independence began, not all Neo-Hellenists, apostles of ancient Greece, became Philhellenes, supporters of the Greek revolutionists. The Greek scholar from Smyrna, Adamantios Coraïs, who had lived in Paris since 1788 and had spent his energy and scholarship in a modernization of the Greek language and translations of the Greek classics, early had misgivings. He thought the War was premature and the Greeks lacked sufficient political experience to maintain their independence. Later he changed his mind and became one of the struggle's most diligent propagandists. While every tenet of his art was anti-Hellenist, Delacroix was moved by one of the worst massacres of Greeks by Turks to express in paint a Philhellenic sympathy. Thomas Jefferson, a fervent classicist, declared while the American people offered ardent prayers for the success of the Greeks, he could not endorse official recognition of their efforts by the Government of the United States lest such action lead to foreign entanglements. President Monroe agreed with him, yet in presenting to Congress his Doctrine, which barred foreign intervention in the Western Hemisphere, he expressed wishes for Greek success.

The Foreign Ministries of Europe were equally averse for other reasons to the Greek War. As much as they favored Russia's intention to restrain any expansion of the Ottoman Empire westward, as much did they fear Russia's designs to annex Moldavia and Wallachia (Rumania). It was safer to use diplomacy within the frame of Europe as erected by the Congress of Vienna than to risk an upset of the status quo. In this opinion both the governments of England and the United States were supported by men who were engaged in business with the Levant. English trade with Smyrna — the only

Turkish port open to foreigners — was in the millions of pounds. Between 1820-1822 the merchants of Boston exported goods to the value of $1,500,000 to Smyrna and imported $750,000 worth. Such commerce was possible only so long as nothing was done to antagonize the Sultan.

But these economic and political tides, as beneficial to traders as to Metternich, ran out, drawn by the unpredictable force of popular idealism. The ideas which had fostered the American and French Revolutions, the dreams of nationalism, were too strong for them.

By the end of the Eighteenth Century the Greeks had already begun to bestir themselves and to act to overthrow Turkish rule. Their first attempt failed through lack of judgment. Trusting in Russia's wish to destroy the Ottoman Empire and relying upon the ties of the Orthodox religion shared by Russia and themselves, the Greeks of the Peloponnesus revolted in 1770 on a promise of Russian aid. For no apparent reason than caprice, Catherine II withdrew it. The lesson of the frailty of foreign promises was learned. By the beginning of the Nineteenth Century patriotic societies called, Philiki Etairea, began to be formed wherever Greeks dwelt from Odessa to Athens and across Europe. The first of these was formed in Odessa in 1814. Seven years later it raised an army of Greek residents in Russia which it sent, under the Phanariot, Prince Alexander Ypsilanti, to challenge the Moslems by marching into Moldavia to stir up a revolt. This failed because the Moldavians gave it no support. So a second lesson was learned : revolutions are made at home.

This was a lesson already understood by the Greeks who lived within the ancient boundaries of Epirus and Laconia and on the isles from Aegina through the Cyclades. Ypsilanti's fiasco occured in early March of 1821. On March 25th of the same year, Archbishop Germanos of Patras refused to obey a Turkish order to attend a meeting of the primates of Greece at Tripolitza, and, taking refuge in the convent of St. Laura, raised the standard of the Cross. Two days later, at the head of a mob equipped with old muskets, scythes, and ploughshares, he took the town of Patras. The Greek War of Independence had begun.

The first purpose of the Philiki Etairea was to spread propaganda, but before any of these societies were formed, the plight of the home-land Greeks under Turkish rule had been revealed. Chateaubriand, returning to Paris from his journey to the Near East, wrote, in 1811, in his *Itinéraire de Paris à Jérusalem,* of Athens under the rule of negro eunuchs of the Seraglio, of the Peloponnesus a desert with villages abandoned or burned, and the inhabitants, reduced to rags and to huts better suited to animals.   If, he wrote, had he ever believed absolu-tism to be the best of all forms of government, a few months in Turkey would have entirely cured him.   A year later, after his first visit to Greece, Byron published in London the first two cantos of *Childe Harold* and in 1813, *The Giaour.*   The last stanzas of the Cantos and the opening ones of the second poem were the laments of a Neo-Hellenist over subjugated Greece, over

> *...that sublime record*
> *Of hero sires, who shame thy now degenerate horde!*

Within months, wherever the English language was read, and it was read by educated Europeans as well as by Englishmen and Ame-ricans, these verses were known and quoted.   Harold Nicholson, writ-ing of the last months of Byron's life, says by 1821 they had done more than the intricate energies of Greek intellectuals such as Coraïs, or the intrigues of Phanariots such as Ypsilanti, to awaken European opinion to the existence of the Greek question, and to prepare men's minds for the upheaval which was so shortly to follow.   They became « the literary stimulus of the Philhellenic movement in Europe ».

Despite the Duchess' Anglophobia, it would have been impossible for her not to have known of the popularity of these verses, yet no records show she was moved by them.   Nor do any show she respond-ed to those other manifestations which were prompted later by the first Greek victories and which multiplied after the massacre on Chios in 1822 and Marco Botzaris' death in 1823 at Missolonghi. The slaughter of twenty thousand men, women, and children aroused horror and revulsion throughout the Christian world.   Sharing these feelings, Delacroix painted *Scènes des Massacres de Scio* which was hung in the Salon of 1824 and purchased by Charles X for the French nation. The death of Botzaris, the Souliot commander at besieged Missolonghi, quickly became a legend. David d'Angers carved a monument for his grave, a reclining figure (now in the Ethnological Museum in Athens) of a young girl resting on one elbow with the forefinger of her free hand pointed at Botzaris' name. In a letter to James Fenimore Cooper, the sculptor wrote he had put a Phrygian cap on her head to strengthen the symbolism, « thus she shall be a child of liberty, who exalts the great name of a hero who has died to defend her ».

In the United States Fritz-Greene Halleck was inspired by Botzaris' death to compose a poem which became one of the most popular in English in the Nineteenth Century. Beginning,

> *At midnight in his guarded tent,*
> *The Turk was dreaming of the hour*
> *When Greece, her knees in suppliance bent,*
> *Should tremble at his power :*

and after describing the hero's death, ended,

> *We tell thy doom without a sigh;*
> *For thou art Freedom's now, and Fame's —*
> *One of the few, the immortal names,*
> *That were not born to die!*

In a less rapturous frame of mind the young Victor Hugo wrote in *Orientales* a poem in which he asked a little Greek girl whether she preferred the gift of a flower, some delicious fruit, or a marvelous bird. The child replied, « Powder and shot ».

The same practical sense governed the men and women who, further inspired by Byron's death, formed Philhellenic Committees in Europe and the United States. Their purpose was to support volunteers from their own countries to the Greek army and navy, and to succor the Greek victims of the war. Those in Germany, Switzerland,

and France cared for Greeks who were expelled from Russia and Austria in retaliation for Ypsilanti's foray.   A group of German volunteers, among whom were Colonel Delaunay, Baron von Quass, and Lieutenants Kindermann and Fels, manned artillery at Missolonghi. In addition to a loan to the Greeks which Byron negotiated before his death, English Philhellenes supported General Gordon and Sir Richard Church in their reorganization of the Greek army.   They also raised £150,000 to build a fleet for Greece and paid Lord Cochrane £57,000 to command it.

Coraïs sent to Edwart Everett his translation of the appeal sent out by the Greek Assembly at Messina asking for aid « to purge Greece of the barbarians and to banish ignorance and barbarism from the home of freedom and the arts ».   Everett, who was also editor of *The North American Review*, published it in that magazine. There were Philhellenic Comittees formed throughout the United States from Maine to Louisiana and their donations to the Greeks were the first of the many which Americans have since given to foreigners in distress.   In 1827 alone, the Boston and Philadelphia Committees sent goods and money representing over $76,000.   The most famous American volunteer was Dr. Samuel Gridley Howe, who later married Julia Ward, author of the Battle Hymn of the Republic.   In 1824 Dr. Howe went to serve as a surgeon in the Greek navy.   Three years later he returned home to lecture for the Greek Cause and with the nearly $70,000 he so raised he went back to Greece and started an experimental farm, including a hospital, near Corinth.

With customary flair, the Greek Fever in France was a mixture of the fashionable and the practical.   Images d'Epinal depicting Botzaris' heroic deed sold by the hundreds.   Figures of Greek soldiers adorned clocks, ink-stands, and match-boxes. « Greek » songs were written and sung — marches, and even lullabys.   The French Academy set the subject of a poetry prize as *L'Indépendance de la Grèce*.   At dinner parties Greek caps were passed to receive donations from the guests.   Ladies wore dresses of a color called, Raisin de Corinthe.   At the same time the Philhellenic Committee in Paris collected 1,142,317 francs for arms and supplies for the Greek insurgents.   Yet despite these sights and sounds, despite the fact that two of Barbé's friends, the Duc de Broglie and Villemain, were founding members of the French Committee, the clamor over Greece remained for five years no more than a noise to the Duchess.   One can easily imagine her to have dismissed the French attitude as a fad.   Her tastes leaned neither toward republicanism nor toward social foibles. Besides her egocentricity, there was another reason for her lack of response : she was never influenced by ideas or causes unless they were personified for her by an individual, by some one she was certain she could trust with her allegiance.   Napoleon had won this from her for the Empire; Charles had won it for marriage. The only other person whom she ever so trusted was a man she met in Paris during the winter of 1826, John Capodistrias.

Born in Corfu in 1777, Capodistrias left the island after the French seized it in 1807 and entered the Russian diplomatic service. As a representative of the Tsar in 1815, he helped to negotiate the Treaty of Paris; in 1821 he was the Tsar's Prime Minister.   Because of his Russian sympathies he refused in that year to head the organization of non-resident Greek patriots.   Later, however, he acknowledged the justice of Greek determinism, and when the Duchess met him he was the revolutionary government's representative in Europe.   A man as stern in manner as Barbé, he gained her admiration by his single and profound dedication to Greece's welfare.   The selflessness of his endeavors was above suspicion.   He asked no recompense for himself; it was sufficient for him that the suffering of Greece be relieved and the example of Greece be honored.   These were percepts to which the Duchess was, of course, prepared to respond although unconsciously, since she made no identification of her personal gropings toward independence with those of Greece.   It would never have entered her mind to consider substitutes as solutions for verities.

Still the Fever took hold of her slowly, and it was not until her return from Rome in February of 1827 that she acknowledged the first call to freedom she had heard.   Then she did so spontaneously with those traits she was also indulging toward Charles — egotism, impulsiveness, and extravagance.   She forwarded to the Revolutionary

Greek Government 9,000 francs. Eliza, who was as impressionable as her mother, sold her jewelry to raise money for the Hellenic cause. Of the 14,000 francs which she received from the sale, she sent 2,000 to the Government of Greece and the remainder to the French volunteer, Colonel Fabvier, declaring, « I should rather help the Greeks than wear jewels for the rest of my life. » Thereupon the Duchess added 3,000 more francs to her own contribution.

In acknowledgement of these gifts, the Greek Foreign Secretary sent an effusion of gratitude addressed to The Most Philhellenic Ladies, Sophie de Marbois, Duchesse de Plaisance, and Her Daughter, Eliza, which read,

> *The Greek Nation, supported in its great and just struggle for Liberty by the contributions of Philanthropic Christians, and reinforced by their warm wishes, and having nothing else to offer, declares its eternal gratitude to its Benefactors, whose honored names will one day occupy a glorious place in its much afflicted history.*
>
> *In its list of Benefactors, the Greek Nation will rightly add your noble and praiseworthy names, grateful for your genereous gifts of money you offered, moved by sympathy for the sufferings of much afflicted Greece.*
>
> *It is natural that such philanthropic and noble feelings should characterize your persons. My Government offers you, through me, and from the Greek Nation, the warmest thanks and assures you that it will always consider you as its benefactors, and your honorable names will always be uttered with gratitude and respect by the present and future generations.*
>
> *Poros, May 13, 1827*
> *Foreign Secretary, G. Glarakis.*

In June, after receiving a promise from Capodistrias that he would visit her in Rome, the Duchess, with Eliza, separated herself from Charles by going to Euse to take the Waters. They took with them all the books they could find about Greece past and present, and a white Pyrenees dog named, Baris. After spending the summer in Switzerland, they crossed the Simplon in September and went down to Rome.

Along her route and while in Rome, the Duchess bombarded friends at home with letters denouncing Charles. At the same time she privately examined the alternatives she had. So long as Charles refused to free her, France as a place to live was out of the question. Apart from Naples where the Bourbons were again ensconced, she had, until now, enjoyed Italy. Over its landscape and ruins her knowledge of history and literature spread a pleasant luster. At Queen Hortense's salon in Rome she met creators and sponsors of the arts whom she considered interesting people to cultivate. Madame Mère, the Cardinal Fesch, and the Queen of Westphalia were also there. Guérin had succeeded Horace Vernet as head of the French school. Chateaubriand was the French Minister. But the two men she had particularly wished to see in Rome were not there. The United States Governement had retained Gallatin at his post in London, and Capodistrias, who had been elected by a new National Assembly the first President of Greece, wrote her in November that he was unable to join her. A few weeks before the Duchess had given another 14,000 francs in Eliza's name to the Greek Government and Capodistrias included his personal thanks in the same letter :

Bologna, Nov. 6, 1827.

It is not my fault, Madame la Duchesse, if I have not kept my promise to you and went instead to Agona. I well know that last year, when I was honored with your acquaintance in Paris, I promised to come and pay my respects to you in Rome, but other matters have interfered, and your most kind heart will not disapprove of the reasons for which I devote all my time to them, and in favor of which you have also shown a generous interest.

I have just received from Mr. Rhodokanaki information about your orders and I am answering him that I should like to receive the 14,000 francs here and in cash, the sum namely which your daughter donates to sweeten the very bitter sorrows of Greece, and I hope to be able to give you an account of the use we shall make of it, hoping it will satisfy and give pleasure to your daughter. May she kindly accept my gratitude, and you, Madame la Duchesse, my admiration and deep respect.

John A. Capodistrias.

It was following this letter that the Duchess made her choice. With no freedom to be had in France, with the arts of Italy and exiled compatriots already familiar, with an accelerated need for independence, she made up her mind to take Eliza and go to the font of freedom and the arts, to the well-spring of civilization. She wrote to Capodistrias of her intention to go to Greece in the autumn. She and her daughter, she informed him, wished to establish a home for War Widows in Athens.

It was a unique option stimulated as it was as much by misconception and optimism as by idealism. Greece in 1828 bore no resemblance to ancient Greece. Athens was still held by the Turks. Centuries of separation from Byzantium, and of neglect and pillage by foreign conquerors had turned the mainland into a country whose inhabitants subsisted on an eroded soil and whose only heritages from their pre-Christian ancestors were a passionate individualism, recklessness, and heroism. Seven years after the uprising at Patras, Greece and the Greeks were exhausted by their subsequent efforts to gain their freedom. The land lay wasted by foe and insurgent; the people, reduced by carnage and the hot-headed expenses of valor, were prostrate. There were still some of the Khedive's troops in Morea. After the rout of the Moslem ships at Navarino, England negotiated with the Porte for the withdrawal of the Egyptians. To make certain this was effected, France, whose army had hitherto been engaged in bringing Algeria to French terms, sent a task force to expedite the departure of the Moslems.

However, it cannot be forgotten that the Greeks won their own independence. Despite jealousies, intrigues, perfidy, despite needless waste of lives and land, the Greeks freed themselves and paid the cost with their own blood. Had it not been for their endurance, the governments of Europe would not have recognized their cause and would not have sent them aid. Their first examples of suffering and sacrifice won them the sympathy of freedom loving people in Europe and America. Byron's friend, Trelawny, gave an estimate of 3,000 foreign volunteers who fought in Greece. The names of those Philhellenes who died for Greece, which are listed on the wooden stele in the Roman Catholic Church in Nauplia, total 276. The number of Greek dead was uncounted thousands.

But the image of Greece free increased Philhellenic fervor. Madame de Staël's daughter, the Duchesse de Broglie, found the French expedition admirable. She wrote to Guizot, « I should like to be twenty years old, a man, and to go; it is a superb destiny! » Neither age nor sex deterred the Duchesse de Plaisance : she and Eliza were the only Philhellenic women who went voluntarily to succor Greece.

Their embarkation, however, was delayed. So far the Duchess' tactics to force Charles to institute a suit for a separation had been based upon her belief that fear of dishonor would paralyze his resistance. These having failed, she now decided to go to court herself, and she made known her plan by writing to friends in Paris, « with a rogue like the Duc de Plaisance, who knows no other restraints than the pillory and the scaffold, it is absolutely essential for me to have legal guarantees ». Such an action required her temporary presence in Paris, but despite her decision she postponed her return to France until she had dealt with an arrangement that meant more to her than either Greece's or her own independence — Eliza's engagement of marriage.

Two years before, while he was still in Italy, Casimir Delavigne had introduced the Duchess and Eliza to the Swiss painter, Léopold Robert. Now Léopold was again in Rome with his brother, Aurèle. The son of a peasant watchmaker of La Chaux-de-Fonds near Neuchâtel, Léopold was thirty-three in 1827. He was short and solidly built. A slight cast of his left eye was offset by his broad forehead and nose, by the luster of his eyes, and by his delicate mouth. A pupil of David in Paris during the Empire he had since become famous for two of his canvasses, *Brigands* and *La Madone de l'Arc*.

At the end of December he renewed his acquaintance with the Duchess and her daughter by calling upon them. It was an auspicious visit since both women found his simple, diffident manners charming, and he wrote the same evening to his mother and sister in Switzerland to say he liked them both. He found that they enjoyed Italy as people who knew how to obtain simple enjoyment which meant, he said, true enjoyment. « They are infinitely witty, » he wrote, « a thing which would annoy me were it not accompanied by an imagination in keeping with that which painters must have. » But he hastened to warn his family not to read into his interest any attachment of sentiment. On the contrary, they should consider the French ladies' rank and their connection with all that was greatest in France, and that Eliza would bring an income of 200,000 francs to anyone she married. They had invited him and Aurèle to go with them in the autumn to Greece. They knew Capodistrias and they would be completely at home in Greece, but Léopold added, there would have to be some very positive advantages for him before he consented to accompany them.

The Duchess set about to guarantee these for him. She lent Léopold newspapers; she sent prospective buyers to his studio in one of whom, the Duchess d'Istria, acclaimed a great beauty in Paris, Léopold saw nothing extraordinary. To a painter, he said, her looks were of no interest. Within three days in February of the new year, he received six notes, plus invitations, requests, and explanations of various kinds from the Duchess. She took him to a ball; she extracted a promise from him to go with her and Eliza to Orvieto after Easter. As her attentions multiplied, she used tact and flattery to coat her demands. In her letter introducing the Duchesse d'Istria to him, she explained the visit as a result of Léopold's fame, denying that she would think of sending anyone to him without first asking his permission since she hardly dared to suggest he go on outings for fear of appearing indiscreet in asking him to give precious time even to those with a taste for beautiful painting. In concluding her note she was equally sly asking Léopold to accept her distinguished sentiments and to believe that she and Eliza would profit with pleasure as always from any moments he might wish to give them.

She commissioned two paintings from him, for one of which she agreed to pay him 60 louis, and for both of which she dictated the subjects. One was to be the scene from the life of St. John in the Abbé Fleury's *Histoire Ecclésiastique* in which a hunter is surprised to see St. Francis of Assisi stroking a bird. The other was to be of Apollo consoled by the Muses after the god had been chased from the sky and has sought shelter with Admetus.

Of the two pictures only the *Apollo* was painted, and although it has disappeared some of its details are known from the diplomatic cajolery the Duchess addressed to the artist. The picture was to be a surprise for Eliza, and if Léopold spoke about it to anyone except Guérin, who was discreet, he was not to mention the Duchess' name. She wished the painting to contain eleven figures, one of which was to be her dear Baris, « a worthy dog of a shepherd god ». The muses were not to be larger than those of Jules Romain (whose painting of the same subject was in the Pitti in Florence), and the background was also to be similar to Romains'. She agreed that only Léopold could determine the proper size of the picture. « And, in any case », she wrote, « he can be assured that in stating my observations frankly to him, I should nevertheless be most willing to submit myself to his judgement; if I am unable to make him share my ideas, I have enough good sense to know that he knows infinitely better than I what is correct in painting. » In the conclusion to her letter she used two more ploys : she intended to hold him to his word about making excursions with her and Eliza after Carnaval; and she begged him to follow the example she was setting him and to drop formalities. Titles, she told him, were for Court where she no longer went and for the company of Princes and Ambassadors which she rarely frequented.

Aurèle, who observed these machinations with amused detachment, wrote home that Léopold now dreamt only of duchesses.   Léopold sent home descriptions of the two women.   The Duchess was
a woman of medium height and very thin, who had never been a
beauty.   However, her features were rather lovely and her face was
most expressive.   She was extremely intelligent, a fluent talker with a
quick wit.   She was so superior to other women of her acquaintance
that she was often annoyed by them and pretended she had no affi-
liations with them, an attitude which had gained her a reputation of
a great eccentric and had made her a figure of ridicule.   Léopold
admitted that she encouraged this attitude not only by being different
from other people but by her extraordinary ideas about the betterment
of the human race — ideas which she realized were inacceptable to
the old world of Europe.   Both mother and daughter were maniacs on
the subject of Greece and the Duchess' arguments about Greece had
made him a passionate Philhellene.   Gossip, he repeated, set the sum
she had given to the Greek cause at something like 100,000 francs.
She dreamt only of going to Greece to see it herself believing she
would find there the Golden Age.

It was the only time anyone even hinted that the Duchess might
have been a Bas Bleu.   She was intelligent and she enjoyed intelligent
conversation, but she was not an intellectual trading in ideas for their
own sake or for the sake of inviting attention to herself by her know-

Léopold had misgivings about the Duchess' notions and believed,
if she went to Greece, she would return with very different ideas and
settle in or near Rome.   As for Eliza, he said she was not at all good-
looking, but she had a sweet, childlike expression and, like her mother,
was a great talker.   She was a competent woman with a knowledge
superior to her mother's — perhaps to any young woman of her
class.   She knew Latin and ancient Greek perfectly and had definite
ideas about beauty of all kinds; but he thought she rather lacked
imagination and reflected her mother's opinions and based her entire
manner on that of the Duchess.   However, he insisted, the two women
were not Molière's Femmes Savantes, only enough like them to invite
ridicule.

It was the only time anyone even hinted that the Duchess might
have been a Bas Bleu.   She was intelligent and she enjoyed intelligent
conversation, but she was not an intellectual trading in ideas for their
own sake or for the sake of inviting attention to herself by her know-

ledge.   But she was capable of intrigue, as in her current dealings
with Charles and, as Léopold suspected, in her plans for him.   Under
the influence of her Philhellenism, he transformed the large figure
he was painting of a Roman sharpening his sword into a Greek,
describing it as, « the final thrust I am keeping for my Duchess ».

By the middle of March, the Duchess had confirmed his suspicions
by beginning to discourse to him upon the subject of marriage.   She
made it clear that, above all, her son-in-law should exhibit personal
merit.   She spoke frankly of her family and of her rupture with Charles.   But Léopold did not take the hint, and his relations with Eliza
and her mother remained those of a formal companion at dinner and
on the excursions they began to take together into the Roman countryside.

The dinners were long and rich : soup, several kinds of fish,
hot and cold veal with truffles, roast turkey, quail, *beccafini*, timbales,
puddings, ices, and sweets.   The trips were made by carriage by all
except Eliza who rode on horseback.   The first one was to Castel-
gandolfo, Albano and Ariccia.   If was an early Spring day and, although the trees were not yet in leaf, the ground was colored by
violets, periwinkles, and daisies.   The party halted to make bouquets
and to eat cakes and drink Trevi water.   The Duchess read aloud
some of La Fontaine's fables.   Léopold, a poor rider, dared to mount a
horse to ride beside Eliza, but the animal threw him and he continued
the trip in the carriage.

Such expeditions troubled him.   He enjoyed them but he resented the time they took from his work; and he justified his attendance
by the fact they would soon be over.   The Duchess and Eliza planned
to spend a month in the country on their way back to France and,
although they invited Léopold and Aurèle to go with them, Léopold
looked forward to their absence as an opportunity to finish his Greek
figure.   « I do not wish », he wrote home, « to step out of my
character. » But a tincture of Roman Spring and the temptation of
pleasure weakened his will.   Every Thursday and Sunday, he and
Aurèle accompanied the women on excursions.   A young Greek named
Simos, joined them and sat with Aurèle and the driver and the coats

on the front seat of the carriage while Léopold and the Duchess sat
behind.   The Duchess was delighted with her guests and said they
constituted a Republic of which she and Léopold were the executives
and the three others the citizens.   Each decision as to where to stop
or what to do was put to a vote which, through good nature and
politeness, was always unanimous.

Aurèle disdained this playfulness but, like his brother, he enjoyed
himself.   Eliza was taciturn, yet he admired the noble dignity of her
manner and respected her distinguished bearing. He found her prettier
than Léopold did; and her voice, almost as low as a man's, was
soft and gentle, and her inflexions added a charm to the purity of
her speech.   She was intense but not cold.   The Duchess, Aurèle
thought, was much livelier, precise in her diction and movements,
and very perceptive.   Her imagination got the better of her at times,
but her reminiscences of the Napoleonic court never failed to distract
him.

The Republic went to Monte-Rotondo where seated on the grass,
the Duchess taught Léopold the Greek alphabet.   They went on mule-
back in the pouring rain to Veio.   They spent two days at Tivoli
and at night, by torchlight, they climbed down into Neptune's grotto.
By day they visited the monastery of St. Nil where the Duchess read
the story of the founder from Fleury's book.   They talked of the
comet which could be seen in the night sky and was currently suppos-
ed to augur the end of the world, and the Duchess expressed a hope
that they would all be together at the moment.   Back in Rome they
visited the Rospigliosi and Colonna palaces, and one day the Duchess took them to call on Madame Mère's halfbrother, the Cardinal
Fesh, to see his noted collection of art.   Good Protestant that he was,
Aurèle summed up the Cardinal as a fine man which, he said, meant,
without malice.   Aurèle's religious reservations did not, however, deter
him from going with the Republic on Easter to see the illumination
of St. Peter's.

Two days later, preparatory to starting their journey home, the
Duchess and Eliza paid their official farewell calls upon Madame Mère,
Queen Caroline of Westphalia, and Chateaubriand, the French Ambas-

sador.   On Wednesday evening they dined with the Roberts and saw
a study (now in the Geneva Museum) which Léopold had just finished
of Baris, « the best », Aurèle called him, « the noblest, the bravest,
and at the same time, the most sentimental of dogs » who was equally
remarkable by being able to obey when his mistress addressed him
in Greek.   The next morning the entire Republic started north to
Orvieto.   At Sutri they rode donkeys to see the rock cut amphitheatre
where they were overtaken by a cloudburst and it was voted that
Aurèle should build a fire and serve some soup.   Baris became
enamoured of one of the donkeys and Léopold made a sketch of him
baying, whimpering, and licking the donkey's head.   They stopped at
Viterbo to see a Sebastiano del Piombo in the church of S. Francisco
and at Banagna to visit Lucien Bonaparte's villa.   They spent a
night at the inn at Montefiascone whose keeper, having learned of the
Duchess' advent, so raised his prices that the executive branch of the
Republic was forced, in order to obtain reasonable rates, to engage in
what Aurèle called, « Chinoiseries ».   Later in the evening they climbed the town's hill to watch the sun set.

Apart from arranging that Léopold and Eliza should be together
as much as possible, the Duchess had not lately made any references
to marriage.   At Orvieto, her tactics and tact brought success to her
desires.   Léopold and Eliza had fallen in love.   Just before they were
to part, Eliza encouraged Léopold to speak.   Love gave him elo-
quence and, as he wrote his family, the heavens opened for him when
Eliza vowed that she loved him.   He took her in his arms where she
was overcome by emotions.   The Duchess then appeared to bless their
union by placing Eliza's hands in his.   « What », Léopold asked his
mother and sister, « do you say to that ? In all the annals of history, has there ever been such an extraordinary event ? »

Yet as extraordinary as the event might seem, it was not, Léopold
added, either an impetuous or an irresponsible act.   Eliza was of age;
she was twenty-three and he was thirty-four.   She had refused to
marry the Marquis de Dalmatie, the eldest son of the Maréchal Soult,
and others of her own rank lest they could not share her ideas and
tastes.   She consented to marry Léopold only after mature conside-

ration.   For him, he said, the last days had been a dream of happiness.
Eliza was without doubt the best educated young woman in France
but her education placed no restraint upon « the vivacity of her
deepest feelings ».   If he had at first recoiled from marriage, it was
the better to leap into it.   He was well aware that the Duc de Plaisance would either place or try to place serious obstacles in the
way of the marriage, but Eliza had no great respect for her father
and had sufficient character to act as she pleased.   Moreover, the
Duchess, taking advantage of the acclaim which had been given in the
Paris Salon to his painting *Retour de la Madone de l'Arc*, was
attempting to secure the Cross of the Legion of Honor for him.   She
told him that she knew he did not care whether or not he received
the decoration but she thought he should accept it for his family's
sake.   He thought the Cross would not lessen the Duc's opinion of
him.   The wedding was to take place in six months, after the Duchess and Eliza returned to Italy and after Léopold had met them in
Milan to tour the Italian lakes before they all came back to Rome.
Ever timid, Léopold was now superstitious and begged his mother
and sister to keep his engagement a secret; he was so close to seizing
happiness, he was afraid that, being so near, it might elude him.

Leaving Orvieto, the Duchess and Eliza went on alone to spend
two weeks in Aix-les-Bains.   From there the Duchess wrote to Léopold
in Rome to enquire if he had gone home and, if not, would he join
her and Eliza for a tour of the Chamonix Valley and its glaciers ?
Léopold had not gone to Switzerland, and since he had begun work
on his painting *Moissonneurs*, he asked to be excused.   The women
went to Paris where, with Eliza's future assured, the Duchess intensi-
fied her campaign to force Charles to free her.   His only interest,
she said, was to get her money.   He had seized a house belonging
to her and she called it a swindle.   She brought forth the old memorandum of charges she had drawn up against him and consulted a
lawyer as to the means she might take to use it to her best advantage.
The lawyer found her imputations were grave but her facts were insuf-
ficient to support them.   Yet that years' assault was repulsed only
when it was pointed out to the Duchess that the scandal she was

creating could have obverse results; it could seriously embarrass Eliza.

At the same time, a sadder humiliation was in preparation for Eliza for without her presence and the Duchess' executive ability, Léopold began to have second thoughts about his engagement. He passed hours in self-doubt, torn between grief and joy. To the doubts of a peasant's son of the fitness of a marriage to a Duke's daughter, were added the fears of an artist for his independence. If he were certain, he wrote home, that he could bring happiness to the one he loved, he would devote himself wholly to that happiness; but the distances between Eliza and himself were not only of wealth and position but of upbringing. She was so fine, so rare that she frightened him. The few happy hours they had spent together were no promise of a longer happiness — of so long a one as a lifetime. Both she and her mother were convinced he could be the greatest artist of the century. This idea, he thought, was the real cause of their kindnesses and warm friendship, but these could well be destroyed and leave him bereft of the power to regain them. There was the Duc, too, to be considered. The Duc was most vain about titles and wealth, and Léopold was certain he would violently disapprove of such an irregular marriage for his only child. Certainly he would disinherit her, and this meant that Eliza would have only a third of the family fortune. This would still be more than 100,000 pounds of income and might satisfy the cupidity of other men, but Léopold asserted that money had nothing to do with his happiness. His anxiety was lest he acquire bonds that would make him dependent. He wrote, « I who have always sought to make my own way, in such an event should betray my character. » As for painting, « the charm of his life », he would be obliged to neglect it a great deal since both Eliza and the Duchess were so used to travelling it would not be easy for them to decide to remain in one place for six months.

Did this mean he was not in love ? Of course, he declared, he was in love, but above all there must be reason when one could still listen to it. Eliza was not beautiful — most people would say she was less than beautiful, however, she suited him « a genio », with

her merits and qualities he had a longing for her. A month later,
in June, he repeated these thoughts in another letter to Switzerland
and added that while he had not been given the Legion of Honor,
his *Madone* had been purchased by the French Government and
hung in the Luxembourg (it is now in Neuchâtel). « It is true »,
he remarked, « to call me a happy mortal. All my work is acclaimed and better received than I at first anticipated; my future looks
very bright but... with all this I am not happy. It seems to me if
death were to appear, I would not flee it. »

Some of this melancholy was pathological, the result of a lack
of self-confidence and of a sensitivity too weak to endure its weight-
iest stimuli. As his biographer, Dorette Berthoud, points out, Léopold
was intelligent enough to realize that his talent was limited, that « his
genius was without wings ». Upon this self-knowledge, the bitterest
burden for an artist to bear, was imposed the struggle between ambition
and love. In the summer of 1828 some of his pessimism was also
the effect of overwork which he had forced upon himself. He no
longer mentioned marriage or the visit which for two years he had
promised to make to Switzerland. Aurèle said he worked in a veritable
euphoria which he only broke out of when word reached him of his
mother's ill health. Then Léopold left Rome alone in late June for
La Chaux-de-Fonds. His mother, although very feeble, was able to
take a walk on the day of his arrival with him and his sister. Both
relatives were disturbed by what they knew of his engagement; his
mother, in particular, expressed grave misgivings over the success of a
marriage between a man and woman of such disparate backgrounds
and tastes. Seconded by her daughter, she used every argument to
dissuade her son from making what her instincts told her was a mis-
take. She died a few days later leaving Léopold exhausted by her
loss and defeated by her persuasions. Twice he wrote to the Duchess
and Eliza announcing his mother's death and the grief of his mourning and excusing himself for failing to keep his appointment with
them in Milan. To neither letter did he receive a reply.

Both the Duchess and Eliza were insulted by his conduct. First
things came first to them — what they decided were first — and

death was not one of them. To Léopold their silence meant that Eliza had deserted him in his sorrow and had destroyed the remaining hopes of their marriage. The truth, at least for Léopold — for no records exist of Eliza's feelings — was that he had never been truly in love with Eliza. Despite their attestations of his affection, the letters contain the suggestion that he cared more for the Duchess than for her daughter and that it was Aurèle who loved Eliza. In any case, Léopold went early in November to Milan, urged by no more than curiosity, to see if the Duchess or Eliza had left a letter for him there. When he found none, he continued with relief to Verona and Venice.

The Duchess and Eliza were already in Rome. The day after their arrival they wrote to Aurèle asking if Léopold were there and saying that they would be at home between noon and three in the afternoon to receive him. Aurèle went with trepidation in his brother's stead. The Duchess received him alone, complaining of a headache. She ordered Baris to be brought in and spent the rest of the call speaking of only the most casual topics. Aurèle had been prepared to face an angry Duchess since she had written him a few weeks before in a peevish tone of her intention to pass the winter in Naples, a city he knew she disliked; he was not, however, prepared for her icy dismissal. Although his pride was hurt, he was thankful he did not have to defend his brother's actions and he left heart broken over the effect the final rupture would have upon Léopold.

He need not have worried, for when Léopold arrived in Rome shortly afterward and learned of the visit, he cried, « What do you want me to say ? » He had had, he said, enough difficulties with the two women to make the discharge seem slight, and added that he had guardians in heaven who had upset a plan which would have confined him to a slave's life. He held no grudge and assured Aurèle he could put himself in their place. Such a marriage would have meant a complete break between Eliza, her relatives, and friends. Léopold had never thought her love for him strong enough to deprive her of her ability to think clearly. Her absence from him had given her the occasion to reflect and to reconsider. « If », he went on,

« I had not left her, the separation might have been different. It is infinitely better that it has happened now than later. »

Even Léopold's scars from pride were not deep and any sting they held was quickly soothed by work. He set out with Aurèle through the Pontine Marshes as far as Terracina to make sketches for his painting, *Halte de Moissonneurs dans les Marais Pontins.* Back in Rome in early December, he began a group portrait of the daughters of the Ambassador to Rome from the Low Countries, who were also the great-granddaughters of Madame de Genlis. Through the auspices of Chateaubriand who, in his *Mémoires d'outre-tombe,* listed Léopold among the best painters then in Rome, dignitaries of all nationalities began to visit the studio. The Princess Charlotte Bonaparte, the wife of her cousin, Prince Napoléon-Louis, asked to meet Léopold. Her curiosity was not entirely aesthetic. Her mother, the former Queen of Spain, accompanied her to the studio and on leaving enquired, with simulated innocence, if Léopold had had any news of their friends, the Duchesse de Plaisance and her daughter. The Queen said she had written them several letters but had received no reply. They were, she knew, somewhere in the Roman countryside and, understanding that Monsieur Robert was in touch with them, she begged him for their news. At this point Léopold noticed Princess Charlotte standing behind her mother with a malicious expression on her face, and at the realization that his private affairs were so well known, he blushed and answered that he had no precise nor recent news. The Bonapartes left in a huff.

The Duchess, of course, had not, as Aurèle guessed, gone to Bourbon Naples. During the winter of 1829 she and Eliza moved from town to town in other parts of Italy. In the Spring they returned for a few days to Rome, long enough to permit the Duchess to go alone to see the Roberts. Aurèle received her and listened while the Duchess told him that she and Eliza both realized that a wife who wrote and a husband who painted all day could never understand one another. She then withdrew her commission for a painting which Léopold had never started, and requested the letters Eliza had written to Léopold as well as a little gold box encrusted with mosaics which Eliza had given him. Two days later Léopold returned letters and box through his banker. And so ended the pathetic-comic idyll of a Roman Spring.

The Duchess and Eliza went back to Paris. Although Capodistrias had informed the Duchess it was inadvisable for her to try to go to Athens since the Turks were still there, the Duchess made preparations to go with Eliza at least as far as Nauplia, one of the few liberated towns in Greece and the one in which the President of Greece had set up the new country's capital. At the same time, she made a final onslaught upon Charles' reputation. Her tactics were the old ones of slander and misbehavior and they were no more effective than they had ever been. Charles remained unmoved. Friends pitied him and belittled her. Fortunately for herself and her family, the lure of Greece was stronger than her need to regulate a separation. It led her away. She set out to place herself at a greater distance in space than ever before from the Duc de Plaisance and to seize, for herself and Eliza, a province that was at an even greater distance in experience from anything they had yet known. She was convinced that Greece would be a new world, a fresh scene which she and Eliza would be free both to enjoy and to embellish. In the middle of October mother and daughter took ship for their new frontier. It was their final departure from France.

IV

NATURE STILL IS FAIR

Apollo still thy long, long summer gilds,
And in his beam Mendeli's marbles glare;
Art, Glory, Freedom fail, but Nature still is
fair.

Childe Harold LXXXVII.

On their way to the mainland of Greece the Duchess and Eliza stopped at Corfu. In accordance with custom before Travel Agents existed, the French Consul on the island, the Chevalier de Cussy, was apprised of their visit and, in keeping with their rank, he had invited them to be his guests. What he was not prepared for were certain aspects of their clothes and of their tastes. For travelling clothes, the Duchess had designed for herself and Eliza, flowing white robes and high, white conical hats from which depended long white veils. Eliza's skirt, because she rode horseback astride, was divided. In these Commedia dell'Arte costumes mother and daughter debarked, late in October at Corfu, attended by a retinue of servants, the precocious Baris, and, for some unknown reason, a pony which was not much larger than the dog.

The Consul soon found both women tiring and tiresome. Besides the originality of their dress, somewhere between the dinners they had served the Roberts in Rome, and Corfu, they had added to their ideas for the betterment of mankind, vegetarianism. Like all converts, they were also proselytizers, and they informed Cussy that they found it contrary to nature that their stomachs should serve as sepulchres for animals. Unchecked by conventions and inflated by adventure, they were dictatorial, and the Consul could never be certain what expression their lapses from orthodoxy would take. Learning that the Consul had only one child, Eliza observed, « if all men behaved like you and my father, the world would not last long; for if two only make one — admitting the book of Genesis to be correct — it is easy to calculate exactly when the earth's inhabitants will be reduced to the same number there were at the time of creation ».

The discomfited man's worse trial was the Duchess. Her notions of the actual state of Greece filled him with despair for what he was certain would be a painful disillusionment for her. But no one, least of all a consul on an island which had had no warfare, could tell the Duchess, the friend of the Greek President, the Philhellene who had spent the last three years acquiring all the information available about Greece, anything about conditions on the mainland. The bravery of the soldiers, the inspiration of the leaders, the suffering of the peasants, the dedication to freedom equal to the example set at Marathon, she knew better than he. She permitted no insinuations of personal bickerings among heroes, of civil strife, military incompetence, and above all, of Capodistrias' fallibility. She closed her ears to her host, and with Eliza spent most of her time exploring the island from horseback.

On these excursions the Duchess experienced what she had expected. Eliza riding astride in her billowing divided skirt, the Duchess on a side-saddle, both wearing their high conical hats, and accompanied by their attendants, the pony, and the dog, were greeted with respect by villagers and peasants. At first these apparitions struck the Corfiots dumb. They had not been granted a free show like them since the days of the Doges. But silence and wonder changed when word spread that the two women were on their way to aid Greece. After this knowledge, their public appearances were greeted by cheers.

In December, by order of Capodistrias, John Miaoulis, the son of the great Admiral, brought his father's flagship the *Ares,* to Corfu to take the Duchess and Eliza to the mainland. While the

Consul expressed the formal words of parting required by the
ladies' rank, the citizens staged a demonstration in their honor.   Four
thousand of them lined the harbor's ramparts and waved goodbye.
As many others as were able crowded into boats and escorted the
Ares out to sea shouting, until the ship was out of sight, « Vive la
France! Vive la Grèce! »

At the Duchess' request, the *Ares* made for the scene of
the first uprising of the War of Independence, Patras.   Again, following the custom of travellers of the time, the Duchess had informed
the French agent there of her arrival.   She also asked him to find
a small house for her to occupy during her stay, which would have
a court and a garden.   To this request the Agent had replied by
explaining that, owing to canon fire and a conflagration set by the
Turks in 1821, most of the buildings of the town were in ruins and
the remaining ones offered no accommodations such as she desired.
It was even impossible to find a habitable room.   As usual, the Duchess was undaunted.

The *Ares* passed between Troukis and Papas at dawn one
morning.   Missolonghi lay too far off and too low to be visible, but
to the Northeast the heights of Varassova stood out guarding Aetolia
and the Corinth Gulf.   Ahead were the slopes of Panakhaikon with
the remains of the Frankish citadel; and what was left of Patras lay
at its foot.   A little later in the morning the *Ares* tied up.   The
French Agent was on the mole to greet the travellers surrounded
by a large, idle crowd of Albanians in goat skins and Greeks in
fustanellas.   The crowd gawked at the two foreigners, at the peculiarity of their dress, at their animals, their servants, and at the old
Admiral's son.   It stared without speaking at a parade, led by the
Duchess and the Agent, until the figures disappeared among the ruins
and a commotion on the ship brought its attention back to the water-
front.   As shouts in Greek and in French were exchanged between
the *Ares* sailors and some of the Duchess' men, pieces of furniture
and numbered sections of a wooden roof and walls were unloaded.
During the day, while the crowd muttered and the seamen and servants
continued to bawl, the sections were joined together.   When the Du-

chess returned in the late afternoon, her prefabricated house was ready for her.

Patras, however, was a disappointment. Although it was the first soil of Greece upon which the Duchess had stepped; although it was holy ground as it were, each in its way, Missolonghi across the bay and the butts of Zeus' temple up the Alpheus at Olympia, the town was unrewarding. It was in ruins. The weather also was unfavorable, being cold, rainy, with gusty winds. In late December, the Duchess left and sailed for Nauplia.

Keeping the shores of Cephalonia and Zante to starboard, the *Ares* moved south past Navarino (ancient Pylos), across the Messanian Gulf, by the tip of Mani, past Cytheria, and north into the Argive Gulf. As the New Year began, the wild coast of Arcadia stretched to port, then came Spetsai, and, as the bay narrowed, Larissa marked the beginning of the Argive plain facing the Palamidi. Finally there were Burdzi and hill-borne Nauplia. It had been a voyage of refreshment and preparation. The coasts with their wrench between promontories and valleys, the dominion of graven mountains over graven shoreline, were a revelation of Time's long tax on Earth. The name of each locality was an identification and an inspiration... whether it was Navarino and meant Nestor or Lord Codrington; whether it was Mani and meant Mavromichalis; whether Cytheria and meant Helen or Watteau; whether Nauplia was Nauplia and the hope of Greece. Whether the Duchess' responses to them were clues to her own partiality to plain dealing and elegance, to her susceptibilities to egotism and aspiration, clues to what had brought her where she was.

On January 3, 1830, the Duchess and Eliza debarked at Nauplia. At the request of President Capodistrias, the Mayor of the capital received them on the jetty and escorted them to his house. The *General Newspaper of Greece*, published at Aegina, announced a few days later,

> *The Duchess of Plaisance arrived at Nauplia with her daughter from Corfu on December 22 (O.S.), after a long*

voyage on the brigantine Ares, *commander, J. Miaoulis
which was put at her disposition by the President.*

*Among those who have assisted the Greek Struggle with
generous contributions we must mention this French
woman whose name evokes the most lasting virtues of the
mind with the most humble benefactions. The Greeks are
delighted to have among them these two noble foreigners.
The great memories of which our fatherland has so many
and their desire to be present at the first attempts Greece
is making toward a national renaissance have inspired them
to come to Greece.*

*Our struggle, we hope, shall justify the aid they would
care to offer Greece hereafter.*

In antiquity, Nauplia had been under the control of Argos.
When Pausanias saw it about 145 A.D., it was deserted, but under
the Byzantine Empire, and under the Franks and the Venetians,
who called it, Napoli de Romania, it regained its prominence as a
port. The Turks captured it in 1715; the Greeks won it back
in 1821. As the new capital, the town covered about a third of
the space occupied by the Twentieth Century one. Structures, made
of stones from all ages, pushed against each other down the hillsides.
Many others were hovels of wood and mud bricks. Here and there
a tall and pompous edifice, once the home of a wealthy Turk or
an earlier Frank or Byzantine, rose above the jumble. The streets
were zigzags of rutted mud occasionaly leading to a small square;
and, in accordance with revolutionary custom, some of the old streets
had been renamed for new heroes such as Ypsilanti and Miaoulis.
There were three cafés offering coffee, fruit punch, and narghiles.
Small traders did business in the Turkish manner from open stalls.
Pedlars spread an assortment of wares on the ground : string, flintstones,
needles, thread, sulphur, and firearms. The most attractive stalls
sold fish, fruits, and bread. In Plane Tree Square public scribes
wrote for the illiterate; a German had opened a bookstore for the

educated. Three or four tailors repaired European clothes and all made fustanellas.

Into houses which for centuries had sheltered a population of three thousand, now sixteen thousand people attempted to cram. The original inhabitants were lost in a cosmopolitan host in which members of the government formed the smallest part. Soldiers and sailors from the French task force were still about. Foreign legations had arrived; Phanariots had moved in. The Philhellenic Committees had established headquarters in the town; and a large number of non-Greeks sat about hoping to be employed by the new administration. Now and then there were incidents reminiscent of an American frontier settlement; duels were fought and at least once, a thwarted lover took a shot through a window at the lady's husband. More prominent than the black coated officials, and foreigners, of Klephts in billowing trousers and fustanellas, were the ragged refugees.

While Morea had been cleared of Moslems, fighting continued in Acarnania and Attica. Athens was still not free. The refugees stayed on preferring the miserable safety of Nauplia to the risk of worse horrors at home. They slept in tents made of mats. There had been no harvest of any size from 1826 to 1828. J. R. Lieb, who made a report on the refugees for the American Philhellenes, wrote that their children were naked and discolored. « How they live, Heaven alone knows; probably *upon grass and a few berries,* cockles, and the little leavings of those less hungry than themselves. »

Upon her arrival the Duchess immediately sought to solve her own housing problem and, previsibly, succeeded in securing almost an entire house by renting most of the rooms in a small hotel. The hotel was not much of a place since nothing was in Nauplia. Comforts were not to be had. A few people owned a sofa and mattresses; most had a rug to sleep on, a wooden table, and some wooden stools. Many had no stools. Before leaving for Greece, Capodistrias sent his furniture to Nauplia. It was uncrated and in place when he arrived, but the amount and quality appeared so pretentious, in constrast to what the most fortunate people possessed, that the President had it put back in its cases and the cases stored.

The idea that it could be in bad taste to be more comfortable than the people about her never troubled the Duchess. To deprive herself because others were deprived was not a matter of taste but of sense : to do so did not relieve poverty, it increased it. She had no feeling of responsibility for destitution, and philanthropy, in the meaning of a desire to help her fellowman merely because he was poor or weak, was offensive to her. She hated squalor whether of a beggar or of a refugee, and ignored those who were frail of body or of mind. It was apparent to her that the hope of Greece lay with men and women, whether poor or fortunate, who were talented, healthy, and clean; and immediately after her arrival in Nauplia, she began to sift the worthy from those she considered to be unfit.

Her task was made difficult as much by political reasons as by the limits of her preference. The Greeks were still divided among themselves. In 1823 after the first Greek victories over the Turks, the War of Independence had been hampered by an internicine struggle for power between factions of which one was led by the Phanariot, Mavrocordato, and the Souliot, Marco Botzaris, in Missolonghi, and the other by Colocotronis and the Petrobey in the Peloponnesus. Even in 1830, the mainlanders and the islanders remained distrustful of their kin, the Phanariots. Those descendants of the Greeks of Byzantium had been relegated by the Turks to the district in Constantinople called, the Phanar, where, while allowed religious freedom, they were deprived of most civil rights. As a consequence, they exploited the limitations of their ghetto existence and became traders and by reason of their ecclesiastical dealings with the Sultan, they became diplomats. Contacts with the West permitted them to obtain European educations and to develop European manners and tastes. Although they were of Greek blood and were united by their religion, language, and patriotism with the people of Greece, differences in experience threatened a mutual understanding with the homeland Greeks. The latter found the Phanariots arrogant; the Phanariots found them uncouth. A man like Petro Mavromichalis, the proud, rugged chieftain — who as leader of the clans in Mani had paid tribute to the Turks by presenting the gold on the blade of his sword —

had little in his character in common with John Capodistrias and Phanariots in the subtleties of law and diplomacy. George Finlay, the Scots historian, who upon his arrival to serve in the Greek navy had startled Byron by his resemblance to Shelley, wrote, « The small stature, voluble tongues, turnspit legs, and Hebrew physiognomies of the Byzantine emigrants excited contempt as much as their superfluous splendor awakened the envy of the native Hellenes. »

There was also the factionalism introduced by the European Powers. Even after Greece had been cleared of Moslems, England, France, and Russia, still wary of the Sultan, recognized the Ottoman's rights to Arcarnania and a part of Aetolia. The Duke of Wellington, then Prime Minister of Britain, justified the action « so as not to be a vassal of Russia, she (Greece) should be as small as possible so as not to be a danger to Turkey ». After which each of the three Powers hastened to send an agent to Nauplia to further its own interest. The result was inevitable : the Greeks, already divided for historical reasons, became sub-divided for political ones; and there grew up an English, a French, and a Russian Party.

To these divisions, Capodistrias added another harmful element. By training and by experience, he was pro-Russian. Even more disturbing, was his disdain of his electorate's qualifications for self-government. He had no confidence in their training for democracy; and in conversations with the Duchess shortly after her arrival, he informed her that he would never grant a constitution to Greece. « To be able to govern this country », he told her, « all Greeks over forty years of age should be dead. » Since he fitted his actions to words, the Greeks separated themselves into those who were for and those who were against the President.

The Duchess reacted to these varieties of revolutionary behavior in terms of her idealism. Capodistrias' attitude puzzled her, but she did not permit it or the other manifestations of discord to discourage her. She had not come to Greece to engage in politics. Nor had she come to enjoy with Phanariots, the amateur theatricals, musicals, and card playing with which they filled their time when not manœuvering for power. Nothing but proofs of what she considered to be unqualified devotion to the future of Greece satisfied her, and these she found to her satisfaction among the former fighting leaders of the Revolution : Islanders and Klephts, the Admirals Miaoulis, Canaris, Tombazis, the mainlanders, Zaimis, the primate, Costa, the brother of Marco Botzaris, and above all, the Petrobey and his family, the Mavromichalis.

She was stringent, and in her own terms, she was right. There was everything to be done for the future of the country from education to rebuilding towns, to planting fields, to caring for war orphans, to cleaning the streets of Nauplia; and she quickly made another choice. Phanariot women had had the opportunity of education — the wife of John Caradja, who was in Nauplia with her husband, had been educated in Paris — but from long custom, native Greek women were illiterate. To correct this the French Philhellenic Comittee had sent Madame Volmerange to Nauplia. In keeping with her prejudices, the Duchess decided to educate only exceptional girls of the old fighting families; and in keeping with her idealism, she almost wore herself out trying to choose them.

Two weeks after her arrival, she took Eliza — who thought her mother's discriminations were exaggerated and surreptitiously gave money to assist all refugees — to Aegina to sift the war orphans in the home Capodistrias had established for them there. Back in Nauplia, Eliza occupied herself by reading her grandfather Lebrun's translation of the *Iliad*, and by riding among the victims of the war to find traces of those Hellenic forces which once had conquered Trojans. Accompanied by an interpreter, the Duchess spent her days making enquiries into the fitness of orphans and in sorting hundreds of children. At night she returned to the hotel exhausted, but she forced herself to read whatever literature was at hand that dealt with the regeneration of Greece — until she fell asleep.

In March she made her selection. She chose twelve girls for whose instruction in Greek and Greek history, and in the French language and in French history, she would pay. A decree, dated March 19, 1830 (O.S.), issued at Nauplia and signed by the President and the Minister of Education, read,

To the Duchess of Plaisance who has undertaken the education of twelve Greek girls and has engaged a teacher for the purpose, the virtuous widow of the late (Professor) Cleovoulos, we give the proper thanks of the Government and assure her that we shall continue her work, which future generations will always remember was undertaken by the Philhellenic and charitable Duchess.

Tired by her exertions and beginning to be disturbed by political events, the Duchess with Eliza, made a tour of Morea in the early summer of 1830. Even with the supplies and servants at their command, it was not an easy trip. The horses they rode were small, lean, tough, with the short, uncomfortable gait of their size. There were no roads; ancient tracks cut across mountains and through gorges. The guides knew the countryside, the river fords, and here and there a villager who might part with some food. If there was no chieftain to whom the Duchess carried an introduction, the party camped out, sleeping on mattresses. The sun was hot; the air on the heights, thin and dry. There was no shade, and the dust blew through the veils of the conical hats. Only at night, by a stream or a river, among willows, poplars, and oleanders, was it cool. Yet the land was its own recompense and revelation.

The Duchess had already made excursions from Nauplia to the silent theatres at Epidaurus and Argos, to the battlements of Tiryns, and to the Lion's Gate at Mycenae. Now she passed Lerna where Hercules wrestled the Hydra and Dimitrios Ypsilanti repulsed Ibrahim Pasha. Riding over steep Ktemias, she went down into Arcadia. Hermes oaks gave a sheen of brownish green to the mountains; the ravages of war had left the plain of Tripoli a limbo. Nothing remained of the city itself for Colocotronis had massacred the Turkish population in 1821, and the Egyptians left no remaining wall or inhabitant when they retook it in 1824. But to the North was the site of Mantnia where Epaminondas died, and to the South, Tegea, where Orestes fled. Beyond Lake Taka the track led to Laconia through broken stumps of vineyards and olive groves, across high open valleys and into a narrow gorge. To the east was Parnon and opposite it the lowering might of Taygetus. A stretch of huts bore the name of Sparta whose original site no one then knew. To the West, across the valley, hung forsaken, Christian Mistra.

At Mistra, the caravan turned back to Nauplia. The Duchess was thoughtful. The scenery explained much about her Klepht friends. Roaming the vast, spare mountains, they had become hardened, self-reliant, and suspicious of men less rough-hewned than themselves. The expanse of landscape, the strength of the mountains, the immutable splendor of earth and sky had acted for centuries upon them as a goad to freedom. No other country had so effected her. Everything about it, air, light, forms, the broken columns of antiquity, the ruins of the recent war united to quicken her own longings. Greece had begun to extract its allegiance. All symbols of its ancient and modern ideals were now symbols of her own. She was positive that the nation's future was safer with the raw intentions of the old leaders than with the craft of the new politicians. She returned to Nauplia to acknowledge her distrust of Capodistrias.

One hundred and thirty years later opinions remain divided about the President. Historians differ; and among modern Greeks there are those who defend him and those who denounce him. On one quality only is there agreement, the one which first attracted the Duchess : Capodistrias' lack of self-ambition. He believed, with Coraïs, that the Revolution was premature and he never hesitated to express his opinion that « the Powers should destroy the Greek Revolution by establishing a monarchal government in order to end the scandalous and sanguinary scenes which make humanity shudder ». At the same time, Finlay noted, Capodistrias never failed to insinuate that he alone was fit to govern Greece. He considered himself to be the best of patriots and, within his unfortunate limits, he was. He wished Greece to be free; he felt his mission was to see it was free; but by his aloofness and tactlessness, he betrayed his mission. His reform measures in banking, currency, taxation, local government, and education proved futile because the two foundations of stable government were missing : law and a strong civil administration. The police were allowed to be tyrannical, and the press was throttled. The President packed the Senate with his henchmen, and in July, 1829, he opened the National Assembly wearing a Russian uniform. Men, elected to the Senate, like Mavrocordato and the Islanders, refused to take their seats.   When word reached him that the Powers had named Prince Leopold of Saxe-Coburg to be King, Capodistrias, determined not to share his power, frightened off the Prince by writing him alarming descriptions of chaos and intimating that the Protestant Prince would have to change his religion.   Léopold resigned, and later chose to become the King of Belgium.   The result in Greece was a President-Dictator and a police state.

The Duchess showed her discouragement.   As a foreigner, as a Philhellene, she admitted to herself that there was little more she could do to correct the situation in Nauplia.   Therefore, after giving money to support the Opposition, she took Eliza and went to await a shift in events in the more congenial atmosphere of Aegina.

Aegina had been a refuge since 1821 for the Greek population which was driven from Athens by the Turks.   During the Revolution it became the cultural center of Greece.   Capodistrias used it as his first capital before moving the government to Nauplia; but few of the writers, poets, or journalists followed the President and most of the writing and publishing in the country continued to be done on the island.   Another attraction it held for the Duchess was that many members of the Opposition lived there.   In addition, the flats around the town still held a pleasant stand of olives, figs, almonds, and vineyards.   Tracks led upward across the island to the ruins of what was then thought to be a temple of Athena, the storied ruins high above the sea, known since 1901 to be of a more ancient goddess, Aphaia, whose sculptures were those sent to Munich in 1812 by Prince Ludwig of Bavaria.

Accommodations on Aegina were as poor as those of Nauplia, and again the Duchess took rooms in a shabby hotel.   Their meanness did nothing to improve her frame of mind.   She complained bitterly to the visiting English Captain Trant of « wretched living conditions »; and Trant gained the impression that she was « terribly deceiv-

ed in her classic dreams ».   She had intended, he wrote, to spend the
rest of her life amid the ruins of Athens. However, Trant observed,
« Should she remain, it will be in her power to do a great deal of
good; but she must turn her attention to the living, not the dead. »

Although unaware of what the Duchess was doing for the living,
Trant was correct about her attachment to Greece.   Her idealism had
not been destroyed by political rot.   Her faith assured her this condition could not last forever, and the proof of her faith was her
purchase of land in Athens.   It is not known if the Duchess went
to Athens at this time.   The Turks still occupied the Acropolis, but
owing to the Peace Terms between the Powers and Turkey, their
tenure was coming to an end.   The city was safe enough for Capodistrias to visit it incognito and for him to send there the Greek architect, Cleanthes, with his German friend and colleague, Schaubert, in
order to study the extent of the devastion and to draw up plans
for its reconstruction.   In these circumstances, and given, the Duchess'
character, it is not likely that she brought real estate sight unseen.
Be this as it may, records show that early in 1831 she owned parcels
of land in and near the city and had signed a contract with Peter
Mertrude, a relative of the French Consul, to act as her agent.   Under
this agreement, the revenue of her land was to be divided into three
equal parts : one third to be paid to the Duchess and Eliza, another
to the agent, and another to the cultivator of the land.

Even so, the Duchess was restless.   She was physically uncomfortable and impatient.   The President was increasingly ruthless and had
begun to throttle the press and to throw his adversaries into jail for
indeterminate periods.   Under the rival influence of the English and
French Chargés d'Affaires, the political factions were encouraged in
their disagreements, and the Maniots were in open revolt against the
government.   She realized that their future, like their past, the Greeks
must make for themselves, but the time they were taking to learn and
understand what was required of them irked her.

On May 31, 1831, she and Eliza sailed for Zante where,
after seventeen months of makeshift lodgings elsewhere, the Duchess
found a house to her taste.   It was on the coast, surrounded by

trees of lemon, oranges, pomegranates, palms, and eucalyptus. It had a garden which the soft sea air kept in a glory of color and scent. But Nature, at last fair, was not enough. In July the Opposition met on Poros to set up a separate government. In August the old Admiral Miaoulis, disobeying the President's order to surrender his frigate, *Lias* to a Russian admiral, with courage and pomp, burned it. Yet Capodistrias remained in office, and in his latest affront to justice, he answered a plea for a truce from Petro Mavromichalis on behalf of the Maniots, by throwing the Petrobey into prison.

This act chastened the Duchess; and it was in depressed spirits that the Chevalier de Cussy found her when he made a trip from Corfu to Zante in September. Word had already reached him that the Duchess now admitted what he had told her about Greece to have been correct, yet on the day he called on her in Zante, neither she nor Eliza was inclined to make any formal admissions of error. The Duchess went only so far as to say, « There is, in fact, a great deal still to be done about and improved in the habits and political education of the Greeks before they become a people among whom one would wish to spend one's life. » It was the statement of a proud woman and it gave no hint that the same woman could swallow her pride and swallow it quickly. As a consequence, Cussy was unprepared the next day, when he boarded the boat to return to Corfu, to find the Duchess and Eliza with their boxes and retinue already on deck. Before he could speak, both women admitted to him without embarrassment, that they had had enough of Greece and the Ionian Isles and were returning to France. Eliza astonished him by adding, « Life is only a series of illusions. » Eliza was twenty-seven, and her broken engagement and her Greek experience had left their marks.

Instead of going to France, the Duchess and Eliza went to Rome for word had reached them which made any return to Paris unnecessary. Desertion had proved to be mightier than calumny. The Duchess' absence of a year and a half finally convinced Charles that she would never return to him, and in May, while the Duchess was

on Aegina, he instituted legal proceedings in Paris for a separation
on the grounds of defamation.   Witnesses at the final hearing included
the Duc de Valmy and the Comtesse de Plancy who testified to
the Duchess' invidious behavior; and in August while the Duchess
was on Zante, Charles received an uncontested separation.

The Duchess received the verdict as if it were an anticlimax.
Although she had won control of her share of the assets she and
Charles' had held in common, she was too engrossed with Greece
to consider her economic independence as more than a technicality.
In Rome, in mid-October, the more important news reached her of
the assassination in Nauplia of Capodistrias by two of her friends,
George, the second son of Petro Mavromichalis and, Constantine, the
bey's brother.

The deed was an act both of political and personal revenge since,
in his efforts to centralize power in his own hands, Capodistrias
had removed all members of the Mavromichalis family from official
positions and, goaded by jealousy of the clan's influence in Mani,
had endeavored to render three of its leaders incapable of acting
against him.   By a series of double-crosses Petrobey was again arrested, accused of insurrection, and locked up.   His son and brother
were also arrested and taken to Nauplia where, although prisoners,
they were allowed the freedom of the fortified town.   This was a
concession which permitted them on the morning of October 9, 1831,
to be able to stand, each on one side of the door of the church
of St. Spiridon, at the hour when Capodistrias usually attended mass.
As he approached the church, the President noticed the uncle and
nephew : he hesitated as if puzzled by their presence, then started
toward the door.   At the threshold, a bullet entered the back of
his neck.   He swayed, and as he fell a dagger was thrust into his
chest.   Constantine Mavromichalis was instantly slain by fire from the
gun of one of Capodistrias' orderlies and his body dragged to the
Square in front of the President's house where it was exposed to
public abuse.   Later it was thrown into the sea.   George, after escap-
ing to temporary asylum with the French Resident, was arrested, tried,
condemned, and executed by a firing squad.

The Duchess accepted the event as the final act of the liberation of Greece and the justification of herself. To her Capodistrias' death could only be a good riddance. The Klephts had confirmed her confidence in them as the true leaders of Greek Independence. They had been harried and duped once too often and had destroyed their country's second despot, the man who threatened to betray the freedom they had wrested from the Turks.

To the majority of Philhellenes Capodistrias' death came as a shock and as a surprise. The shock befitted the nature of the deed; the surprise arose from lack of knowledge. Impartial reports on conditions and events in Greece had been almost non-existent since the beginning of the War. From the moment he arrived in Greece Capodistrias began to develop an effective publicity in his own behalf by sending his own reports on his work to friends in Western Europe. His success became evident a few weeks after his death in a long letter, published in the *Journal des Débats*, which was written by his old friend the Franco-Swiss banker who had headed the Swiss Philhellenic Committee, Gabriel Eynard. In his communication, Eynard reviled George and Constantine Mavromichalis as murderers, extolled Capodistrias' virtues and achievements, and quoted a denial by Capodistrias that he had ever dismissed honest men from government service. Eynard ended by asserting his obligation to defend « the memory of one of the most outstanding characters of the age », and added. « the murderers of Capodistrias murdered his fatherland ».

When the Duchess read the letter, her Philhellenism erupted, and she composed a reply to Eynard which she paid to have printed and circulated in Paris. She gave as her qualifications for writing it, her recent presence in Greece, her knowledge of the Peloponnesus, and her friendships with the Mavromichalis, Deliyannis, Zaimis, Benizelos-Rufos, Costa Botzaris, and the Admirals, Miaoulis, Sahinis, Kriezis, and Tombasis. She denied that Capodistrias, because of his Corfiot birth, was a Greek, and she compared his killers to Harmodius and Aristogiton and to the heroes and descendants of Leonidas because of their heroism during the War of Independence and because they knew their act meant certain death to themselves. She wrote in part (the complete text of her letter is lost) :

Rome December 9, 1831.

I have read a letter from Monsieur Eynard in the issue 7.XI of the journal called le temps (sic). I am going to try to reply to it.

Monsieur Eynard impugns, under the pretext of partiality, the accusations of the Greeks against Count Capo-d'Istria. Is not this comparable to impugning a complaint by Monsieur Eynard against people he might accuse of destroying his house ?

Monsieur Eynard tells us that Count Capo-d'Istria was the only link between Greece and civilized Europe. Could it have been out of consideration for Count Capo-d'Istria that Admiral Codrington aided Greece by the victory of Navarino ? He would have to say that himself before I should believe it. Was this link not made by the heroic actions of the Greeks of that country and by their illustrious ancestors who have bequeathed to the world such noble examples of all kinds of beauty ?

I have personal knowledge of the state of affairs and of what people of all classes thought of the head of the government.

Monsieur Eynard repeats confidences made to him by the Count of his love for Greece. To me, he spoke of the Greeks and here is what he told me at my first meeting with him (in Nauplia) : ' Well, what do you think of this country ? In order to govern it, all Greeks over forty years of age should be dead... '

On another visit, after having explained his motives or what it pleased him to allege were his reasons for not granting a constitution to the Greeks, he declared ' As for me, I shall never give them one. '

ANNE-CHARLES LEBRUN, DUC DE PLAISANCE
By Van Brée
Louvre Museum Paris

FRANÇOIS BARBÉ DE MARBOIS
Museum of Petz

I have always attributed this exposition of his ideas to what I had said a few days before to the director of the public school at Aegina, « Count Capo-d'Istria had the opportunity to place himself beside Lycurgus and Numa; he has missed his possibility of glory. »

It seems pitiful to me to speak of the creation of an experimental farm, of carriage roads, of schools, etc., in referring to a man who threw into his prisons, attempted to have assassinated, forced to leave the country, reduced to rebellion, the most distinguished liberators of an unfortunate nation, which, exhausted by so many heroic efforts to free itself from the Turks, finds itself, through the treason of this Count Capo-d'Istria to whom it had confided its destiny, *reduced to defend its independence against other more powerful and more deadly barbarians. Monsieur Eynard calls the heroic action of Konstantin and George Mavromichalis* a dastardly assassination. *It is an act of justice that could be done only by those who have no other power than the strength of their souls...*

If the prince who bestowed victory at Navarino was familiar with the nation, I cannot believe he deliberately turned it over to the cruelty of Russo-Tartars and all the monsters they have unleashed upon it. I venture to say that the avenger and protector of Greeks and Poles should be showered with the blessings of all noble and generous souls...

I ask all honest men, would it ever enter the mind of a man with the least feeling of virtue, to make a traitor of the intrepid incendiary of the Turkish fleet.

Sophie de Marbois,
duchesse de Plaisance

During the winter of 1831-1832 a series of articles appeared, written by the son of the Maréchal Soult, whom Eliza had refused to marry, which denounced all Greeks as thieves and bandits. With

greater oratory and more dubious syntax, the Duchess again made a
public protest.   From her villa near Florence, where she was living
in September, 1832, she wrote and again had published, a rebuttal :

Villa Galli at Coreggi near Florence

September 12, 1832

*The son of the Maréchal Soult, Duc de Dalmatie, has
written a series of articles against the Greeks.   Happily,
he has decided, contrary to his own judgement, that independent Greece should not be limited on the continent,
only to the Peloponnesus : thus I shall say nothing on
this point.   Nor shall I speak of all military matters; for
one must speak of only what one knows.   What I had
printed in reply to Monsieur Eynard was only on behalf
of the Greeks, and it is still to defend them that I am
determined to publish this; but, for the present at least,
I shall answer only one of the Marquis de Dalmatie's accusations.   He treats all Greeks as thieves, as bandits; it
appears there are no exceptions.   I do not pretend that
that country should have the privilege, which would
indeed be extraordinary, of producing none; but I think it
is necessary to make a distinction between those who have
enriched themselves and those who have pillaged in order
to exist and to allow their stratiotes (troops) to exist, in
a war of insurrection, in which, so to speak, it was
necessary to wrest from the Turks the arms which they
required to free themselves at last from their abominable
domination.*

*The Marquis is very severe on this point of pillage.
I am persuaded that the Maréchal, his father, would not
be so vigorous.   He has commanded armies.   I shall therefore rely upon his sense of enlightened justice instead of
his son's opinion.   It is he that I ask if, in waging war
— to judge fairly, one must put one's self in the place*

*of the Greeks, since France, thanks to God, has only been
temporarily at the prey of barbarians — and lacking
supplies for himself and the men under him, would not
have taken them or whatever could be procured for him;
and if he does not find there is a great,* an immense
difference *between this kind of pillage and that which has
for its purpose the accumulation of riches for one's self?
Now, it seems to me that among the Greek fighters one
can cite, and the Marquis himself names as a bandit and
a thief only* Kolokotronis *— son of a Zante butcher and
now the Tsar's principal agent among the Greeks. I am
willing to believe there are others who have done well
for themselves; but which is the nation, in which probity,
scruples, honor, noble and generous feelings are shared
by all or the greatest number? All I maintain is that
these fine qualities are no rarer among the Greeks than
among the French themselves; and to show that they are
still to be found in the country of Aristides, and among
the descendants of Leonidas, Cleomenes, and so many
other men illustrious by their virtue. I shall name only
those generous Hydriotes,* MIAOULIS, KONDOURIOTIS, TOM-
BASIS, SACHINIS, KRIEZIS, *who, not content to expose their
lives and employ their talents in the service of that renascent
country, have also placed in it their ships and their fortunes; André Zaimis, one of the primates of the Peloponnesus contracted on his own security, a loan which,
in temporarily sating the cupidity of the Turks, diverted
their suspicions from the insurrection they were in the
position to have foiled, if they had discovered the plot
before it came to light; and those heroic Mavromichalis
who, lacking fortunes, gave themselves as hostages to the
Turks, and spilling their blood in a war whose success,
in assuring the independence of the Greek Nation could
only take from them the privileges they had once enjoyed
among those worthy descendants of the Spartans, who,*

taking refuge, since the Barbarian invasions, in the moun-
tains of Taygetus, made these impenetrable and knew
how to preserve there that independence which lofty souls
prefer to the enjoyment of riches.

Signed :   Sophie de Marbois,
duchesse de Plaisance

The letters reflect much that had happened to the Duchess' character during the time since she had made up her mind to rid herself
of Charles and had made her decision to go to Greece.   The young
girl eagerness, which marked her outpourings of the Napoleonic Wars,
had disappeared; the feeling from which they sprang, while equally
strong, had become deeper and fuller.   Her impetuosity was un-
dampened, but the tentative, undefined gropings of youth had cohered
in middle age into a mature, less personal idealism.   She was as
strong willed as ever, and inclined at times to be pompous and to
strike a mental pose not unlike the affectation of her clothes; but
the logic in the later letters was sound for her forensic purpose, and
the clarity of her perceptions balanced her yearnings with common
sense.   At forty-seven, although no more introspective than she had
been at twenty, she displayed both the exaggeration of certain atti-
tudes as well as the development that is the strength of character.

Her hopes for Greece were further renewed after Capodistrias'
murder, by the Powers' selection of Otho, the eighteen year old son
of King Ludwig of Bavaria, to be the ruler of Greece and by
their recognition of the country from Arta to Volo as an independent
kingdom under their protection.   In her opinion, there was nothing now
which could impede the destiny which the country deserved.   With the
settlement of her own affairs, she had an income between 100 —
300,000 francs with which she could do more than ever before to
encourage the future of the new nation. Early in 1833, about the
time the young King reached the capital of Nauplia, the Duchess and
Eliza debarked at Pireaus.

The port was almost deserted.   The ruins known as Themistocles'
Tomb stood on the point of Alate, and along the shore spread a

dozen or more broken shafts of antique columns. A few wretched houses and two or three Turkish khans comprised the town. The khans, all equally filthy, offered the only haven for travellers and consisted of one room in which natives and strangers slept with the inns' owners and servants. Their walls were enhanced by gaudy lithographs depicting allegorical scenes of the newly appointed monarch watching Greeks trample upon Turks. There was no furniture; mats covered the floors, and guests slept in blankets they provided themselves. Neither food nor drink was served.

Owing to the late hour of their arrival, the Duchess and Eliza endured a night in one of the khans, and the next morning in a file of rickety hacks, they, their servants, dogs, and boxes took off for Athens. The weather was cold and wet. The conveyances were infested with bugs. Screaming dragomen clung to the carriage doors and to the horses' bridles until lashes from the coachmen's whips flicked them off like flies and the procession climbed the rise to the ancient road between the Long Walls. Parnes, Lycabettus, Hymettus... the Acropolis marked their destination, signposts to a renewed optimism that needed such reminders to sustain it, for Athens was a shambles.

At the beginning of the War of Independence a thousand houses formed the city; in 1833 only three hundred were standing — for the most part around the northern base of the Acropolis. A town of 20,000 inhabitants had become a ruined village of 6,000 people choked by the rubble and rubbish of war. Maize stalks and straw thrown over opened cellars made houses for most of the population. Paths led over and through the debris and so criss-crossed that people who ventured on them at night by candle and lantern light, stuck high sticks along them to point the way back. Wider passages were sogged in mud and filled with garbage on which roving pigs and half-starved dogs fed. From Hadrian's Gate past the Temple of Zeus, the ground was open to the Ilissus where the Callirhoe Fountain served as a basin for washerwomen. On the Acropolis, the Florentine Tower covered the southern wing of the Propylea, and although Greece was a sovereign nation, the Turkish Governor and his garrison still lolled in the buildings on the rock, and as Athenians stumbled among their city's devastation, the voice of the Muezzin still called the Faithful to prayer. Beyond the town limits brigands roamed the countryside.

But in Aeolus Street, the only thoroughfare, with Pireaus, to bear a name, there was a structure called, Hôtel de l'Europe, which possessed a few stark bedrooms and no servants. Its food was questionable yet its owner — possibly because he was French — had enough taste to send his guests at bedtime some honey from the Ceropean bees on Hymettus. His only other activity during the day and most of the night was to engage in resounding altercations with his wife. Since the hotel was the only one in the city, the Duchess was obliged to go there and to find compensation for its mean shelter in the comfort of being able to make herself understood whenever she could interrupt connubial arguments.

Contrary to habit, she did nothing immediately about better accommodations. She had only two alternatives : to build or to leave, and she was too certain of the country's development to do the latter and too good a business woman to do the former. Athenian exiles were returning from the islands; the Russians had started to construct an embassy; an American missionary, Dr. King, had already built a house among the ruins of the old Agora; other missionaries from the United States, Mr. and Mrs. Hill, had opened a school for girls. Although it was too early to be certain, these were all signs that the city would become the nation's capital, and they were reinforced when, shortly after his arrival in Nauplia on February 2nd, the young King, with his three Bavarian Regents, his Bavarian troops, and his Bavarian General dined with the Turkish Governor in the Parthenon. The Duchess and Eliza were presented to Otho.

The King was not handsome : he was short, his brown hair was straight; his nose was flat and his cheek-bones high and heavy; but his figure was slight and he carried himself in a manly fashion. He pleased the Duchess by his modest manner and by his fluent although accented French. He returned to Nauplia, however, without saying anything about a new capital.

The winter was cold and wet; yet despite the weather and the hotel, the Duchess stayed in Athens. She busied herself with a lawsuit against a young man who had not returned money she had leant him. Two public events also brightened the season. On March 2, the Turkish Governor, symbol of nearly four hundred years of Moslem domination, decamped with his troops from the Acropolis. A month later, on Easter weekend, the bells of St. Nicolas Rangava rang for the first time since 1203 when, under Frankish rule the ringing of Orthodox church bells was forbidden — a rule which Moslems' with a religious horror of bells' strictly enforced. The King's appointment of Petrachis to be his antiquary and to care for the Acropolis was taken as another sign of Athen's importance; but June came without any change in the city's status.

Later, when the heavy thyme scented heat descended the Duchess chartered a boat. With Eliza, she sailed to Sunion to examine what was called Minerva's temple on the promontory, and leaving the mainland shore, voyaged through the Aegean Islands. Back in Athens in the autumn, she bought horses and she and Eliza started to ride into the country — to Marathon, across the Attic plain to Kifissia, to Amaroussi and beneath the great quarries through the pines of Pendeli, along the loveliest slopes near Athens and from which on clear days they could look over the city and the Saronic Gulf to see Cyllene where Hermes was born.

The winter began quietly. Petrachis had begun to sort the antiquities on the Acropolis. The so-called Theseum, the temple of Hephaestos, stood neglected and among the dank weeds of its eastern porch, was the grave of the Duchess' friend who had brought her from Corfu to Nauplia. It was a pathetic memorial for John Miaoulis had died two years after the Revolution for no other reason, as Cambouroglou said, than « there was nothing more for him to do ». Then in February, King Otho paid Athens another visit. This time he gave clear indications of his intentions by sending members of his suite to sleep in various sections of the city to determine which was the healthiest. They chose the high land at the easterly end of Hermes Street; and six months later, in September, 1834, Athens was declared the capital of Greece.

The effect of the edict turned the city into a boom town. A

land grab started that was distinguished by the usual elements of such phenomena : rapacity, frenzy, and rumor.   The German architects of the young King played Cleanthes' plan for the reconstruction of the city against several of their own.   No one was sure where the center of the new city would be, nor how far nor where the city would extend — indecisions that caused many speculators to make and lose money over night.   Since only the site of the new palace was known, houses were hastily erected in open spaces in its direction in the hope that their presence would increase the value of the land around them. Other houses, besides Dr. King's, were put up in the Agora. Rubble was cleared from the streets and sorted to be used for building material; existing structures of all ages, including ancient ruins and Byzantine churches, were torn down for the same purpose.   Although a few historically minded people protested the irresponsible destruction, they prudently limited their dissent to monuments of antiquity.

The Duchess watched these operations with a mixture of distaste and perspicacity both of which she could afford since her own holdings comprised lots in the center of the old town as well as many acres in the country along the Ilissus, a mile beyond the site of the palace.   It was one thing for a poverty stricken people to wish to prosper; it was something else for the champions of the glorious past to sacrifice its evidences for land speculation.   It was again something else, when, as the richest person in Athens, the Duchess was approached for loans and began to take mortgages on the finest of the houses.

She also decided to build a house for herself since, in general, Greece was fulfilling her expectations.   The human shortcomings revealed in the scramble of reconstruction, could be dismissed as growing pains.   The new capital of a new nation, rising amid the ruins of the beginnings of civilization, presaged only good for that country and the world.   In such surroundings her Philhellenism, endowed by her wealth and rank, would be of greater use than ever before. What she called, « old Europe », France and Italy, had never encouraged such hope or happiness.   The only questions to be answered were where and what to build; and she answered the first with acuteness by choosing land she already owned at the junction of Aeolus and

Pireaus Streets just below Ludwig — now Omonia — Square which became the center of the city. She solved the second with prejudice and independence.

The Bavarian and, therefore, fashionable taste, was neo-Hellenic. Ludwig, Otho's father, having undertaken the new Munich in that style, ordered Kleutze, Otho's architect, to draw up plans in it for the young King's palace. It was not the Duchess' taste. She had no desire to live in a pseudo Greek temple, and she saw no reason for Greece to be rebuilt by foreigners when there was an architect at hand who was both Greek and more versatile than they, namely, Cleanthes.

Stamatis Cleanthes, a Macedonian, had studied in Berlin and built a house for himself in Athens in 1831, which was in the simple, old Athenian style. Later he and Schaubert designed houses for the Austrian consul and art collector, Gropius, for Sir Pultney Malcolm, Admiral of the Malta Fleet, and for the Duchess' banker, Paul Skouloudhis. Resourcefulness being a quality the Duchess always found worthy of encouragement, she contracted with Cleanthes to do a large house for her in wood, a material which did not rob ancient ruins and which was readily available on boats that brought it from the north to Pireaus. During the Winter of 1834-1835, she took much of Cleanthes' time in instructing him in her own very decided ideas on architecture. One of them was for an observatory on the roof of her house from which by day, she could look at the view and by night, scan the heavens. Only Cleanthes' insistence that the wooden foundations of the house could not support such a weight drove that notion from her head.

After Otho took up residence in Athens in November, 1834, he, too, received her attention. With him came his soldiers, his regents and their families, his staff and their families, Greeks, native and Phanariot, officials, politicians, and hangers-on. Nauplia devoid of them, was left to become a pretty little port; Athens swollen by them, became the center of a foreign administration, of intrigue, and gossip — especially gossip. Having served at the Court of an Emperor whose orbit ringed Europe, the Duchess regarded Otho as an amiable child to whom chance had granted the opportunity to restore Greece to pre-eminence among modern nations. As an experienced, older

9

woman she believed the self-effacing, slightly deaf, slightly stupid boy, could profit by her counsel. The King acknowledged her solicitude by presenting her with a bracelet on which was mounted a miniature of himself — the gift of a well mannered youth to a respected friend.

The gossips of Athens gave another interpretation to the friendship. To them, a Duchess of fifty, without a husband, and with an unmarried daughter could have only one purpose in cultivating a relationship with a bachelor King — a marriage between him and Eliza. That Eliza was twelve years older than Otho was not considered. No mother, it was pointed out, ever gave up hope of marrying off a daughter. The odd little Duchess, for all her trappings of idealism, was no exception. Her very Philhellenism was reason enough to prompt her. Nor was the unlikelihood mentioned of a rich young woman, related by blood and marriage to the Napoleonic nobility, whose tastes were literary and aesthetic, trying to catch a minor, not too bright, princeling on a precariously new throne. In popular opinion her mother was no different from any other matchmaker.

Since the only rules of behavior the Duchess recognized, were of her own legislation, this tattle, like all tattle about herself, she ignored. She had become accustomed to being a figure of rumors. The Lebrun family enjoyed saying that she and Eliza had left Paris to come to Greece riding upon asses and had fortified themselves on biscuits and raisins. Since it was the occupation of empty tongues to feed on their own concoctions, at her age she could neglect them. It was an attitude to goad the Athenian gossips and in early 1835 they made most of a near accident the Duchess and Eliza had in their carriage.

Talk began when the Duchess purchased a carriage before the King owned one. Owing to the condition of the streets, a carriage was an ostentatious superfluity; to the Duchess it was a pleasanter means of getting about at night or in bad weather than of stumbling along with a footman bearing a lantern or an umbrella. Of course there were risks to such a novelty since horses, freshly broken to shafts, were unreliable. And one afternoon, shortly after the Duchess got her four-wheeler, while she and Eliza were being driven along the banks of the Ilissus, her horses bolted. Fortunately, one of the King's adjutants was riding nearby and, seeing the danger, spurred his mount, and seized the bridle of one of the runaways — thus stopping the pair and saving the women from being thrown into the river bed. The gossips immediately set to work on a tale of love at first sight, of heartbreak and hysterics. They insisted that both mother and daughter became enamored of their rescuer and that both pursued him with such ardor he was made desparate by the double siege and begged the King to send him to a foreign post. According to gossip, Otho acceded to the request and the adjutant left Athens — whereupon Eliza became so overwrought the Duchess was forced to take her daughter on a soothing expedition to the Levant.

What is known of the truth is less elaborate. The man was Elias Katsakos Mavromichalis, a nephew of Petrobey. Like all the male members of his family, he had been a leader of Maniot rebels during the War of Independence, and, like those who were not killed in battle, he had served a jail term for his patriotism. From his great grandmother, whose enchanting beauty had gained her the nickname, Fairy, he inherited a handsome face and a graceful figure. At the time of the runaway, he was thirty-three, a widower with three children, Captain of the Gendarmerie, as well as one of Otho's aides. The Duchess and Eliza had known him in Nauplia and it can only be wondered if they would have waited six years to succumb to his charms ? In Nauplia both women were in a more susceptible state of zeal and idealism than they were in Athens, and it is not in keeping with the impetuosity and self-assurance of either of them to have suddenly found an adroit horseman more alluring than a young hero of the Revolution. What also of the designs upon the King ?

The certainties are stronger contradictions of the rumors. The Duchess presented Katsakos with the bracelet Otho had given her, an appropriate reward for his gallantry and her life. In April, 1836, Katsakos went with the King, in his regular line-of-duty, as an Aide to Munich. There in November of the same year, he died of cholera. But in November of 1835, six months *before* Katsakos left Athens, the Duchess and Eliza were already in the Levant travelling lavishly and vigorously without showing any signs of hysteria.

V

THE LAST CAVALCADE

> *... behold, and see if there is any sorrow*
> *like unto my sorrow.*
>
> Lamentations.

There are no records giving the reason for the trip to what the Duchess called, « Asia ». In the letters remaining of those the Duchess wrote while there, she mentions only her intention to stay through the summer of 1837. However, at least three explanations are possible, any one of which would have been sufficient. Both women enjoyed travel and curiosity could have led them. The house in Athens was not completed, and Syria offered a novel, instructive way to pass the time until it was ready. It may equally have been that Eliza was upset and a change of scene promised a cure, not from heartbreak over Katsakos, but for an older wound which had been re-opened by word of Léopold Robert's suicide.

In the years since the engagement to Eliza, Robert's fame as an artist had steadily increased. His genre paintings, executed in a classic style contributed to the fashionable taste. His large canvas, *The Arrival of the Harvesters in the Pontine Marshes,* when hung in the Louvre in 1831, had won him the acclaim of the critics and the adulation of the Parisian public. But his success was embittered for him by the frustration of another love affair. Although there were similarities to his experience with Eliza, his affections this time were not encouraged. The woman also belonged to the Napoleonic hierarchy, at a step even above Eliza's rank, being the Princess Charlotte, second daughter of Napoleon's eldest brother, Joseph, ex-king of Naples and of Spain, and of the ex-queen who had so embarrassed Léopold by her question concerning the Duchess and Eliza. Charlotte had married her cousin, Napoleon-Louis, the second son of Louis Bonaparte and his wife, Hortense Beauharnais, ex-sovereigns of Holland.

In Rome, during the winter of 1828, Charlotte became interested in Léopold's work and had asked to have him presented to her. After meeting her, Léopold fell desperately in love. His old struggle with the question of differences in social rank subsequently beset him; his tact in not declaring his feelings tormented him; but his severest trial was the fact that Charlotte showed him no special consideration. He attempted as before, with Eliza, to find solace in work and, as before, he overworked to the point of exhaustion. For seven years he was torn between elation and melancholy until in Venice, on March 19, 1835, he surrendered to despair and, taking a razor, cut his throat.

The effect upon Eliza of his death and his kind of death could not have been mild. Yet whatever this may have been, all that is known of her at this time is that she was with her mother in Lebanon as early as November, 1835, staying with Lady Hester Stanhope at Djoun.

Granddaughter of William Pitt, first Earl of Chatham, and niece of William Pitt, First Lord of the Treasury, Lady Hester, during the previous twenty-five years, had created a legend which was known in Europe, England, and America. Just before her departure from England for the East in 1810, she had the misfortune to believe a « prophet » who told her she would someday be Queen of Jerusalem. To await the fulfillment of the prophecy, Lady Hester built a house for herself in the hills at Djoun eight miles from Sidon. To encourage the prediction, she learned Arabic, studied the religious and occult mysteries of the Orient, and with obstinacy developed her own gifts of augury, and with pride dissipated her fortune in good works, and gifts to neighboring Pashas. Djoun was a complex of small cottages separated from one another by courts and gardens, an oasis in a lonely valley amid desolate mountains which were ranged by marauding Be-

douins.   It was unfortified and unprotected yet, owing to the Arabs'
belief that Lady Hester was the King of England's daughter and that
she was mad and, therefore, holy, Djoun was seldom molested.

Its owner's notoriety prompted every European visitor to Lebanon to seek an invitation to visit it, but as she grew older, Lady Hester
became selective of her guests and refused to see most of those who
applied.   One of her exceptions was Lamartine whom, although she
told him she had never heard his name, she invited to spend half
a day and a night with her in 1832.   Following her custom, she let
him wait after his arrival for hours in solitude in one of her cottages;
then, after having him served a delicious supper — still in solitude —
she received him near midnight.   First pleased by his willingness to
listen to her discourses upon a variety of metaphysical subjects, she
became bored near dawn by his doting attentions to his lap dog and
dismissed him.   Several other guests, the length of whose visits were
not defined, when they bored her, were served a black concoction to
cure the inevitable physical disorders of the Orient, which produced
a nausea her guests were happy to avoid by taking their departure.

At the time she consented to receive the Duchess and Eliza, Lady
Hester was sixty, lonely and impoverished.   She was ill and gaunt,
suffering from violent attacks of coughing which were not eased by
her addiction to the « tchibouk » (a pipe whose long, slender stem
rose from a tiny bowl that rested on a saucer on the floor) which
she smoked constantly and so carelessly while lying in bed that its
cover was riddled with tobacco burns.   She wore a loose, white linen,
surplice-like dress and her face was blanch beneath a turban made of
pale cashmere shawls.   The Duchess and Eliza in their flowing white
robes and white conical hats, arrived to find her surrounded by cats
and dogs, absorbed in astrology, magic, and charms.   Despite her illness, Lady Hester firmly believed she would live to see the Second
Coming of the Messiah and for this event she kept two Arab mares
of a particular breed each of whom had her own groom whose only
duties were to wash and exercise the sacred animal.

Too level headed to be tempted by clairvoyance or the message
of the stars and too practical to approve of Lady Hester's careless

munificence, the Duchess could still find much to admire in her hostess. Like the Duchess, Lady Hester had educated a number of girls, young Arabs with no more opportunities for learning than the Greek girls in Nauplia; and she had also protected and maintained at Djoun seventy-five families of Arabs whose lives were threatened by a blood-thirsty Pasha — a reaction to tyranny the Duchess could equate with her own stand against Capodistria. Except for money, she was as positive as the Duchess about the details of her affairs, such as the building of houses; and when she wished to unbend she could be amusing in her mimicry of men like Byron and Lamartine. Her greatest attraction for the Duchess was her independence, not so much for what she had done with it as that she, too, had seen fit to become independent, to have chosen to leave an old world to go to a far country in order to seek a new site for her own freedom. No potion could have distorted that personal appeal.

In May, 1836, the Duchess and Eliza went to Damascus and Baalbec, a journey Lady Hester had made twenty-two years before. They went to and from ancient Heliopolis over the barren mountains and whatever the ruins may have meant to them was diminished by the two women's discomfort. They suffered cruelly on the heights from the cold; and the food was bad. The only places to sleep were in peasants' houses which the Duchess found to be worse than stables in other countries.

Upon their return they went to Dayr el Kamar on the side of the mountains above Sidon. Dayr el Kamar was a town of some four thousand inhabitants, the capital of the Druses, and a miserable place. The Duchess called it a forlorn desert. Only the air and water were any good. There was nothing in it or near it to look at, and the accommodations were very bad. In despair she wrote to Monsieur Henri Guys, the Fench Consul in Beirut, asking what she should do. Were there rooms to be had in a convent; and would he send her a loaf of decent sugar ?

Her solution was to rent a house; and she again wrote to the Consul asking him to find her one near Beirut which would have a stable for two horses, a donkey, a room for a groom, and two others for an interpreter.   She wished it, she said, from September 5, 1836 to July 6, 1837.   Within a few days she contracted, through Guys, for a house belonging to a man named Saussa, and paid the rent in advance.   Her conditions were that Saussa clean and whitewash the whole place, repair the roof, heighten the chimney flues, do over the kitchen and install a fireplace in it, and divide a small room at the end of the garden horizontally to make a small stable with a hayloft above it.   A bathroom was also to be added which was to be completed before the end of July so that its walls and wash could dry during August and be ready for use in September.

The inconvenience of all this was that it did not solve the immediate problem of what she and Eliza were to do during the summer. They had never been so poorly lodged and fed for so long a time as at Dayr el Kamar.   Fruit did not exist; the only vegetables were zucchettos, old onions, and chick-peas.   The bread was bad; and the meat was excessively tough coming, the Duchess thought, from old animals.   The only decent things to eat were milk and eggs, and a jam she had bought in Damascus, and a cake made of semolina.   She and Eliza only lingered in the place for fear of the plague which had begun to break out elsewhere.

Besides these discomforts, the Duchess had servant trouble. Of those servants she had, only her valet, Kalil, and his wife were satisfactory and she even wished that Kalil would use a handkerchief instead of, as he occasionally did, blowing his nose in his fingers.   Her groom she never wished to see again; and she asked Guys to find her a new one able to take care of her horses and her donkeys, to follow her when she rode out, to cultivate a small garden, and to take a donkey once a day to fetch water.   She also wished a maid who could iron.   Her linen was simple, without pleats and the important thing for the woman to know was to try her iron first so as not to burn anything, and to clean it well so as not to dirty anything. Her requirements for a new cook were stricter; she had kept her last one, a liar, who was light-fingered, and dirty, only because she spoke French.   She did not suppose there were many trained servants to be had, but as she paid more than was customary, she thought she could expect the Consul to find a cook who would be obedient, respectful, and quiet, and besides cooking, who would wash her own clothes as well as those of Kalil and his wife, and who would know how to wash, scour, and milk a cow. For these accomplishments, the cook would be lodged and paid 15 francs a month. Should the Duchess dismiss her, she would receive extra wages for three days; should the cook give notice, she would be paid only to the last day of her work. « Nothing more than that. » Moreover, the Duchess needed another donkey, and would Monsieur Guys kindly find one for her ?

The Duchess even wrote of her tribulations to Madame Guys excusing herself for what had become daily letters to the Consul which might have overwhelmed him and perhaps abused his kindness. But she made it clear that the sooner her wishes were met and she left Dayr el Kamar, the better. She was copiously bored in the dismal place which was nothing more than a shanty town.

As usual, she got what she wished. The Consul, learning that the Papal Legate was absent from his house at Zouk, put it temporarily at her use. He suggested that from Zouk she could inspect a house that was available at Antoura at the end of August. Because of the heat, he offered to meet her with his tent at the Spring of Pseba where she would have to spend the night on her way from Dayr el Kamar to Zouk. The Duchess of course accepted : Monsieur Guys had already found her a new groom, Kabour, a new maid and a cook, and had even sent a male and female donkey for her choice. She chose the male in order not to excite her « dear stallion » who would share the stable with the new donkey. As for the groom, she had heard he was lazy and at times insolent, but she kept him because he was honest and intelligent. He also spoke French, and she hoped he would learn respect and break himself of his lazy habits. In replying to the Consul, she begged him to bring another loaf of sugar to Pseba and a sack of the best white flour that she might have bread made in her own house. Brown bread was fairly good, she said, but what she wanted was pure white flour, very dry, yet not too old to taste like dust.

On the 12th Day of the Moon, July 20, a caravan left Dayr el

Kamar. Kabour started out at dawn, riding a large ass and accompanied by a porter and two camels bearing luggage. Later, but still early in the morning, the Duchess and Eliza left on horseback with four porters and more donkeys carrying more paraphernalia.

All Consuls in the early Nineteenth Century expected to be taxed by the personal demands of visiting notables, and while Guys' duties were not exceptional, even Lady Hester who used him when she wished, found him more obliging than most of his kind.   His only recompense from the Duchess seems to have been copies of old Paris newspapers which she sent him and asked him to pass on to the Greek Consul. For this, besides acting as a real estate agent, a donkey dealer, a grocer, and an employment agent, he served as the Duchess' banker, taking care of her exchange, and as her postmaster, forwarding letters from her to Italy, Crete, and to her lawyer, and Barbé in Paris.   When she needed tables for the house in Zouk, the Duchess sent him orders to have them made with their dimensions : one was to be 4'4" long and 3' wide; the smaller, $3^1/_2$' by $2\text{-}^1/_3$'.   There was likewise to be a sideboard to measure 3' high, $4^1/_2$' long and 20" deep.   These, she added could be stored later with the French Lazarists until she decided whether she would take a house for the summer of 1837 at Broumana where some American families lived.   Guys heard from her when she had a headache from eating watermelons which upset her stomach; and he also received a request to omit all formal conclusions to his letters and to end them as the Duchess did hers, which was the best way of all, by merely writing, A Dieu.

Despite the Consul's goodwill, the Duchess' housing problems took over three months to settle.   Mr. Saussa procrastinated, and Guys was told that while the Duchess did not know what Moslems were like, Syrian Christians seemed in general to have neither honesty nor good faith.   The Legate, learning that his house was being occupied, was displeased; and the Duchess was forced to move quickly to Antoura. Mr. Saussa made further trouble about the new bathroom which the Duchess was paying an extra sum to have installed and therefore, in her mind, to improve the Syrian Christian's property.   While it was more important, she wrote to Guys, that the chimneys did not smoke, and she could only expect to enjoy the bath in the warm weather of the Spring, she did not intend to have the bathroom made too narrow because Saussa was quibbling over fifty francs.   When, at last, house with bathroom was ready and the Duchess moved into it in September, she sent one more letter to the Consul : he was to see that Saussa plugged holes in her bedroom and in the salon, and put a wooden shutter on the small window in her bedroom to keep out the winter cold.   The Consul was also to see that Saussa removed from her bedroom an old wooden chest that was filled with ants.

There are no further letters to Guys — perhaps the nearness of her house to Beirut allowed the Duchess to present her persistent demands to him in person ? — and the next record concerning her is of February 1837 when word reached Beirut of the death of Barbé on January 12 in Paris.

Barbé had retired, because of near blindness, as President of the Cour des Comptes in April 1834, two months after the death of Madame de Marbois at Noyers.   Yet his remarkable stamina allowed him, until shortly before his death, to continue to take part in the debates in the Chamber of Peers.   The only man to have served France so long in an official position, seventy-one years, beginning under Louis XV, through the reign of Louis XVI, under the Directory, and the Consulate, through the Restoration, under Charles X and Louis-Philippe, Barbé was one of those men whose patriotism led him to sustain law and order, not to venture to overthrow them.   A moderate in politics and an incorruptible civil servant, Thiers wrote of him and his friends, « they were not those extraordinary men who shine at the outset of revolutions, but were men of solid merit who succeed genius in the career of politics as in that of the arts ».   Barbé's finest eulogy was by his friend and former colleague, Guizot, who wrote, « He belonged to that old France which in a spirit of generous liberality, had adapted and upheld, with enlightened moderation, the principles most cherished by the France of the day. »

His funeral was held in Paris at the Church of the Madeleine which Charles was the closest member of the family to attend.   His body was taken to the little cemetery at Noyers in which Madame de Marbois was buried. Because his wife had remained a Protestant, Barbé had had her body placed just outside the center of the westerly wall of the cemetery. Before his own death he had the wall broken at the site of his wife's grave and a towering, stone obelisk erected in such a way that its base was half within and half beyond the line of the wall. After his death, his grave was made directly inside the wall so as to touch his wife's. The monument still stands, as stern and rigid as Barbé's principles, separating consecrated from unconsecrated ground, and boldly joining a man and wife in death. On its outer base is carved the simple notice of a sad and faithful marriage : Elizabeth Moore de Marbois *Uxor Carissima Nata* 1764 *Decessit* 1834. On Barbé's side is carved beneath his name, *Vita Brevis Si Bene Agendo Vixit Longa Nimium Si Vixit Inutilis.*

These stolid virtues which were so admirable for Barbé in public life, were those which first alienated his daughter from him in private life. The Duchess reached maturity only after she had left him as well as Charles; and the final break with her past came when she went to Greece for the first time. The death of her mother was but as a shadow gone. Barbé's death left one less figure in a half-forgotten landscape.

Eight months before his death, in June, 1836, from the habit of his long life, Barbé attempted to regulate the last untidy ends of his family affairs. He wrote to his lawyer in Paris, Masson, who was also the Duchess', that because his daughter no longer wrote to him, he wished Masson to urge her to make a will and to make her understand what rights collateral relatives would have to her estate if she did not do so. The lawyer was to stress the necessity because « she was living in a country in which the plague took frequent tolls ». Following Barbé's instructions, Masson wrote to the Duchess and, because of his letter, she wrote from Beirut in July, 1836, to her father for the first time in seven years. But she did not make a will. She risked the plague for whomever it took, whether it took her or Eliza, one would be the other's heir; and if it took them both, what happened to worldly goods was of no interest.

The plague made its choice : in Beirut on June 18, 1837, aged thirty-three, Eliza died of typhoid fever.

For want of information, her character remains as indistinct as her father's. Spirited and intelligent as a child, she grew to be a lively, erudite woman. Léopold Robert found her unimaginative and homely; his brother thought her dignified, gentle, and fairly pretty. She confounded de Cussy at Corfu by her wit, and she regarded her mother's actions at Nauplia with amusement. But, on the whole, she seems to have been her mother's daughter, not so much spoiled as over-shadowed by a more aggressive parent, a beloved offspring whose special talents were encouraged as much as her fondest wishes were respected.

The Duchess' reaction to her death went far beyond any reasonable grief for the loss of an only child. For the first time, the Duchess seems to have become aware that Eliza had been the axis of her life. During her engagement to Léopold Robert, the question of a separation, of the daughter leaving her mother to go with her husband, never arose. All three, the Duchess, Eliza, Robert took for granted that they would make a joint household. Now, shocked, bereft, alone, the Duchess suddenly realized the magnitude of Eliza's meaning to her; and with this sense came an irresistible determination to keep her with her even in death. Eliza, herself, before her death, had expressed a wish never to be separated from her mother, and had told her mother that she eventually wished to return to Greece. Impetuously, erratically, the Duchess set about fulfilling both their desires. Contrary to custom, she had Eliza's body embalmed. Then it was settled into a glass coffin filled with alcohol which was placed for travel in a lead box. After which, taking ship, the Duchess took it with her back to Greece.

VI

WHAT IS NEW

*Will you stroll forever asking one another,
'What is new'?*

Demosthenes.

*For all the Athenians, and strangers which
were there, spent their time in nothing else
but either to tell or to hear some thing new.*

St. Paul.

The ship from Asia deposited its lonely passenger and somber cargo at Pireaus whence they were taken to the new house in Athens. It was a large square house, a barn of a place which, in the ten years she lived in it, the Duchess did little to refine. A few tables and chairs sufficed for the public rooms, beds, a chair, and a table in the sleeping quarters — for in her current state of mind, the Duchess sought only a refuge for her sorrow and a fortress for her privacy. To her the important thing about the house was it was where Eliza had wished to be : it was in Greece. This, like all details of her private life, she considered to be nobody's business but her own, and whenever some one dared to question her about these matters, she showed her displeasure by a turn of wit. Asked, why she had returned to Athens instead of going back to France or Italy, she replied, « Those who look back run the risk of turning into pillars of salt. » This was a habit of tongue which furthered her seclusion and increased her stature as a figure of gossip.

Her appearance also helped her legend for, while she was still slender, and her eyes were as blue and as bright as ever, her soft brown hair had turned white, and she wore it parted in the middle, cut short to her shoulders. Over it she wore a long, white veil, and on all occasions, a white robe, like a chiton, with a white girdle. The robe fell straight to the tops of curved, red Turkish slippers. Out-of-doors, she put over the veil a broad brimmed, high crowned hat that gave her the look of a Tanagra figurine. Athenians immediately identified the garb as a copy of Lady Hester's clothes — none of which they had ever seen. N. Dragoumis later said the Duchess called it Ancient Hebrew, but for the moment, she gave it no name.

Her own interest was Eliza's body. As soon as she was installed in the house, she turned one of its rooms into a mortuary chapel. There, with windows darkened, the coffin was placed surrounded by lighted candles and fresh flowers. On week days, the Duchess spent several hours alone beside it, and often passed an entire Sunday in praying and talking to her dead. Upon occasion, she reported with joy to her friends that the corpse had spoken to her. « Thus », Raoul Malherbe, the French diplomat, wrote of the Duchess whom he met in Athens in 1843, « she seeks to cheat her sorrow. Men may speak of her in various ways; some may even smile at her, but there is no mother who will not understand and admire her ».

This refusal to acknowledge death and the insistence that a corpse could talk, if not from the grave, at least from behind sealed glass, could well have produced serious morbidity, but the Duchess possessed in her restless disposition sufficient resilience to withstand such a tendency. Long ago she had written to Charles of her fear of becoming like her mother; now, under the weight of Eliza's death, which could have snapped the mind of a less balanced woman, her extraversion saved her. Like her father under the stress at Sinnamary, she began to stuff her days with occupations that would give her little time to pay attention to her loss and little strength to lie awake at night to suffer.

In keeping with a long interest, she turned her efforts to the education of young girls. If she could do no more for her own intelligent daughter, she could do all in her power for the most gifted daughters of others. To the brightest she could find, she would give personnally her own knowledge and taste. Her choice, of course. was daughters of the heroes of the War of Independence, four of them : Panayotika Mavromichali, the daughter of Petrobey, Photini Mavromichali, her cousin, Maria Yanitzi, daughter of the Admiral from Psara, and Elena Kapsali the daughter of a cousin of Christos Kapsalis, a hero of Missolonghi in whose house Byron had lived and died. Besides their intellectual endowments, all four girls gave promise of that other attribute which never failed to attract the Duchess; physical beauty. She called them her Little Friends, and through their parents arranged for each of them to take turns in coming one day a week to study and to lunch with her. On the fifth day they came together. Within a few months they became so familiar with Greek history and literature, and with the French language and literature, that foreigners and members of the Court and the Embassies expressed surprise at their attainments.

To fortify their knowledge, the Duchess composed a prayer for them to recite every morning in French, a prayer that also reflected her abiding Philhellenism :

Dear God, I pray Thee to protect the Greek Nation which Thou hast miraculously delivered from the Turks. And may Thou never permit it to fall under the domination or protection of any other nation. Grant us virtuous and able leaders to direct us readily in the paths of justice. And cause us, the possessors of our fair fatherland, to be more pleasing than all other nations and more worthy of Thy holy favor.

At times the Duchess puzzled the children. Her Asiatic experience with food had modified her vegetarian practices. In Syria she observed that for strengh « one needed good food in small quantities », but she insisted to her Little Friends that, ' Man does not live by bread alone '. Consequently the lunches she served them were frugal for growing girls. More difficult for them to understand at their ages (they were between twelve and fifteen) was why often after the Duchess had been with them awhile, she suddenly left the room and retired to the side of Eliza's bier. Lefka, meaning White Poplar, the Pyrenees who had succeeded the late Baris in the Duchess' esteem, went with her and stood guard in the hall by the door of the chapel until his mistress came out and, with tear stained cheeks, returned to her pupils.

To receive more intensive instruction, the Duchess took a young Maniot boy to live with her, Elias Dimitrios Karakar. Personable and intelligent, Dimitraki, soon learned to act as her host, greeting callers and entertaining them until the Duchess appeared. For these efforts in his behalf, a grateful Athenian public insisted he was the Duchess' lover. If he was, he was the only lover the Duchess ever snatched from the cradle. It was he who greeted the French diplomat Raoul Malherbe, when he first called on the Duchess, and the Frenchman's description of him and the Duchess makes no such insinuation,

> *Upon entering,* Malherbe wrote, *we were received by a young Greek man with a lively, intelligent face, wearing the Greek national costume. He was a Maniot living in the house to whom the Duchess was giving an European education. Indeed, she could not do better for Monsieur Dimitraki is an accomplished youth.*
>
> *He showed us into a large square room on the second floor, furnished with the greatest simplicity, and chose to remain with us while the Duchess was informed of our arrival. She soon entered, accompagnied by two Pyrenees dogs of enormous size. Her dress was a kind of white smock, held about her neck by a drawstring; her hair was cut rather short and, parted in the middle, fell to her shoulders, and a large white veil, thrown off her face, was the only ornament she wore on her head. We had heard a great deal of talk in the town of the eccentricity and oddity of her conduct; but the charm of her conversation quickly caused us to forget what there might have seemed*

*to Parisians to be slightly extraordinary in her completely
ancient costume.*

*She received us with a courtesy both gracious and melan-
cholic, the usual expression on her face and we saw through
the polished manner of a high social position and of a
familiarity with distinguished people, that this strong and
resigned soul hid a deep sorrow.*

The days spent in education were still too long for the Duchess
and within a year of her return to Athens, she started projects which
became her principal diversions for the rest of her life : the construc-
tion of houses. Again she called in Cleanthes and, offering a number
of confusing blueprints of her own devising, she commissioned him to
draw up plans for a marble residence with gate houses and dependencies
to be built on the lands she owned lying along the banks of the
Ilissus beyond the King's palace. At the same time, in the autumn
of 1838, she began negotiations with the monks of the monastery
on Pendeli, to buy property belonging to them on the slopes below
their priory. These were those lovely hills and glens, ten miles from
Athens, where she and Eliza had so often ridden together, where there
were clear brooks, and stands of pine and olive, of oleander and of
myrtle, where heather and shrub arbutus grew, and the summer
heat was never oppressive. Here, there were to be a château, two gate
houses, and several guest houses, stables, carriage houses, and kennels.
Before any of them was started, a small Maisonette was to be built
in which the Duchess could live while she superintended the work
on the other buildings.

Ground was broken in 1839 for Ilissia, the town house. Begun
in 1840, the Maisonette on Pendeli was sufficiently habitable to allow
the Duchess to spend the next summer in it. But Ilissia was not
finished until 1848 and, while one gate house and two guest houses
were eventually completed near the château, the roof of Rhododaphne
was not on at the time of the Duchess' death in 1854. Some of
the delays were unavoidable; those on Pendeli were caused by lengthy
bickering with the monks over acreage and terms. On October 11,

1839, a year after her first verbal offer, the Duchess composed a letter in French to the Prior which the fifteen year old Elena Kapsali precociously translated into Greek :

> *Having learned that the monks of the Pendeli Monastery, besides owing debts, are desirous of having money with which to repair their building, I am renewing the offer I made verbally last year for a certain amount of ground on the mountain and for water for the purpose of constructing our tomb (mine and my daughter's) and a château with gardens in an environment where the air and water agree so well with my health. I join with this proposal, which my architect, Monsieur Cleanthes, has consented to transmit, my respects to all the monks and the Prior.*
>
> *Sophie de Marbois,*
> *duchesse de Plaisance*

The written word convinced the monks of the Duchess' earnestness and, believing they recognized a good thing, they drew up an agreement of sale which retained all water rights for themselves and set a price of 30,000 drachmas on the land. Owing to State control of the monasteries in Greece as a result of the Revolution, this document had to be submitted to the Government for approval. The Government, wiser than the monks in the ways of the Duchess and of trade, expressed consternation at the terms and instructed the monks to make others.

Six months later, the Duchess paid 7,512 drachmas (357 of which she capriciously threw in to make what she called, a round sum) for three hundred and forty-eight acres below the monastery. These included one hundred and twenty-six olive trees and two acres of cultivated land. The final terms required her to build a road to encircle her property and prohibited her from walling any portion of the tract except the site of the château and the garden. Since the purchase also included the spring, Skapetos, she was required to build, outside her boundaries, a watercourse for the benefit of passers-by and animals.

On Mondays and Thursdays the Monastery was to supply, free of charge from their reservoir, water for her garden. In return, animals belonging to the monks, which were found on the Duchess' land were to be returned to them without claim of indemnity. Five years later, desiring to buy more water-rights and eight more acres, the Duchess escorted the Prior to point out to him what she wished. The Prior was displeased and annoyed. In his report to the Secretary of State, he called attention to the fact that the water the Duchess wanted irrigated in its downward course the Monastery's land in the nearby town of Kalandri. He ended by asking permission to inform the Duchess to be satisfied with what she already had and to stop bothering the Monastery with new demands. Not until 1846, and only after political pressure was exerted in her behalf, did the Duchess get most of what she wished. Land on which to build a second gatehouse opposite the one still bearing on its lintel the name, Plaisance, was refused her.

Added delays were owing to the Duchess' decision to have her engineer, Georganta, bridge over streams, make a special bridge to facilitate the transportation of marble from the ancient quarries to build both Rhododaphne and Ilissia, cut a new, shorter road, to Kalandri, and construct a viaduct to carry water from Pendeli to Ilissia. She also started to have built in Athens a house near the Observatory, and one in Maroussi Street for her physician, Dr. Raiser.

Public opinion dubbed these postponements further examples of the Duchess' eccentricity. The gossips were certain of their judgment when the Duchess replied to them by her own version of an old Moslem superstition. She said a pythoness had warned her that to finish a house meant death. The pythoness was her own Delphic touch; the Moslems to this day, in repeating the adage, omit her. The truth was that a motive for the delays was purposeful. Except for Rhododaphne and the house by the Observatory, all the Duchess' houses were finished before her death. She took so long to complete the others because she frequently changed her mind about their plans, invented new projects, and was indifferent to time. Her intention was to keep herself occupied. She needed to be busy.

By protracting her enterprises and employing Cleanthes to achieve them, the Duchess made her most visible contribution to Greece. She gave to Cleanthes his broadest opportunity to create a domestic design and in taking advantage of it, he added to his importance as Greece's first, fine modern architect. Each house he did for the Duchess displayed his understanding of setting and living requirements, and extracted the best of his talents and taste for design and the use of materials. The stuccoed Maisonette, with its little balustrade beneath the roof for coolness and decoration, with its charming balance of height, width, and length, remains a model for a country villa for a hot climate — before air-conditioning was invented. For Ilissia and Rhododaphne, he used a similar, rectangular plan, suppressing halls and placing staircases at both ends of the houses. Ilissia with its arches, was an adaptation to local conditions of an Italian palazzo and a bold innovation in a city of neo-Hellenic posts and lintels. He exhibited more courage for Rhododaphne by introducing into Greece the latest European fashion, the Neo-Gothic. Of the four examples of that style in the country, La Tour Reine near Liossia, designed by Theophil Hansen for Queen Amalia, a small house in Mylopotameo on Cytheria, Cleanthes' English Church in Athens, and Rhododaphne, the latter is the most distinguished. Happily all these buildings are still standing, and of those the Duchess commissioned, Rhododaphne and the Maisonette, after too many years of neglect, have been restored. Ilissia on what is now Queen Sophia Boulevard, became in 1931 the Byzantine Museum.

With time still to spare, the Duchess added to her occupations by buying more real estate, and her perspicacity was a clear reflection of the astuteness in business matters she first displayed in managing Charles' affairs. She bought tracts of land in the fertile valley of Levadia beyond Thebes, and large stands of olives at Longos, Koukouvaounes, Kefissia, Amaroussi, Kalandri, and on the Attic plain. She extended her holdings around Ilissia and acquired lots between the Royal Gardens and the Temple of Zeus, where the Zappeion is now. By 1840, her income from her Greek properties was reputed to be 20,000 francs a year. While she undertook the general management of her business herself, for financial and legal requisites, she engaged Paul Skouloudhis to be her banker and Klonaris her lawyer. She protected whatever benefited her and when Metrude, her early agent died, and his heirs attempted to retain his former share of the Duchess' revenues, she did not hesitate in May, 1842, to go to court to obtain her due.

Yet her peculiarities are not to be denied. Her force of character was often as much at the mercy of whim as of conviction. Her clothes, her buildings, her diet, and her wit furnished targets for facile barbs. Nevertheless, there was only one serious attempt to ridicule her in writing during the early years of her permanent residence in Athens, and even it was far off the mark.

In the summer of 1841, the Duchess invited the Greek scholar Rangabe to lunch at the Maisonette with her friends, T. N. Soutsos, D. Boudouris, and the painter, Margaritis. She sent her carriage early one morning to Athens to fetch them to Pendeli where, after two hours of jolting, heat, and dust they arrived to find the Duchess was still asleep. From that moment on, Rangabe found everything about the day to be a farce. Only upon waking and learning of her guests' presence, did the Duchess arrange for anything to be served to counteract the strain of their trip, and then, to Rangabe's dismay, it was a glass of water with some drops of lemon juice in it. He provoked the Duchess by showing disagreement with her, and when he expressed a hope that all Christians would be freed from Turkish rule, she mocked him. The lunch, he said when it finally came, consisted largely of more water, the Duchess explaining it was harmful to the health to have two meals a day and promising a good dinner because her steward had just shot a hare. At dinner soup was omitted owing to the Duchess' dietary laws, and in its place were the cold remains of the chicken from lunch which, since no one touched them, were fed to Lefka. The hare, the Duchess cleverly cut into eight or ten pieces and gave Rangabe the lower part of its jaw. Instead of a cake for desert, also considered harmful, Elena Kapsali distributed a spoonful of jam to each guest. The visit ended by the Duchess, in fine fettle, mounting her horse and conducting her starving guests in the carriage to the highway. Later in writing of her, Rangabe said the Duchess had come to Greece only by caprice and her sympathies were with the Turks.

His account is irrelevant except as some poor threads in the stuff of her legend. Water with lemon juice was an old and well known means of refreshing hot and weary travelers. J. A. Buchon in January of 1841, picnicked with the Duchess on Pendeli without noticeable undernourishment, and in October of that year, Charles Lenormant arrived there to find that, although the Duchess was ill in bed, she had arranged to have his lunch served under the monastery porch, a lunch that was not meager enough to cause him to comment upon it. Had Rangabe known the Duchess better and been a wittier man he could have had the whole chicken and the whole hare. Vice Admiral Sahinis had lunch at the Maisonette a month or two before Rangabe's visit and to the Duchess' question if he preferred the head or the tail of the rouget she was serving, he replied, « What do you think, Duchess ? I want the whole fish. The rouget would be offended if an admiral disdained it. » For his sally, he was given the whole fish. As for the report of the Duchess' defense of the Turks, it was the repetition of a slur the Phanariots circulated about her in retaliation of her dislike of them.

Old friends knew her better, and only the year before Constantine Levidis dedicated a new edition of his *Greek Chronicles* to, « The most illustrious Duchesse de Plaisance, born Sophie de Marbois, a sincere Philhellene, this book is respectfully dedicated by the author. » In his preface, Levidis wrote, « The Duchesse de Plaisance, who has taken up residence like an affectionate mother among the Greeks and who has bestowed her benefactions in a multitude of ways upon them has graciously permitted this present edition of the Chronicles to be dedicated to her. The names of all true Philhellenes are associated with all that relates to the rebirth of Greece. The Duchess considers herself highly honored to be counted among them. She has authorized us to say this. »

Anything the Duchess did made tongues click, and she made them sputter when, after Eliza's death, she began to expound upon a religion of her own invention. That she might seek consolation out-

side Roman Catholicism perplexed minds adhering to Orthodoxy which
had never been disturbed by scepticism or reformation.   That she could
contrive a creed of her own, seemed to them preposterous and absurd.
But in the Duchess' childhood during the French Revolution, religion,
denounced in the name of Reason came to rest lightly on men's souls.
Like many Catholics, she was taught to respect the ritual of the
Church without profound consideration for its doctrine.   Not, then,
until she knew a desolate sorrow did she search for a solace in Faith.
Precisely what she believed is unknown since her own statements on
the subject were vague and other information was hearsay.   Gossip
ran a gamut from declarations that she thought herself to be another
Lady Hester, to assertions that, while in Lebanon, she had become a
Jew.   The former, to describe a woman who never copied anyone and
who, owing to the strength of her own individuality, never thought of
doing so, was a grave misconception of both the Duchess and Lady
Hester. As much as they shared traits of character, in the matter of religion, as of dress, they were independent.   Save for the Messiannic touch
there was no Judaism in Lady Hester's religious brew.   Indeed, she
once pronounced Judaism, « defective ».   Both women, it is true, were
monotheists, but there was nothing of astrology, face-reading, or sooth-
saying in what the Duchess believed.   The nearest she was even said
to have come to the esoteric was a Pantheistic hope that her beloved
dogs and horses would appear with her in Paradise.   Nor was she
tempted by the Messianic.   Elena Kapsali, who grew up to become the
Duchess' friend and companion and who knew her better than anyone
in Greece, dismissed the reports of the Duchess' conversion to Judaism
as gossip.   After the Duchess' death she told Dora d'Istria, « By the
finesse of her mind, by her very conscious prudence, by the firmness
of her judgment in ordinary matters, she (the Duchess) was a daughter
of a Voltairean epoch; by the exaltation of her ideas, by her invincible
partiality for all that was unusual, she was linked to that remarkable
movement which produced *René, Adolphe, Childe-Harold.* »

The Duchess' library contained books on all religions, and the
one book she read constantly was the Old Testament. Edmont About,
who knew her well toward the end of her life, thought that perhaps the

assiduous reading of the Bible had thrown her into a religion that belonged to her alone because she had no followers and was at once its priestess and prophetess.   She believed in a personal God, she told him, whom she consulted and who inspired her to build a great altar on Pendeli, and this she intended to do as soon as she could find a spot worthy of God and herself.   The best that About could make of what he heard was that her belief, while far removed from Christianity, was closer to Judaism without being of it.

Certainly the most positive expression of this religion was the Duchess' concern for Jews.   She wrote to the editors of the *Archives Israélites* an explanation of it which she asked them not to reveal but which the editors felt at liberty to say went back to her birth and to remark, « Although born into a Catholic family she has been tolerant in regard to Jews, and without having changed her religion, she has returned to the source of faith, to the Bible. »   Whether or not the Duchess retained particular memories of the first days of her life in Philadelphia or of the following four years in Santo Domingo, is also unknown; what is certain is that her benefactions to Jews started upon her return from Syria and continued throughout the rest of her life.   Two years after Eliza's death, she began to talk about memorials to Eliza and to herself, something like colleges that were to aid Jewish women of Greek and French origins, and her intentions were taken seriously enough by the Chancellor of the French Consulate in Athens to prompt him to request her to outline them for him on paper. With a mixture of egotism, Philhellenism, financial restrictions, and poor syntax, she wrote :

> *My motives are : to perpetuate the memory of my daughter and myself, to aid women of Jewish origins, Greek or French, who are distinguished by their intelligence, the elevation of their feelings or the goodness of their characters, to give them some possibilities to cultivate these happy attributes, to offer them some means of existence which will surpass all others and through my two foundations, to join all these ideas in an inseparable manner*

*since it is the members of our sex who are most eminently
fitted by their moral and intellectual qualities in our nation
and in the two best which have existed on earth that I
entrust the care of perpetuating some souvenir of myself
and above all of my daughter my only and beloved child.*

*Monsieur the Chancellor of the French Consulate hav-
ing asked my motives, I send him these lines which express
them all.*

*I have already made a donation of land I own at Patissia
and which I consign to the Elisane or Museum of Eliza
and of fifteen stremas (three acres) along the Ilisus and
near the house in which I propose to establish the
Sofiane of the Atheneum of Sophie. To complete this
donation I wish to add that of my large farm at Noyers
near Gisors Department of the Eure, Dist. of Les Andelys
(Vexin normand) guaranteed to yield twenty thousand francs
a year.*

*These twenty thousand francs of income and in time
the proceed from the olive trees, lands and waters at Kefissia,
Maroussia, and in the Athens plain will serve to pay for :*

Two Lady Custodians of the Elisane at three thousand six hundred francs for each, a total	7,200
The Lady Custodian of the Sofiane	5,000
The Administrator in Greece of the estate I shall leave in Greece for these two founda- tions as well as to those I may establish in the the future	3,000
To the Elisane a ball on the first of Novem- ber the day of my daughter's birth	760
To the Sofiane a ball on April 2, my birth . .	700
To contribute to the celebration of the fête *of the* Insurrection *of the Greeks against the Turks in 1821*	300
Upkeep	5,040

But in making these donations of my farm at Noyers and of the olive trees and waters that I own at Kefissia, Maroussia and in the Athens plain, I reserve for myself as with the donation of the fields, the entire and full benefits during all my life. To name while I live, or by my will the lady incumbents, two at the Elisane with titles of custodians and one at the Sofiane with that of Custodian and to make all the regulations governing these Institutions dedicated to the arts and to letters and to preserve the memory of my dear child and of myself.

Observations.

*So long as the farms at Noyers are not sold, the tax will be (*illegible*) and paid from the revenues from my woods in the same commune of Noyers; but if this (sic) farm is sold the Institutions of the Elisane and of the Sofiane cannot claim more than the price of the said farm. The Olive Trees.*

The proceeds from the Olive Trees have already been reserved to the end of the year eighteen hundred and eighty and it will only be then that those trees and the land that bears it (sic) returns will belong will be consigned and cultivated to the profit of my Institutions.

The details were clear enough but perhaps because of the entailed funds, the Duchess' plans were never realized. Neither Elisane nor Sofiane was ever started or endowed. However, in 1843, the Duchess' good will toward Jews resulted, through the solicitation of David Pacifico, in the gift of a plot of land in Athens near the Royal Gardens for the site of a synagogue and a rabbi's house. Pacifico, later to become internationally notorious, was even then a shady character. Of Portuguese Jewish origin, he slid at his convenience under the protection not only of Portuguese Legations but of those of Spain and England. He worked upon the Duchess' sympathies in the name of his coreligionists, and although a corner-stone was laid for the synagogue by the handful of Jews then in Athens, Pacifico held on to the grant for the use of Sephardic Jews whom he said would eventually settle in the city.

Once more the Duchess' feelings let her misjudge character. Socially she could succumb to flattery or dismiss it at will, and except for Rangabe's lampoon, the records of how she used this talent are remarkably moderate in tone. She succeeded by shunning those whom she disliked or who bored her, and by charming those who pleased her. Bavarians she continued to ignore no matter their rank. When, under royal patronage, the German archeologist, Ross, founded the Service of Antiquities and started to clean up the Acropolis, the Duchess remarked with disdain, « The donation of a few drachmas gave it (the patronage) the illusion of contributing to the conservation of the most beautiful edifices to come from the hand of man. » When Otho's Bavarian Government sponsored a Polytechnical Institute in Athens to instruct Greek artists and artisans in German methods, the Duchess counteracted this influence by bringing from Rome where he was working in 1840, the French painter, Pierre Bonirote. She paid his travel expenses as well as his salary for the two years he taught at the Institute. Otho the once affable and gracious youth, was a disappointment to her after he brought back from his trip to Munich in 1836, a bride, an Oldenburg princess named, Amalia, under whose domination he fast became an obese piece of putty. Phanariots, as always, were excluded from her consideration. In fact, only the handsome, the young of both sexes, the witty, the well mannered, and intelligent were welcome. Fortunately these were in sufficient numbers in Athens between 1837 and 1846, to give her surcease from her sorrow and her multiple occupations. She saw friends she had made in Nauplia, the Mavromichalis, Levidis, Dragoumis, and Trecoupis. The marriage in 1842 of Elena Kapsali to George Skouzès of an old Athenian family gave her delight for Elena remained her loyal companion and her husband, as the years passed, became her friend and acted as her agent.

She made two exceptions to the Court : Dr. Raiser, a Bavarian, was Otho's physician, and became hers, and one of her cherished friends was Rose Botzaris, the first Greek woman to be Maid of Honor to Queen Amalia. A daughter of Marco Botzaris, Rose was a heroine in her own right since, as a child, she had been taken with her mother and held captive for several years by the Turks. Her beauty was so renowned throughout Europe and the United States that travellers to Athens asked to be allowed to see her, and English and American tourists believed that with what they called The Ruins, Lord Byron's Maid, Teresa Macri Black, Rose was one of three chief sights of Athens. Christened, Catherine, she was given, because of her superb coloring, the name of Rose, La Rose de Seeleide by Otho's father, King Ludwig. Raoul Malherbe, who met her at the Maisonette in 1843, called her, « the charming Mlle. Rose Botzaris, Maid of Honor to the Queen, whose Greek dress set off her grace and beauty », but he added, « I do not, however, know if my phrase is correct, for I still doubt if it were not she who lent an entirely special grace to her costume. »

Foreigners also came to the Duchess' house in town and to Pendeli — her Scots friend from Nauplia, the historian, George Finlay, the German archeologist, Welcher, and Buchon, the French historian, Lenormant, the archeologist, Malherbe. Two of her closest friends were the Count and Countess Théotoki. The handsome Count belonged to an ancient Corfiot family and in 1843 was named Aide-de-Camp to Otho. The Countess was known in England and on the Continent as the notorious Jane Ellenborough whose love affairs had long been a scandal (Balzac called her Lady Arabelle Dudley in *Le Lys dans la Vallée*, and Ludwig, his Ianthe). Her conduct with Hadji-Petros, who succeeded to her husband's position at the Greek Court, soon made her a rival in gossip to the Duchess. As both women were indifferent to public opinion, the rivalry strengthened their friendship. Each enjoyed her own kind of rebellion; neither tolerated conventional people or interests; both were pleased by sharp tongues, good looks, and animals, and each had charm to attract the most disparate admirers. Malherbe thought Jane represented the perfect type of gracious, lovely woman. Charles, Duc de Plaisance, admired her because she rode her horse like a cavalry officer.

For Charles, too, came to Athens, after Eliza's death. His good nature bore no rancor for the manner in which his wife had forced

him to obtain a separation; and once the Duchess was no longer tied
to him or had to see him everyday, it never entered her mind to resent
his patience and his dullness.　Each now lived his own life as he
wished — Charles was content in Paris with the Chamber of Peers,
the management of his estates, his hunting, and a satisfactory mistress.
He and the Duchess corresponded, expressing a friendly interest in
each other's welfare.　The loss of their only child made no definite
rupture possible.　But when he was in Athens, the Duchess arranged
that he stayed, not with her, but in a hotel.

　　So the Duchess' legend grew; and an example of its contents
by 1842 was in a letter written by a woman, who in the spring of
that year, accompanied the Court on a picnic to the slopes of Pendeli
near the Maisonette :

> *After lunch we went to visit the recently completed villa
> of the Duchess de Plaisance which stands on a beautiful
> site.　Perhaps you have heard of this woman whose eccen-
> tricity arouses so much comment.　She lives away from her
> husband who lives in Paris; I do not know whether or
> not she is divorced.　She spent a number of years in
> Anatolia where she lost her only daughter.*
>
> *While she may well have an income of 100,000 francs,
> she leads a frugal personal life, but she is generous to her
> dogs and to certain people in proportion to their political
> ideas or their origins English, French, or Greek.　She
> detests all Germans with the exception of our head physi-
> cian.　Even the King and Queen have never been able
> to gain her favor, outside of Mlle. Botzaris whom she loves
> because she is Greek.*
>
> *To her favorites she is very generous, offering them
> money, land, and horses of great value.　Never does
> she give to the poor.　I am generous, she says, but I do
> not bestow charity.　Every day she rides out and organizes
> excursions to which her favorites are invited.　Her dogs
> are always served first before the guests at meals and receive*

the best morsels. Rumor has it that she embraced Judaism in Palestine. Obviously she does not practice this religion openly, but one is led to believe she is a Jew in listening to her explain her religious doctrines. Because of these opinions, it is quite easy to fall in disgrace from the heights of her favor. This original woman had organized an excursion for the same day; however we had hoped, when we arrived to visit her house, to find her there. We met no one. When the King arrived, the Duchess had left her home.

The insinuation is that the Duchess, having got word of the Court's intention had decamped before it could catch her at home, a slight which adds interest to the moderate tone of the account for its author was Julie Nordenphlycht, one of Queen Amalia's Bavarian Ladies-in-Waiting.

THE KING OF THE MOUNTAINS

Athens in the early 1840s had become an overgrown town of 12,000 inhabitants, a near-city which still displayed signs of a too rapid growth. Hermes and Aeolus Streets were now paved with stones. There was one palm tree in Hermes Street and less than a dozen in the labyrinth of alleys and crooked lanes of the old town. There were still not enough buildings for the population : ministries functioned in rooms above stores, and too many people had to sleep out-of-doors. In contrast, the old Agora was becoming a residential district; toward Patissia and around the Palace, Bavarians and Phanariots lived behind pseudo-classic facades (which in the latter quarter faced an open sewer). Under Queen Amalia's direction, a Royal Garden was coming to life, and along the new streets cypresses, laurels, and mulberries were planted. Otho had founded a university; there was a maternity hospital, and a girl's training school for teachers. Varvakis endowed a high-school, and the Epirot, Rhizaris, a seminary. There were naval and

military academies and mission schools.   The Powers had new embassies, and the English their church.   Orthodox chants had replaced
the Muezzin, and the shouts of newsboys and hawkers, and other loud
Greek voices echoed between houses.   The rags of the poor set off the
black coats of courtier and diplomat, the fustanellas and billowing
trousers of soldiers, and the French plumes of Phanariot women whose
riding habits came from Paris.

Beneath the panoply of noise, display, and smells, there was a
discontented populace.   Otho, who had been hailed as a deliverer
from anarchy had failed to live up to expectations.   First his Bavarian
Regents dominated him, then his Queen controlled him.   The promising
lad had grown to be a vacillating procrastinator who took weeks,
months, even years to come to a decision on the simplest matters his
ministers presented to him.   In an honest effort to please everyone,
he became a pawn of political factions and a prey of all.   The Greeks
might have condoned his childless marriage, had they not been expected to accept Bavarians in all high offices, Bavarian appropriation of
a $10,000,000 loan from England, Bavarian graft in taxes, and the
consequent bankruptcy of the country.   There was no money to cultivate fields, to reforest, or to replant vineyards.   In the twenty-nine
years Otho reigned, he built only seventy-two and a half miles of roads
— none to Corinth, or to Patras, or to Sparta.   Communications, trade,
and internal development were stifled.

Worse, there was no civil order.   When the Bavarian Regents
disbanded the Greek forces in 1833, the soldiers were mustered out
penniless, without the means to return home or to restore their lands.
Without other sources of employment they turned to the one certain
way of survival : brigandage.   They roamed the country in bands,
pillaging, fomenting local strife, and making travel precarious unless
under armed escort.   Fitful attempts were made to suppress them by
employing one or more bands against others, but, once these motions
ceased, those of the bandits who did not ride to safety across the Turkish border, returned to their more stable vocation.   Certain of their
leaders like, Bibisi, Bourdabis, and Grivas became famous through their
presumptions and treachery.   Many murdered; more were calculating

rather than cruel; and while legend transformed the latter into Robin Hoods, for the most part they took few dramatic risks. Owing to the casual anarchy of the country, their pursuits became as much political as larcenal. Politicians who wished to intimidate rivals, willingly paid for their services : a few burnt villages permitted a public enquiry of how long Athenians would suffer a Minister who allowed villages to be burned. Although brigandage was an old and familiar Greek pastime under the Turks, the Bavarians were blamed for the renewed lawlessness. Finlay wrote in his Journal, « Greece bled, starved, fought, conquered and dispaired for what ye Gods — to be trampled on by John Capodistrias and ruled by a German Prince. »

Growing dissatisfaction forced Otho in 1841 to appoint Mavrocordato the first Greek President of the State Council and Minister of Foreign Affairs. Behind the official scenes the old divisions of Phanariots and native Greeks, and of the Powers versus each other were still active. The Russian party, who objected to Otho's non-Orthodoxy, joined the pro-English Phanariots, who sought power for themselves, against the King. Together they raised the issue of a Constitution and arranged for a military demonstration to be staged before the Palace at midnight, September 14, 1843. Without a shot being fired, Otho signed a proclamation the next day in which he promised to summon a National Assembly within thirty days to draw up a Constitution and to dismiss all foreigners from his service except Philhellenes who had seen service in the War of Independence.

It was a moment of double rejoicing for the Duchess. The despised Bavarians had been put in their place, and Greek freedom had gained a second chance. But she spotted dangers, and so intense was her Philhellenism, it not only erupted, in a heat of good intentions, it scorched her. Her prejudice against Phanariots and her Napoleonic distrust of English and Russians threw her into a frenzy of political activity. During the campaign for the election of Deputies set by the new Constitution, she gave her support to the non-Greek Colettis because he headed the French faction. She talked in his favor and gave money which contributed to grease his way to victory and eventual nomination as Prime Minister. She also behaved shamefully. Because her old friend from Nauplia and Aegina, Spyridon Trecoupis — who had delivered Byron's funeral oration, been Capodistrias' secretary, and lately Greek Ambassador to London — supported Mavrocordato of the English party she sued him in an effort to regain money she had given him when the Revolution had made him destitute! In the year before the election she sued her old friend, Anastasios Mavromichalis, a son of Petrobey, because, she said, he had become money hungry and was pestering her for loans. Fortunately, she lost both suits. What she had given them were the incomes from olive trees (some of which the Elisane and Sofiane were to have had) and her original terms for them were allowed to be continued. Trecoupis received his income until his death in 1874, and Mavromichalis and his family enjoyed theirs until 1886.

There is no excuse for her. Since Mavromichalis was helping starving clansmen in Mani and needed more money from time to time for his own family, he appealed to the Duchess as to an old friend who had always been eager to help him before. Her action against Trecoupis was pure spite. Too strict a sense of behavior for herself, and too little leniency toward others mixed with her willfulness and self-indulgence to exaggerate her sense of gievance beyond reason. She had a quick temper, and, as Charles had learned, she could indulge a grudge. She could also, when she chose, let expediency curb her : she never sued for the return of gifts she made to her lawyer, Klonaris, or to her physician, Dr. Raiser.

The only return the Duchess received personally from these political performances was Colettis' assistance, when he was Prime Minister, in forcing the monks of Pendeli to sell her more land on the mountain. As usual, the monks demurred and dilly-dallied, and it took Colettis two years to convince them that the State had no money to give them and the Duchess' offer was a Godsend. While the argument lapsed, the Duchess continued to build there. Work on the château, the guest houses, on bridges and roads all went on at the same time. When she was not in residence at the Maisonette, she drove out from Athens to supervise and to instigate new projects.

It was for these reasons that she started to Pendeli in her carriage on Sunday morning, June 14, 1846, together with Gorganda, her engineer, Sakellaris, her builder, and the architect Gourgaris Denain. On the box with the coachman was her steward, Sekeris. Just before her carriage reached the monastery, the Duchess, looking ahead, noticed another carriage tipped up across the road to bar the way, which contained a constable and three other men. Before she could say anything, her carriage was stopped, and asking the reason, one of her companions replied, « Brigands ». It was a hold-up with the threat of kidnapping the Duchess, and the chief of the gang was Bibisi whose purpose was to extract ransom for her person.

Had the Duchess been of lesser rank and Bibisi an unknown thug, the affair would have been only one more incident in the current banditry. Since each of the principals was already notorious, the episode became a cause célèbre.

Bibisi had his legend too. It was said that, in revenge for being denounced as a brigand, he had once cut off a man's head. It was also said he protected widows and orphans, redressed their wrongs and never broke his word. Unlike most of his kind, he was intelligent as well as wily, and in common with other well known highwaymen, he was for hire and not above blackmail. The enormity of his exploits depended more upon the social position of his victims than upon theatrical effects of daring or mercy. He did not hesitate to burst into the house of the defenseless Demetrios Levidis in Athens to extort his aid in obtaining an amnesty from the King and he did not hesitate, when faced with superior numbers, to take to his heels. The one thing that distinguished him from his confreres of equal gall was that he followed his career, not to live, but to escape punishment for having murdered his wife's lover.

Nothing the Duchess had yet done or experienced — not her separation, her clothes, her Philhellenism, her religion, her politics, her buildings, not her obsession with Eliza's body had given so much occupation to gossips as this encounter.

A few hours after the hold-up, the newspaper, *Vema*, reported that Bibisi, with some of the best known rogues in Athenian society, had captured the Duchess outside the city and had been paid 1,000 Spa-

nish gold pieces to release her.   Although the journal corrected itself
the next day, the mischief was done.   Rumor increased the number of
the Duchess' companions from five to an entourage of twelve or fifteen
rich friends plus an armed escort of three.   The site of the crime was
given variously as « somewhere » to « before her own house door ».
The number of her rescuers went from four to an entire village.   The
ransom demanded was stretched from 100,000 thalers to the Duchess'
consent to sleep with Bibisi.

Two days after the event, the Duchess wrote a letter about it
to Charles in which she inadvertently disclosed some of her admirable
qualities.   She was sixty-one and as courageous as she had been when
she first set out on her travels with Eliza.   It never occured to her,
after driving so often to Pendeli either alone or with friends, and after
riding for so many years alone across its slopes, to think of an armed
escort; and when her carriage was stopped on that Sunday morning,
she was surprised before she was frightened.   Following the first few
moments, she regained her poise and became coquette.   She kept her
head; and it was a cool head under stress with a humorous and delible
mind.   She matched her wits against Bibisi's as if playing a game, all
the while noting with irony the individual reactions of her companions.
Nor was there any affectation in her report for she had enough self-
confidence not to dissemble.   She admitted she had been scared.   Contrary to the Scotsman, William Mure of Caldwell, who said the risks of
brigandage in Greece were no greater than those of fox-hunting, they
were for the Duchess.

The letter was addressed to The General Duc de Plaisance, Peer
of France, Place de la Madeleine N°. 1.   By French steamer to Marseilles, and read,

Athens this Tuesday June 16.

*Day before yesterday Sunday I left Athens with M. Sa-
kellaris, the engineer Gorgandas and my architect M. Gouza-
ris Denain.   Arriving on Pendeli mountain a short distance
from the monastery by my latest route I saw a carriage
stopped and tipped up across the road in which were a*

gendarme and three other men. Hardly had I noticed it when our carriage was also stopped by some men whose skins and clothes were the color of chestnuts or dead leaves.

What is it ?

Brigands, I was told by one of my companions.

Ah, brigands.

While this was being said their chief forced the coach- man to get down next to whom Sekeri had been sitting and were questioning him to make certain the lady in the carriage was really the Duchess and to find out the names and importance of those who were with me. One of the Brigands wanted to take the coachman's watch, the chief stopped him saying, ' No, it's the Duchess who must pay '. Then he went up to M. Sakellari (an employee of the Ministry of Foreign Affairs) and to M. Gorgandas who could act as interpreters. I had a moment of a very sharp pain in the intestines, but it lasted only a couple of minutes. My mouth was dry but I did not tremble and I did not lose my head. I asked one of the Brigands to take a small pitcher I had with me and to get me a drink and he went to look for water in the ravine. I had some raspberry syrup I drank and poured some for the three gentlemen. The two Greeks were more frightened than I especially the engineer whose hand trembled as he held the glass both were pale the architect seemed sad, calm, and resigned. Sekeri kept all his courage, having drunk I asked what the Brigands wanted. Inwardly I said to my God ' You are all powerful if you wish to protect me nothing will happen to me '. M. Sakellaris : the brigands demand that you write a note for two thousands Dubione (pieces of Spanish gold each worth 84 francs) they will send one of us to get the money and when he returns they will set us free. M. Gorganda, sign Duchess otherwise they will torture us.

I : but that is impossible where can I find that money. The King himself could not get it right away.

The Chief of the Brigands 'You are richer than the King Palati in Athens, Palati on Pendeli lands and a village.

' All right, said I, take the lands and the palaces but as for the money I do not have it. I am not so rich as you think and besides my fortune is in France. I have my income come every three months and I expect it by the next steamer. I do not keep any money in my house. My banker himself could not have more than a thousand drachma in his house, he keeps (it) in the big Bank. Today is Sunday, everything will be closed '. Sakellari said to me he would agree to 1,500 Dubione (about 130,000 francs). M. Gorgandas kept begging me to sign saying they will torture us. Sakellari seconded him, the architect remained silent. It was not yet two in the afternoon when I was stopped. It was known that the Chancellor of the French Consulate was at the monastery with his family. The brigands thought they were too exposed waiting there. They had the carriages turned around and conducted us to the side of one of the abandoned quarries. They also forced a builder who had arrived about the aqueduct I am having built on Pendeli to walk behind the carriages also two peasants who were passing. They held them so that they could not report on what was going on. I forgot to say that upon my refusal to sign the note for 1,500 doubloons the chief said he was going to kill us at that I got out of the carriage and faced him and I said to him, ' Very well, kill me and let the others go '; but it was a lot of money and not my life that he wanted. At my refusal because of the impossibility they expressed incredulity and they said what use will your money be if you are killed instead with the money we shall cross into Turkey and bless your name. I go back to the quarry road where they had stopped the carriage at the foot of a fairly high little peak. Soon there appeared at the approach

*to the bridge a builder who was coming to receive ins-
tructions from the Engineer Gorgandas for a road I wish
to complete. At a sign from Sekeri, at the peril of his
life and in sight of the brigands he turned back. The
Chief who had seen Sekeri's sign knocked him down to
the ground and seemed to me to kick him. I got down
right away from the carriage and again said to him to kill
me; me and leave that man alone the contract was again
taken up and frightened probably by the escape of the
builder, Flamborou they consented to a note for a thousand
thalers 5 or 6,000 francs that I signed. The officer Gorgandas offered to take it; but they preferred the writer
Sakellari and made him leave in a carriage drawn by two
horses. Then the chief climbed up the little peak with
the Engineer Gorgandas to discover what was going on in
the plain. When they came down the Engineer came to
tell me that twenty Kalandriots could be seen marching
toward Pendeli that the chief ordered me to send him the
officer Gorgandas to stop them and to make them go back
telling them if they advanced I would be killed. Gorgandas thus to his great pleasure got himself out of the
Brigands' hands. I remained alone with the architect Denain and Sekeri whom I made get inside the carriage
where I believed he would be safer. I had wished him
to go with M. Sakellari pointing out that the Banker accustomed to send me money by him perhaps would not wish
to give it to some one else. The Brigands refused. They
had the carriage climb to the base of the quarry. From
there seeing the Kalandriots getting closer they left me to
flee just as they left. Sekeri gave me 2 coins that he had
in pocket and following his wish I gave them (this was
considered good luck) to the same chief who had kicked
him. In returning I soon met the Kalandriots and some
Maroussiots under the command of a young Frenchman
named M. Armand Boisguilbert. As this letter is already*

very long and here I am released I shall say no more at least today.

A Dieu

You can be assured that I shall go back to Pendeli only with an escort of about five mounted gendarmes. I do not know if I shall spend the Summer there; but it would only be with a guard. Could you send me the two guns that I asked for lately by the steamer.

On July 24 the Duchess wrote again to Charles on the same subject :

You may do with my last letter whatever you please; but when you will receive this one, my adventure with the brigands — except for the very few people who are interested in me — will have fallen into the gulf of oblivion. Isn't it better to leave it there ? Be assured that politics and the opposition do not enter into this affair. I wish I could say as much for the monks of the monastery of Pendeli; but unhappily I am convinced of the contrary. First you will have to know that the monks of the mountain monastery are all more or less friends of the brigands to whom they furnish bread and meat to live on in the desert. And then one circumstance I had noticed although I have forgotten to write it to you is that the brigands who stopped chance comers — as they had to do lest they spread word of my apprehension — were not at all disturbed by a goatherd from the monastery who was nearby with his herd and moved away very softly and quietly. I should like this to be put in several French papers but without letting it be known that this information comes from me The Journal des Débats *particularly.*

I think I wrote you that the gendarme who was in the carriage which was stopped ahead of mine said the chief of our Brigands was Bibisi and he named two or three of the others. I have been told that he had been forced into Brigandage to evade punishment for the murder of his wife's lover. He has protectors among those close to Co-letti above all a certain Mayor or Demarch of Athens with whom you dined at my house. The same is mayor and accused by public opinion of protecting a great many thieves... (illegible) ... But he has or had influence upon the Electors of Attica at the election of Coletti in Athens. I return to Bibisi : one of his Protectors : the monk Taba-kopoulos vicar of the monastery of Kaissariani sent me word, as a piece of advice, some days later; that Bibisi had a daughter seven years old and that if I wished to take care of her I would acquire some rights to his grati-tude ... (illegible) ... — between an adulterous mother and a murdering father one does not find much hope for virtue — I replied that I would have to see the child and before anything else it would be necessary to obtain the father's exoneration — I know that for some time the Government has given him hope of it — and for that I was willing to take some steps. Some days later the monk Tabacop sent word — always by M. Sakellaris — that he had seen Bibisi that he had nothing to do with my arrest and that his exoneration was promised to him my intervention was superfluous. A few days afterwards a farmer from the monastery of Kaissariani appealled to Sekeri on behalf of Bibisi to ask me to obtain his exone-ration. Consequently I have composed a little supplication to the Queen I have had it translated into Byzantine Greek and sent to Bibisi for him to sign last Wednesday 22 of this month.

Thursday July 30

The farmer mediator between Bibisi and me told Sekeri that he had not yet been able to send back the letter to

*be signed not having seen him for ten or twelve days.
However the heat here is prostrating I have entrusted some
one to ask Coletti for five gendarmes for me — four with
the same sub-officer they gave me for my trip to Livadia
— and I believe I shall go to stay at Rhododaphne where
the heat is never insupportable.*

A Dieu.

The letter, however, continued in the handwriting of Elena
Skouzès, copying a long account from the Athens *Courrier* of a political
agitator who had caused, by home-made bombs and other means,
blood to be spilt on the island of Samos.   The Duchess' purpose in
sending the report was to acquaint Charles with some of the ways the
factions of the Powers in Greece used such men and brigands.   At the
end of the account, the Duchess again took up her pen to comment on
it, to say that Bibisi had been exonerated without her assistance, and
to conclude with a family note,

*I hope to learn in three weeks that Jules has been elected
a Deputy.   That will fill his time.   Do you know anything
about the countess ?   Here it is more than three years since
she became determined to give up her daughter!   Does
Jeanne know about her mother ?   Has the latter written
to her since she went off ? (The wife of Jules, Charles'
nephew, had deserted him and their child).*

*In what occupation does the child show most interest ?
Is she made to read history ?   What history ?   and what
authors ?   The first to read are Genesis and Exodus written
if not by Moses at least from notes and documents left
by that man whom Bossuet called, ' The oldest of historians,
the wisest of legislators, the most sublime of Philosophers. '*

A report on the Duchess' hold-up, sent six days after it, by the
French Minister in Athens, Piscatory, to the Ministry of Foreign Affairs
in Paris, expressed the suspicion that the act had been prompted by

politics : why was it that the bandits were supplied with writing paper and a pen ? It was very similar to a hold-up that had been staged a little earlier near Corinth of some carriages belonging to the King, in which the brigands had also first to ask to whom the carriages belonged. A short time ago it had been the fashion in Athens to blame Colettis and his Ministry for all acts of brigandage in Greece. Piscatory wondered if now the Opposition's turn had come. In any case, the Duchess had told him she had less to complain of about her hold-up than she had about law-suits she was involved in against some of her friends.

Both because the Duchess always did what she said and later the brigands of Pendeli came to regard her as a friend, Bibisi's daughter was presumably taken care of. Little Jeanne began to receive many letters from her great aunt; and shortly after the rescue, the village of Kalandri was given a much needed public washhouse by a grateful Duchess. Having done the latter, the Duchess considered the hold-up to be lost in « the gulf of oblivion ». She refused to speak of it and, when queried about it, changed the subject. Others made the most of it and added versions of it to her legend. And, with the coming of new faces and fresher excitements to Athens, it might well have become a dim reference in local lore had not Edmond About joined the French School there six years later. That enquiring and intelligent Frenchman soon heard enough about the Duchess to seek an introduction to her and by his wit and charm, he eventually made her talk of her experience. Two years after her death, following his return to Paris, About used the hold-up in his novel, *Le Roi des Montagnes*. The book was translated into serveral languages and became one of the best sellers in the middle of the last century. Partly melodrama, partly farce, its story of the arrest of a titled woman by bandits in the Greek mountains, spread the Duchess' adventure across two continents.

A PYRE

The encounter with Bibisi tempered the Duchess' enthusiasm for politics, and after the death of Colettis in 1847 she tried to avoid them for safer pursuits.   Had she been a less erratic woman or a less prominent one she might have gained a degree of seclusion from public attention, but her character prohibited it.   Even luck was against her, and during the year following the hold-up only some new friends offered diversions from the consequences of old involvements.

In the Spring of 1847 the French School was opened in Athens, an organization based upon the plan of the French Academy in Rome, where young scholars could spend two years at the expense of the French Government studying Greek history, philosophy, and literature. Its beginnings were inauspicious as its first director, Daveluy, took one look at Athens and developed a crippling case of home-sickness.   He avoided the company of his students and rebuffed their efforts to improve his morale.   Desirous, as always, to tilt with bright minds, the Duchess used his nostalgia as an excuse to meet him and took Dr. Raiser to tend him.   While her call produced no medical benefit, it gave her the opportunity to become acquainted with the students. Among this first group, Emmanuel Roux, Georges Radet, and Charles Lévêque were invited to Ilissia and the Maisonette.   A sensitive young man with engaging manners, Lévêque found special favor with their owner; and it was after the inspiration which the views from Pendeli instilled in him that he composed his *Philosophic History of the Greek Minerva* and his essay on the *Physical Causes of Perfection in Ancient Greek Art*.   Later, Alfred Mézières, who was to become an Immortal of the French Academy, became the Duchess' friend, recalling after her death that she had been the students' most faithful friend who never abandoned them in their loneliness.

One December morning, to thank the Duchess for a gift of two bottles of her best wine, Mézières went to Ilissia, a house he found very large, very Oriental and, without any European comforts.   It was ten o'clock, the hour the Duchess received, and as soon as he was announced, according to her custom, the Duchess had him shown into a small sitting room where there were a warm fire and some newspapers to read. A few minutes later, she appeared and asked, « You haven't had any breakfast, have you ? Good! What would you like ? Tea, coffe or chocolate ? » He chose tea which was served with fresh butter, toast, and small cakes, and the Duchess ate with him surrounded by her dogs.

He remembered that she never appeared without her white veil, her red slippers, and her long, simple, white tunic. « Although she was very small and very thin, the dignity of her carriage and the elegance of her gestures gave her an imposing appearance. After the astonishment caused by her bizarre costume, when she began to speak, the Grande Dame became apparent. » He was impressed, as so many were, by her wit and memory, and he relished an historic anecdote she told him of a time in 1809 when she and her father-in-law, the Archtreasurer, called on the King and Queen of Holland. On the stairs they met a nurse carrying the youngest of the King's sons. Upon the Archtreasurer complimenting the King on the health of his son, the King replied, « My son! Go on! I have no illusions. I am sure that child is not mine. But I do not wish to make a scandal that would irritate the Emperor. What good would it do ? He is not the eldest; he will not succeed me. » The child did not succeed Louis on the throne of Holland but he did become Emperor of the French as Napoleon III.

There was one, however, among the early students at the French School who, like Rangabe, was less susceptible to the Duchess' hospitality. Eugène Gandar found her attentions to be a kind of blackmail by which she was able to fill her own loneliness. Night and day, according to him, she routed the young men out of the School, dragged them to her house, drove them on excursions into the country and bored them with her Biblical talk, her pack of ravenous dogs, and her stories of the Empire. Even those students who at first put up with her because she recompensed them by gifts of that rarest of Eastern delicacies, fresh cow's milk, and by the release from the heat of summer with the cool air of Pendeli, eventually lost patience. Revolted by her stilted character, they refused to set foot in her houses. With the intolerance of youth and without a sense of humor, Gandar wrote from Athens to his brother in France,

> *I am annoyed by this woman who could with her fortune of three millions, give happiness through her charity to whole villages and through the courtesy of her hospitality to the whole colony of bored foreigners. Who better than she could gather in her salon a distinguished society and could create a common center where different circles could come to mix together and could forget the monotony of their isolation? She has never known how to do it because she does not attract others to her house for their pleasure but for her own; because she disgusts everyone in turn by her pedantry and demands; so very few come to her while very many go away; and there remain about her, to listen to her lessons and to submit to her whims only sots who go to be fed or whose compromised virtues have thrown them out of other places, or people with nothing else to do who are on the look out for the crumbs from her table.*

Gandar was bored. He complained that he could not find in Athens a quiet fireside where he could poke the logs, nor a woman whose agreeable conversation gave relief to the masculine conversations of the School which sooner or later got on his nerves. In all of Attica there were only two French women, a little old bitch in Pireaus who only talked about herself and her clothes, and the Duchess — Charybdis and Scylla.

In despair he opted for Scylla and finally accepted to drive with her in her carriage where for two hours he listened to her Act of Faith which, he said, she had written at the foot of Mt. Sinai. She vexed him because she had a distinguished mind which her peculiarities and egoism had ruined. On the same ride she discoursed upon the electoral law, the motto for the Republic, and by fits and starts threw him such questions as, « Are you a Christian ? Do you like Italy ? Will you come back to the East ? Would you like to be a Deputy ? » She interrupted him to pronounce in the grave voice of an oracle, « You are young; believe me when I say, be careful of one thing : do not let yourself grow fat; do not use too much vinegar; sleep on a horse hair mattress; sleep little and follow a meager diet. Rice makes you sleep. »

Allowing for Mézières' generosity and Gandar's resentment, taken together, their accounts give a fair picture of the Duchess at this time. She continued to be open handed to those she liked; and she had grown demanding and unreasonable. She could be witty and entertaining; she could be repetitious and tiresome. She was proud and selective; and the choice of congenial companions was not always large in Athens. The students of the French School made the most stimulating audience she had had since Eliza' death. They were young; they were French. Most of them were graduates of France's strictest school, Normale, with minds as sharp as her own; and they furnished her diversion from an entanglement resulting from one of her acts of generosity three years before their arrival. Within a month after the School opened, her gift to David Pacifico boomeranged; and she was drawn into one of the strangest political manœuvres concerning Greece which was ever staged by the European Powers.

In the 1840s there still existed in Greece the custom of burning The Judas on Easter. A large dummy was made, often bearing the features of some unpopular person, and framed in fireworks. On the day of the festival this caricature was paraded through the streets for Christian derision and deposited before a church to be set afire by the jeering mob. Just before Easter, 1847, Alfred Rothschild, the son of the Neapolitan banker, went to Athens to discuss a loan to the Greek Government, and lest his financial goodwill be destroyed by a religious insult, the Athenian police were given orders to suppress the burning. When the populace arrived at the church to await the effigy and learned of the prohibition, a riot ensued. Further inflamed by a rumor that Pacifico, who lived nearby, was responsible for the order, the mob made for his house, stoned it, forced him to flee, and indulged in larceny and pillage.

When the first word of the inequity reached the Duchess, without waiting for explanation, she expressed contempt for the action in heated words. Her sense of justice and her sympathy for the Jews were both aroused. Despite Pacifico's dubious reputation, she defended him as a victim of unpardonable malice and slander, and reviled anyone who tried to point out discrepancies between the man's character and her notion of his persecution.

Both were soon evident for, in a matter of days, Pacifico drew up a list of claims against the Greek Government and presented it as a British subject. He asked 500 Ls for personal suffering, 5,000 for the contents of his house, 21,000 for legal and financial documents destroyed. He even included an item covering the cost of his bridal bed. The exorbitant sums — for he actually had no assets — were based upon the theory of the higher the demand, the higher the settlement, a theory which was the outgrowth of his dismissal from employment by the Portuguese Government for which he had asked an indemnity of 450,000 francs and received 5,000. The Greek Government understandably refused to consider his claims. Whereupon, Pacifico, pleading destitution, asked the Duchess for money and also appealed to the British Government to support his official demands. The Greeks refused to deal with the English, and the affair dragged on for years because the English saw it as a way to discredit King Otho and the Russian faction which supported him. When Otho stood firm, for once, the English took his attitude as a serious affront. Palmerston, then Foreign Minister, issued an ultimatum demanding all debts to British subjects in Greece be paid. In a speech in the House of Commons, Palmerston justified the demand by recalling St. Paul's arrest in Jerusalem, and the speech is still known by the reply St. Paul made to the centurion, *Civis Romanus Sum.* When this reference to Biblical precedence still failed to move the Greeks, the English reduced the amount of Pacifico's claim but they put pressure on the Greeks for its payment by blocading Pireaus. While this reprisal ruined their trade for a full year, the Greeks remained indifferent.   In the end, the English had to leave the settlement to an international committee. This commission awarded Pacifico 150 Ls.

Privately in 1852, the Duchess sued him sucessfully for the return of the land she had given him for a synagogue, land which had never been used.

In the meantime, eight months after the assault upon Pacifico, on the evening of December 19, 1847, the Duchess drove up to her wooden house on Pireaus Street to find it in flames.   At the sight, her one thought was of Eliza's body, and leaping from her carriage she ran to rescue the coffin.   But the fire was lethal and she was forced to turn away from it.   In anguish she stood in the street begging for volunteers and offering a reward for the recovery of the coffin.   Again the heat forbade entrance, and since there was no fire brigade in Athens at the time, she was compelled to stand helpless and watch her house with her most precious possession reduced to ashes.

Some bystanders said the fire did not prevent the theft of the Duchess' jewels.   Some declared the coffin exploded and its embalming fluids turned the conflagration into a display against the winter sky of red, yellow, and blue pyrotechnics.   Others declared the Duchess kept screaming, « My daughter! My daughter! »   Several people asserted that they had had the decency to lead the Duchess from the disaster and to give her shelter.   In fact, the same young man who had led her rescuers to free her from Bibisi (Louis de Boisguilbert, an attaché of the French Embassy), stepped from the crowd of onlookers and gently steered the Duchess to her carriage in which he took her to a house where he had recently rented an apartment.

The house belonged to John Dragoumis whose six year old son, Constantine, never forgot the Duchess' arrival that night.   He was awakened by a loud pounding which, repeated with the noise of splintering wood, shook the house.   Jumping out of bed, he followed his aroused parents to a window.   Below them they saw Boisguilbert coming from the wrecked door of the apartment which, his servant being away and he being locked out, he had kicked in to reach the latch. Before the door stood a berlin with two stout horses.   By the door of

the carriage stood its liveried coachman and two large white dogs.   At
the carriage window was the face of a woman with a white covering
over her head.   As the family watched, the coachman opened the
carriage door and he and Boisguilbert helped the Duchess and her maid
to alight.   After which the women and the dogs followed their host
into the house and the carriage drove off.

By morning the gossips were busy.   The French Ambassador,
Thouvenel, had his little joke.   It was he, he said, who took care of
the Duchess after the fire.   He conducted her on his arm to the embassy
where, learning from her that Eliza's body was in the cellar of her
house in a cask of malmsey, he offered a reward of 500 francs for
its safe delivery.   An hour later a cart drove up to the embassy and
deposited a cask for which the driver was duly paid.   The Duchess,
informed of its arrival, went to see it and discovered she had been
given a cask of rum.

Greek gossip was more interested in the Duchess' relations with
Boisguilbert, and when their names were mentioned, the town guffawed.
Why had he taken it upon himself to shelter the Duchess ?   Why had
he destoyed Dragoumis' door ?   When asked these questions, Boisguilbert replied it was the only way a man could behave who had a sense
of duty and hospitality.   But the gossips were not satisfied and, when,
because Ilissia was not yet completed and the Duchess remained several
months in the flat, they found in her stay all they wished to believe.
Altough the young man had not moved into the apartment at the time
of the fire and did not do so so long as the Duchess was in it, a love
affair was flushed from behind this cover.

Boisguilbert was thirty, single, rich, handsome, and charming.
He kept horses and spent as much time in hunting as in working.
When not using his gun on game, he peppered the door of his room
with shot.   The very model of a reckless cavalier, he was, in the public
mind, irresistible to the Duchess.   Precisely how attractive a tiny, white
haired woman almost twice his age, done up in a white chiton, was to
him no one cared to conjecture.   Nor is the nature of their relationship
known.   The Duchess never referred to her private life.   She never,
after her separation from Charles, repeated her reasons for it; and she

never revealed the name of a lover. « The tongue », she once told an inquisitor, « cuts off the head. »

The gaudiest patch on her legend was stuck on it as late as 1926 when there appeared in the French publication, *Intermédiaire des Chercheurs Curieux*, information saying that the Duchess had returned to Paris after her first visit to Greece and had taken up residence with Charles in Barbé's house by the Madeleine. The marriage went from bad to worse. She began a love affair with the Prince Belgiojoso, and one fine day in 1843, following a more than unusually violent dispute with her lord and master, she appeared at the handsome, happy Prince's house carrying only her handkerchief for luggage, and said to him, « Let's be off ». They thereupon made their way to Lake Como where they lived openly together for nearly ten years when, breaking with her lover, the Duchess returned to Greece.

This piece of scandal was an interpretation of a paragraph in a letter written by Alfred de Musset to his brother on May 22, 1843 : « I do not know if you know, the rest of you, at Catinia, that the *Principe* has carried off the *Comtesse de ...* For two years everyone in Paris has known they have been living together. It seems the Countess had an argument with her husband; she arrived at the house of the Prince — who should have been singing at a concert that evening — adorned with her handkerchief as her only baggage and said to him, *Let's be off.* They are on their way. »

The interpretation is one of the risks of notoriety. The Duchess, of course, was never a Countess. She became part of the Napoleonic nobility without passing through its lower ranks and her first tiara bore the eight points of that of a Duchess. After her first visit to Greece she was legally separated from Charles. In 1843 she had been living consecutively for six years in Athens after her return from Lebanon. The reference to the Jeanne in her second letter to Charles about Bibisi, refers to the daughter of the eloping mother whom she calls, Countess, for this young woman was married to Jules Lebrun, the orphaned son of Charles' brother, Alexandre, who had been killed on the retreat from Moscow. The Countess did run away with Belgiojoso on April 27, 1843 from Paris to Lake Como. The couple remain-

ed together for five years.   On February 5, 1848 Prosper Mérimée wrote
to the Countess of Montijo, (the mother of the future Empress Eugénie
of France), « The Prince Belgiojoso has left the Countess of Plaisance
or has been left by her, I do not know which, but she is now in Spain
with a new lover. »   The Countess was the daughter of the Maréchal
Berthier, and in the Château de Grosbois near Paris, in the great
salon carpeted with the rug bearing the arms of the Maréchal as Prince
de Neuchâtel, there hang two portraits of her, and one of her husband.
On her smaller one, done in the late 1830s, is painted, « Comtesse de
Plaisance », and on her husband's of the same date, « Comte de
Plaisance. »   It was not until after Charles' death in 1859 that his
nephew and his nephew's wayward wife became by succession, Duc et
Duchesse de Plaisance.

It is possible that Sophie de Marbois had lovers.   Her French
biographer comments upon lack of proof with Gallic incredulity,
« Sixty years of virtue! ».   It is also possible that the Duchess' obsessive
affection for Eliza took the place of another kind of love.   It is equally
possible that this feeling caused the mother to covet whom the daughter
desired.   The Duchess' behavior toward Léopold Robert suggests she
was as taken by him as was Eliza : and it could also explain any
intense feeling she might have felt for Katsakos.   But one of the un-
common things about her in an age of so many women, like her friend
Jane Ellenborough, whose prominence was largely gained by the flaunt-
ing of their love affairs, was a fame independent of sexual adventures.
Loving to the Duchess, like giving, was a private matter, and if she
had lovers they were men of a similar opinion, who remained as reticent
as she.   If they existed, discretion might well have been part of their
attraction to her.   In a very important sense, the question of lovers
is beside the point since no love affair affected the Duchess' character.
None ever modified her resolution, and none altered the course of
her life.

All that could truly have been said of her feeling for Boisguilbert
was that it was strong.   He came into her life when she was in need
of his gaiety and loyalty.   He was the sort of man who was kind
enough to spare her the rumor of the common people of Athens who

asserted that the destruction of her house was the Curse of God fallen upon her for keeping and unburied corpse in it. He was intelligent enough to let her hear the rumor that called the fire arson and declared it to have been set on fire by those who resented her defence of Pacifico. He had sufficient humor to have appreciated the Duchess' own version. The fire, caused in fact by a defective flue, the Duchess said was owing to the combustibility of all human things.

TITLES OF NOBILITY

Ilissia, when the Duchess moved there in 1848 was an unfinished country estate at the edge of the Attic plain. Heather covered Hymettus and Athena's discarded burden, Lycabettus, were its neighbors. Only the two main buildings of the present Byzantine Museum were completed. The arch with the name, « Ilissia » curved above the carriage entrance between the double gatehouse. The gatehouse served on one side as a porter's lodge and on the other as a kennel for those of the huge Pyrenees who acted as watch dogs. The great courtyard was bare except when a carriage rolled across it, or the dogs bounded over it, or the Duchess' flock of white pigeons fluttered down to strut upon it. Behind the palace, the Ilissus cut through an immense, unshaded garden plot where About said the Duchess took pains to see that no tree grew. Edmond About found the house lacked refinement and was underfurnished and uncomfortable; and, by Paris standards, the house was not a model of decoration nor had the Duchess any desire to make it one. It was uncluttered and its few pieces of furniture were in the simpler Empire style which, being few, increased their elegance. Proud of this, the Duchess never tired of taking her guests on a guided tour of the house. She acted, Mézières said, as she showed him things he had seen twenty times before, as if he had returned from a long voyage during which she was afraid he had forgotten their disposition.

She felt differently about Pendeli where Rhododaphne was a sad woman's unfulfilled dream. The only person in Athens to have the sense and the taste to build a refuge on those slopes from the summer heat, she cherished their breezes, their heights, and the panorama below them as a reminder of what she had come to Greece to find — the compensation for history, her hopes for the future. She never ceased to search those heights for a site for the altar to her God; and on them she wished to be buried. In contrast, Ilissia was a dwelling, the only house, since she left France, to give her a feeling of establishment, and she never stopped making plans to enlarge and to embellish it. When David d'Angers went to Athens in exile from the Revolution of 1848, she saw in his presence an opportunity to adorn it and she commissioned him to do a bas-relief of Themistocles in the house of Admetus. Although the plan never progressed beyond a drawing, the Duchess' intention was to have placed the plaque over Ilissia's front door.

Before the destruction of her wooden house, the idea of celebrating hospitality would have been surprising; but the fire had its effects. Eliza's body could no longer tempt the Duchess to fruitless mourning and sap her emotions. Without form, her daughter's ashes conjured no presence. Boisguilbert's gaiety undoubtedly helped to loosen the Duchess' self-imposed constraints. The expression of her pride in Ilissia showed it. Even her gifts were now made with less chance of their being snatched back. On the west wall of the Rhizarios Seminary where the name, Odos Rizari is today, she installed a simple marble fountain. On it was inscribed in Greek and in French, « For Passers-by ». Its water came from her own supply from Pendeli, and the peasants, coming from the long march into Athens or leaving the city to recross the hot plain, were heard to bless The Doukessa, as they called her, while they drank.

In 1848, Sir Albert Denison, the great grandfather of Sir Osbert and Dame Edith Sitwell, spent three months in Athens and, although he did not meet the Duchess, he heard of her benefactions by a curious extension of her legend. The Duchess, it was said, had willed her property to the most virtuous woman in Greece. The plausible part of this gossip was that no English woman was eligible; the implausible part was that the Bavarian Queen of Greece was to head a committee to choose the paragon.   Once again, what people thought the Duchess could have done was contradicted by their ignorance of her prejudices for the whole idea was conceived by others and not by the Duchess.

Yet not even her experience with Pacifico embittered her.   In 1849, she gave outright the sum of 5,000 francs to the Consistory of Metz for a prize to the French Jewish girl of that city who excelled in Hebrew.   She specified, if one of the contestants was not outstandingly successful the judges were to divide the money equitably.   So rare was the knowledge then of Hebrew, that in October of that year only three candidates presented themselves and a committee accorded 2,700 francs to Mademoiselle Céleste Alexandre, 2,000 to Mademoiselle Nathalie Blum, and an Honorable Mention, signed by all the judges, to Mademoiselle Julie Brunschwig.   In September of 1853, the *Archives Israélites* announced another gift under the heading, *A Well-Placed Liberality.*

> *A French lady, living in Greece, and who has so many times proved that Jewish adversities are assured consolations from her, has just forwarded to us the sum of* One Thousand *francs to be given to relieve the unfortunate Jews of Salonika (in European Turkey), who have lately been the victims of the most odious persecutions.   We have lost no time in seeing that these funds reached their destination, and we are happy to thank publicly their distinguished donor.*

Like most changes that come with age, those in the Duchess were of degree not of kind, accentuations rather than differences in character.   While she remained as perverse as ever, she seemed more reposed. There was no smoothing of edges; no softening of feeling; and never any compromise.   She repeated that her calling — in the face of the contradictions to the destitute of the War of Independence, to her Little Friends, to the Jews — was to help the rich and not the poor.   She spent little on her person, yet she lived surrounded by servants, a steward, a housekeeper, a secretary, maids, cooks, grooms, coachmen, gardeners, farmers, architects, engineers, masons, and carpenters, the whole fortification of wealth.

The exigencies of Time she accepted without regret. She watched without flinching people she had known well, makers of an empire and of a new nation, slip into the ghostly role of stock characters for historians : her cousin François-Etienne Kellermann, victor of Marengo and second Duc de Valmy died, as did her Aunt Marguerite, Admiral Miaoulis, the Petrobey, Marco Botzaris' brother, Lady Hester, even Bibisi who was murdered by an erstwhile friend who was hired to kill him. There were some satisfactions : beautiful Rose Botzari married Major George Caradja, the first Greek to head the Military Academy; and Panayotika Mavromichali became the wife of Admiral Salimis. At her request, Elena Kapsali Skouzès, named one of her daughters, Eliza. (There is living today in Athens a great-granddaughter of Elena also called, Eliza.)

Yet the Duchess continued to treat her dogs better than most people she knew and to demand human indulgence both of their behavior and of hers toward them. Not long after the hold-up she recovered from her fright of brigands and, instead of armed guards for herself, she increased the number of her dogs and used them as her guardians. Two, Ouzac and Bourie, in the place of the dead Baris and Lefka, were her compagnions and one always rode on the seat facing hers in her carriage and at night one slept in her bedroom while the second slept in the hall by her door. Constantine Dragoumis and his playmates made a point of going to Ilissia to bait the watch dogs who crouched in the entrance way with eyes fixed on the gate. At the slightest movement by the children, to their delight, the dogs snarled and leapt toward them. The Duchess encouraged this ferocity and even allowed all the dogs the run of her houses. Gossip insisted the dogs tore beggars to pieces without being punished because of the Duchess' distaste of beggars. She was reported to have received an ambassador in her dining room instead of in her salon on the second floor of Ilissia because Ouzac was asleep on the landing of the right staircase and Bourie on the landing of the left one. When the French Admiral, Duperré, visited the Maisonette, the Duchess took him to the funeral of a spaniel on the slopes of Pendeli. While the Duchess was still in Boisguilbert's apartment, Ouzac and Bourie, hearing one of Madame Dragoumis' maids crossing the courtyard, dashed out and viciously attacked her. By the time the Duchess' servants had collared the animals, the girl was unconscious. Although she was ill for several months afterward, it was only under threat of law that the Duchess paid her medical expenses. She never paid an indemnity yet Constantine Dragoumis, who witnessed the incident, said the Duchess' excessive fondness for her dogs « proved her noble heart and high opinion of dogs, which she loved as much as human beings »!

Love is hardly the word to describe the Duchess' attachment to people. She had loved Eliza; in a different way she had loved her father-in-law; and once she had loved Charles. Some people like Jane Digby amused her; some like Mézières, were sympathetic; some she was fond of, like Rose Botzari and Elena Skouzès, and Boisguilbert; but, in general as she grew older she showed no deep feelings. Upon learning in 1849 of the violence of the cholera epidemic in Paris, she wrote to Charles urging him to escape and bring Jules, the Count, and his daughter Jeanne to Pendeli where they would have pure air, pleasant walks along streams shaded by oleanders, vegetables from her garden, plump chickens from her farmyard, milk from her cows, and partridges which her steward would shoot in the mountains. Even warblers. Charles relayed the invitation to his niece asking her to note that fresh vegetables, plump chickens, and above all fresh milk were rarities in the East. He recalled when he had been in Athens, that the Duchess used to send milk to her friends and, he thought, even to the Queen. Charles had already refused the invitation and merely asked Jeanne to add his thanks to hers when she replied to her aunt. The Duchess' consideration for Charles was typical of her attitude to people against whom, once she had settled their score, she harbored no grudge. The difficulty in knowing her was how to anticipate what one's score might be. People talked about her; they slandered her; and some failed her without retaliation as did her banker when he lost 300,000 drachmas of hers in bad investments and she did not complain.

She shrugged off the idea of malice in the destruction of a bridge she had built as she had belittled the cause of the fire; but she could have her joke with those who tried her no matter their rank.

The King and Queen had no summer residence. The royal palace in Athens had cost 10,000,000 francs and the royal purse was light. Otho, however, kept his eye on the progress of Rhododaphne, and although relations between the Court and the Duchess had not improved since the picnic, the King one day ventured to Pendeli without the Queen. This time the Duchess was there, busy directing the men at work on the Château. After a few formalities, the King began to admire the beauties of the location and finally expressed a desire to live there. The Duchess immediately offered him her unfinished building.

« Sire », she said, « take my Château. Finish it. You can have it for 50,000 francs. »

Knowing that the Duchess had already spent 300,000 francs on it, the King was delighted to accept.

« Furnish it any way you like », the Duchess continued. The King nodded.

« Live in it as much as you like », she went on, « and at the end of ten years return it to me as it then is. »

Seeing Otho's face drop, the Duchess remarked, « If this arrangement is not satisfactory, I would take the liberty of offering another idea. »

« Do », the King begged her.

« This one is a true gift that I am about to make to Your Majesty. »

« Make it, Madame la Duchesse. »

The Duchess led the King to a piece of land adjoining her property which still belonged to the monastery. She pointed out its advantages as a building site, the excellent air, pure water, and admirable view. The King would be able to see a large part of his kingdom from his windows. The Duchess paused. The King waited.

« Well, Sire », she finally said, « I give Your Majesty, if you condescend to accept something from me, the advice to take this land from the monks and build a summer palace on it. »

The King bowed, departed, and dreamt no more of Pendeli.

Despite closing her doors to Bavarians and Phanariots, the Duchess saw many more people after 1848 than formerly, and even held soirées at Ilissia. At these, and surrounded by her dogs, she recited poetry and prose, suggested topics for general discussion and served a goodly number of her anecdotes. She permitted debate even though her comments on expressed opinions were pronounced before those of her guests. Hours that might have been tedious she at least tried to enliven by jokes. One of her favorites she remembered having heard in 1814 when Louis XVIII was said to have asked Pope Pius VII why His Holiness had consecrated the usurper, Napoleon. The Pope chided Louis, « What can you expect ? You were not around ». « But », Louis protested, « Holy Father with my legitimacy, I reign even where I am not. » To which the Pope replied, « But, my dear son, with my infallibility, I am right even when I am wrong. »

Her most constant guests were old Greek friends who had escaped her displeasure, the Levidis, Dragoumis, Botzaris, Sahinis, Zaimis, Soutzos, and Skouzès. Madame Thébaut, the sister of Madame D. Levidis and Madame N. Dragoumis, who had married and separated from a Frenchman, was particularly admired for her physical courage and wit. She lived in a house on the Patissia Road as isolated as Ilissia and as open to danger from bandits. It was a location her family deplored, but which Madame Thébaut minimized by saying no harm could come to her since she slept with an icon above her bed and a pistol under her pillow. Of the Duchess' Little Friends only Photini was absent. The Duchess never forgave her for becoming a Lady-in-Waiting to Queen Amalia. After the Queen read in Photini's diary of her secret passion for Otho and dismissed her, the Duchess added trouble to shame by asking Photini to return a gift of money.

Dr. Raiser, Boisguilbert, and George Finlay among non-Greeks remained her friends. Finlay sent her copies of his articles on Greek history and politics; and after Sir Thomas Wyse became English Ambassador in Athens in 1849, the Duchess forgot her antipathy for « our eternal enemies » and saw something of him — probably because he had married, although not for long, the Princess Letizia-Christine

Bonaparte, daughter of Napoleon's brother, Lucien.   She introduced
About to David d'Angers in 1852, and About, in turn, took Théophile
Gautier to see her during Gautier's brief visit to Greece.   The perma-
nent French residents numbered two landowners beside the Duchess,
two storekeepers, a baker, an innkeeper, Monsieur Bareaud, one of the
Queen's gardeners.

Of the volunteers who had borne arms for Greece only three
settled in the country after the War of Independence, Sir Richard
Church, Colonel Touret, and Baron Frederic Eduard von Reineck.
The Frenchman, Touret, became a self-appointed Aide to king
Otho and was responsible for erecting the wooden columns bearing
the names of the Philhellenes who were killed during the War in the
Roman Catholic Church in Nauplia.   Von Reineck was a Saxon
whose valor as a soldier had early won him an honorary Greek citizen-
ship, an award the Duchess could not belittle however much she
might have deplored his marriage to a Mavrocordatos.   Adding
her antipathy to English, Germans, and Russians, it was not a large
group from which she could choose friends.   The American colony,
the smallest of all the foreign ones, was not composed of people with
more attractions.

It is largely forgotten now that the first Americans to reside in
Athens after 1829 were missionaries.   It had not been enough for
Philhellenes to support the cause of Greek arms and to send food
and medical supplies to the victims of the war, in the minds of many
of them, it was their equal duty to sponsor education in a land of
illiteracy.   The intention was admirable and its results were extensive
and laudable.   The men and women from England, France, and the
United States who opened schools on the Greek Islands and on the mainland in the 1820s and '30s toiled with zeal from the highest motives.
Their only handicap was a Protestant bias, a blend of bigotry and
dedication, inappropriate to an Orthodox nation.   The most prominent of them were clergymen and their wives who were employed by
the Protestant Missionary Society of France, the Church of England
Missionary Society, the American Board of Commissioners for Foreign
Missions, and the Episcopal Church.   Their pedagogy was thus naturally

inspired by their sectarianism and they became anachronisms — Christian missionaries to a Christian country.

The Reverend Pliny Fisk reported to the American Board in 1825 that both Greece and Russia presented extensive missionary fields because the Orthodox Church did not admit several of the important errors of the Papists. In 1828, the Reverend Jonas King of Amherst College, having made a survey of Greece with Fisk, found that schools should be started at once in that country and added, « With this the Bible must be distributed. If something is not done Greece will be lost. » (It was Mr. King who, with Dr. Samuel Gridley Howe acting as grooms-man, married The Maid of Athens, Teresa Macri, to James Black on Aegina in January, 1829.) In April, 1831, while the Turks were still in Athens, Mr. King with his Greek wife, opened a school in their house in the Agora. Two months later, for the Episcopal Church, the Reverend John and Mrs. Hill opened another school in the Plaka — that still exists as a school for girls. In both establishments religious services were held, and while the Greek Church at first welcomed the educational efforts of the missionaries, by 1835 it began to take exception to their proselytism. An Orthodox bishop preached against the schools in Athens, and in 1846 Mr. King was taken into the Criminal Court there on charges of reviling the Greek Church. When Julia Ward Howe visited Athens with her husband, the doctor, in 1867, she found « the religious quiet of the city somewhat disturbed by the presence of several missionaries, supported by funds from America, who persisted in teaching and preaching ». The author of the Battle Hymn of the Republic added that, while « the missionaries cannot compete in polite learning with the *élite* of their antagonists, they are much better informed than the greater part of the secular clergy and represent, besides, something of American freedom, and the right and duty of doing one's own thinking on religious matters ».

In a city the size of Athens — it had twenty-seven thousand inhabitants in 1851 — it would seem unlikely that the Duchess did not know the Kings and the Hills, yet no record connects her name with theirs or with any American travellers to Greece. Mr. King was a friend of George Finlay, but a woman who could elude a monarch, could have eluded a clergyman if she so wished. Evidently she so wĭshed. The missionaries' belief in mass education must have tried her patience; their cordial relations with the Palace and the Government would have been no recommendation to her; and their evangelism would have seemed to her absurd. Similar causes separated her from the laic visitors from the United States, differences in sophistication, in points of view, and in tastes. American travellers to Greece in the early Nineteenth Century were people of cultivation, from Nicholas Biddle through N. P. Willis to C. C. Felton and Henry M. Baird, the latter two professors of Greek, one at Harvard and the other at New York University, yet their books, journals, and their letters show them to have been singulary pre-occupied with self-improvement of a serious nature. Their lives were real and very earnest, and they regarded any signs of detachment as suspicious luxuries. Professor Baird, the only American to mention the Duchess — and he never met her — reported with condescension from hearsay which was kinder than usual, « The amiable old lady now confined her attention to her buildings and to half a dozen dogs of various kinds, which she took out on an airing every afternoon. She enjoyed among the inhabitants the reputation of being a millionaire, from having an income of 15 or 20,000 dollars, which was lavishly expended. »

The American sense of humor was a sense of fun, an exaggeration notably lacking in the subtlety of French wit and satire. Proud citizens of a new republic, the American travellers all sought invitations to the Greek Court and in its stodgy rituals — receptions and balls at which male and female guests, separated by their sexes, waited until the Grand Master, the Grand Mistress, and Aides ushered in the Monarchs, and made a circle around the King and Queen — they found much to impress them and nothing to laugh at. Among the souvenirs Professor Felton took back from Greece to Harvard in 1853 were, a fragment from the Parthenon, pebbles from Demosthenes' beach, and a jar of olives which had been pickled by The Maid of Athens. The hundred and fifty little scholars at the Hill School were trained to sing a hymn to the tune of *Home Sweet Home*. The Duchess could offer only partridges, and she never found a site worthy of her altar.

About reported that she craved new faces, and any man who appeared at her door, provided he wore gloves, could boldly present himself and be welcomed. The Duchess would submit him to a drive in her carriage in the company of one of her dogs and invite him to dinner with the pack of them. Although it was known that her interest was apt to wane quickly, every European stranger to Athens ran the risk. Early in 1850, when the Princess Cristina Belgiojoso, the wife of the Prince with whom the Duchess did not elope, came to Greece, the Duchess invited her to stay at Ilissia. There were many reasons for the visit to be successful since the Princess was a devotee of liberty, her own and her country's. As a young girl, twenty years before, she had gone into exile in France owing to political disturbances in her native Italy. In 1848, she returned to Milan to take part in the insurrection there and had been rewarded by the confiscation of her property and a second exile. During her first sojourn in France, she became notorious, prospering under the auspices of several distinguished elderly men including General Lafayette and Barbé de Marbois, and by a series of love affairs among which were those with Heine, with Liszt whom she lured from Madame d'Agoult, and with Alfred de Musset whom she snatched from George Sand. A tall woman, she had black hair and a gaunt ashen face which she set off by wearing a white robe and a Rennaissance turban. She had entered strenuously into the Paris fashion for religion, receiving callers as she knelt at a prie-dieu with stacks of large, dusty Bibles and a skull at her feet. She also published an essay in four volumes on the formation of Catholic dogma.

Her arrival in Athens offered every advantage to gossip and to the Duchess' experience in dealing with it. Its greatest possibilities for the Duchess were opportunities to deliver to a fresh audience her opinions of history, religion, and diet. The Princess had another attraction : she had come to regard Barbé before his death much as his daughter had. A visit to Noyers had so bored her, she described it as « a hell ». Yet within a few days of the Princess' arrival, the Duchess quarrelled with her and packed her off to stay with the Countess Théotoki. Whether from guilt or not, the Princess bore no resentment against this lapse in hospitality, and after her return to Paris she published in the newspaper, *National*, a long and kind account of the Duchess which, after speaking of her separation from Charles, of her eccentricities, of Eliza and Bibisi, she ended,

> *The Duchess succeeds however in overcoming her sorrow. Now she lives, so to speak, outside herself. She gives herself objectives for the pleasure of attaining them; she devises plans; she is passionately for or against certain people; she talks well; she keeps up a correspondence with a number of friends; she behaves like a woman whose feelings have never been struck by those three scourges; illness, old age and death.*

Between the Duchess and Jane Digby Théotoki there was a strong confidence, and it was on the Duchess' recommendation that Jane commissioned Cleanthes to build a house for her in Socrates Street. Jane had stayed in the wooden house on Pireaus Street while her own was being built; but the friendship between the two women was sealed after Jane became the mistress of Hadji-Petros and was banished by Queen Amalia from Court and consequently shunned by Athenian society. While it was well known in Athens that Jane had been Ludwig's mistress for a short time, Amalia took offense at her conduct with Hadji-Petros because, gossip said the Queen had her own eye on the soldier. In 1846, when the affair began, Jane was thirty-nine and Hadji-Petros was nearly seventy, still a tall, handsome, vigorous creature, resplendent in a gold covered Albanian costume, Commander of the Pallikars, and Governor of Lamia. To Bavarian dismay, not unmixed with envy, Jane went off with him to spend an idyllic interlude among his warriors in the wild mountains of Lamia. Upon their return to Athens, only the Duchess had the courage to receive them; and she did what she rarely did to others, she went often to call on them.

The calls had certain limitations since Hadji-Petros spoke neither French nor English and the Duchess spoke little Greek; but she and

Jane shared an abundance of vitality, quick minds, a love of horses and dogs, and a taste for reading the Bible. They had, too, the gift of style, the ability to mark whatever they did with their unique personalities. The Duchess was Jane's confidante and it was she who insisted that Jane divorce Théotoki, neither as a moral nor a social rectification of the liaison with Hadji-Petros, but as a financial safeguard. The Duchess refused to condone an unprofitable investment, and she found the fact that Jane was still giving the Count half her income, a monstruous extravagance. Divorced, she told Jane, and Spyridon could not claim a penny from her.

Singularly good-looking, witty, cultivated, and with habits as rakish as Jane's, Théotoki bore the Duchess no grudge for the advice which Jane took. Through his introduction and recommendation, in an interview at Ilissia on January 19, 1852, the Duchess employed Demosthenes Vratzanos to be her secretary. The meeting took place in a small salon lighted by an open fire and a single window, and furnished with a few straight chairs and one armchair. The Duchess sat in the armchair and gave a performance worthy of those with which she used to greet guests in the old house on Pireaus Street. She inclined her head as the men entered and extended her hand to be kissed. After some seconds of silence spent gazing at the ceiling, the Duchess said, « Be seated », and pointed to the chairs. Although she listened while Vratzanos gave an account of himself, she behaved as if he was not there. Her questions concerning his qualifications and her stipulations of lodging, board and salary, she addressed to Théotoki. « Ask the young man if he wishes to work for me », she instructed the Count. « Tell the youth I shall give him 80 francs a month. » Vratzanos was hired without once being spoken to.

The Duchess made up for this neglect a few days later when Vratzanos arrived at Ilissia to take up his duties. Anxious to exhibit his resolve to please, he drew up at the gate in a public hack at nine-thirty in the morning, one half hour before the time stipulated via Théotoki by the Duchess. The Duchess was already in the courtyard, a blue-print in her hand translating its contents to workmen. Noticing the porter about to open the gate, she enquired who was without.

Upon being told, she pulled a watch from her girdle, looked at it, and informed the porter, « It is not yet ten o'clock. » The porter asked if he was to tell the secretary to wait. « Tell whom ? » the Duchess replied, « The secretary ? My secretary ? I like that! Now I have two secretaries, one at nine-thirty, the other at ten. What shall I do with two ? Certainly the man who came before his time is not my secretary so I cannot receive him. Here, take my watch and see that you do not admit my secretary before ten. »

Vratzanos waited and had the hack wait because it contained some furniture for his future bedroom. Connoisseurs of Ilissia had told him that all its rooms were so sparsely fitted, if he wished to live there he had the choice between discomfort with any complaints being met by the Duchess with, « My house it not a hotel », or supplying some furniture of his own. If he did the latter he ran only the risk of being accused by the Duchess of transporting microbes into her house. Vratzanos risked the microbes; and when Ilissia's gate was opened at ten, two porters began to carry his belongings toward the house. At this sight, the Duchess, who was still in the courtyard, asked, « What are those red things my men are carrying above their heads ? » « Two shabby chairs », Vratzanos told her. « Oh, » the Duchess exclaimed, « they look like guillotines. Burn them! Burn them! » « Fire! » she cried. Vratzanos begged her mercy; he explained they were family pieces; but she was not dissuaded. « Burn them here in the court- yard! » « At least », Vratzanos pleaded, « change the sentence to exile for life. » « Fire! » the Duchess repeated; and the chairs were burned. Yet no sooner were they reduced to ashes than she showed remorse. « Of course », she apologized, « I have caused you sorrow. » « It does not matter », Vratzanos replied, « The table is left me. » Whereupon the Duchess cried, « The table! It looks like a sepulchre! Burn it! » The finale to this scene was the Duchess' direction to Vratzanos to pick up a handful of ashes of his beloved property adding, « I too have a handful of ashes and I keep it... oh, I keep it. »

Eventually Vratzanos was led by Maria, one of the Duchess' maids to his room which was all he had been led to expect. In it were an iron bedstead, a wooden table, two chairs and an armchair.

The air for lack of ventilation, was stale.   Vratzanos objected about the room to the maid.   Maria assured him he would have better accommodations, perhaps the next day, because she knew the Duchess was well disposed toward him.   In any case, she asked him, didn't he know he was dealing with an ill-tempered old woman ?   She herself, she said, had been subjected to much worse.   She had been with the Duchess for several years and only remained because she was friendless, an abandoned orphan.   Look at her cropped hair.   Until the day before her hair had been long, and fair, falling to her heels. Every one had been jealous of it; even the Countess Théotoki had offered to buy it; but Maria had refused to sell because her mother had kissed it just before she died.   But her hair reminded the Duchess of her daughter's, and only yesterday morning, while Maria was in her room combing her hair, the Duchess had suddenly appeared with two of her dogs, and silently raising a pair of scissors had grabbed her hair and cut it off.

These episodes of the burning of the chairs and of Maria's hair were among others which Vratzanos published fourteen years later in sixteen pages of fiction he called, *Three Months by* (sic) *the Duchess of Plaisance.* In his preface he announced that he saw no reason not to prefer the attractive style of romantic narration to that of dry and direct historical presentation; and his intention, he said, was to be a poet and idealize the Duchess.   « Here », he wrote, « is Dumas, here Féval of our poor Greece.   Salute him, maidens, he comes disguised as a strange old woman, the Duchess of Plaisance. »   Her age did not stop him from also hinting that he had been the Duchess' lover.   But Vratzanos was known to be unscrupulous, an opportunist, and an addict of purple prose; and his episodes contained enough plausibility to make them seem true and enough distortion to make them popular.   No doubt, the Duchess did have his chairs burned. They were suspiciously shabby and soiled, and the Duchess loathed unclean things as much as unclean people who blew their noses in their fingers.   She may well have cut off Maria's hair, not because it reminded her of Eliza's but because the maid refused to wash it and it was filthy.   Jane's offer to buy it was a teasing reflection of a common cus-

tom among poor women of the time who sold the crowning glory of
their heavy braids to women less hirsutely endowed. Jane was irresponsible at times; she had deserted two of her children. At times the
Duchess was hard-hearted; she had no pity for the Dragoumis' maid.
But neither woman viciously concocted mischief. Vratzanos' accounts
are out of focus; and his sights were perhaps irreparably joggled when
the Duchess dismissed him by whacking him off her premises with
her cane.

His reports are also suspect because Edmont About, who was
often at Ilissia at the same time and who searched for tattle about
the Duchess, never mentions Vratzanos or his adventures. About was
a brilliant, cynical, gifted young Frenchman whose clear eye caught
the Duchess' character with more comprehension than anyone else who
wrote of her. Her character, About said, was as sound as few men's
are, with a firm will, not without depth, and with a lively wisdom all
of which was tinged by her invincible taste for everything out of the
ordinary. The exaltation of her ideas and the peculiarity of her faith
had in no way altered the finesse of her ideas nor the soundness of
her judgment. She had a prodigious memory which, although good
journalist that he was, About had difficulty in making her share with
him.

It was hard to draw the Duchess out and she refused to criticize
anyone, preferring to answer About's questions by anecdotes or reminiscences. « In my time », she told him, « we loved stories and those
who knew how to tell them were welcomed everywhere. Your novelists
are poor story tellers; they know only how to discourse. Is there one
who is the equal of Delille ? And have Monsieur de Lamartine and
Monsieur Hugo written anything as perfect as those verses ? » She told
him the joke about the Pope and Louis XVIII. « I have forgotten
nothing », she said, « I have learned much. I know everything
that has taken place since my arrival in Greece. I know, wait! I
know too many things and several I should like to forget. One above
all... would you believe it in this country they sometimes bury people
alive ? One man who was subject to fainting spells that could last
twelve hours, had one that lasted twenty-four and he was believed dead,

so he was buried.   The next day, the grave-digger heard a noise from the grave.   He did nothing, but a day or two later he met the widow and told her that evidently her late husband did not like the next world for he was making enough noise to wake all his neighbors... the grave was opened and it was found that he was dead but after frightful convulsions. »

She spoke to About of the altar she wished to live long enough to build on Pendeli, and made vague references to her religion.   She was explicit only about her fear of being buried alive.   No one, she said, would do that to her if she could help it.   She had, she said, left instructions in her will that she be placed on a couch in a well aired vault with two doors, one in front and one at the rear.   A bouquet of fragrant flowers was to be placed on her litter to help her regain consciousness and also a bottle of Bordeaux to restore her strength.   And lest brigands come to slit her throat, she was leaving a pension for life to a robust shepherd to spend his life on the first floor of the monument to watch over her.

About's greatest difficulty was to make her speak of the hold-up.   Again and again he asked for her account only to have his request ignored.   He even resorted to telling her about a hold-up in the Peloponesus, but the Duchess was not to be decoyed.   Finally one afternoon when Jane was with them, he asked once more.   The Duchess insisted the incident was not worth talking about, but Jane, playing up to About, began to describe it.   The Duchess interrupted her and proceeded to give an abridged version of it which she ended by saying that Bibisi had taken his leave of her in tears.   « I gave him ten francs which he accepted with thanks. »   Then she added, « There is some good in those people. »

In a woman with less flint in her character, the Duchess' tribute to the brigands could be construed as sentimentality, but the Duchess' flint never softened.   Her plans for her burial showed that some fear of them lingered and her reticence that the hold-up belonged to her private life about which she never wished to speak.   « I know too many things. »   She never learned resignation to sorrow, but she knew how to substitute activity for repining and how to adapt her resources to what her life had become.   She knew the cost and reward of her freedom — mockery and independence — and she knew how to protect her feelings.   She dismissed servants who refused to address her as, Madame la Duchesse, and when asked, why, replied, « Old as I am, what have I left but my titles of nobility » ?   When Jane discovered Hadji-Petros' affections were really for her maid, she rushed off in shame and hurt to the Near East and rushed back to tell the Duchess she had found a Sheik she intented to return to.   The Duchess told her the idea was insane and the Duchess quarreled with her.   But the Duchess' true reason was her realization that with Jane gone, she would lose her friendship and she did not wish to miss her.

At the time she said farewell to Jane, in 1853, the Duchess was sixty-eight.   She had lived longer than the average woman of her day who died young from repeated childbearing and lack of medical knowledge of endemic diseases; and she showed her age.   She was old and ill, so frail she looked to About as if a breath of wind could blow her away.   Her face was lined and as white as her hair and her robe.   But her eyes were as blue and as bright as ever, and her beautiful French made up for a lack of teeth.   Eugene Gandar who had once mocked her, returned to Athens in the Spring of 1853 and was shocked and grieved by her appearance.   « What kind of life », he asked, « does she lead here in utter solitude ?   It is still worse; one is never alone when one is sixty-eight and has two millions and no heirs.   The memory of her kindnesses to me during my first trip and a feeling of just compassion, which renders me more sensitive to the poor woman's qualities and distress than to her eccentricities, as pronounced as they are, forces me to mix from time to time in her dubious entourage.   The Duchess herself feels grateful to me for my attentions.   I could not vouch that those about her feel the same way; and who knows if there are not some kind souls in Athens who suspect me of having reformed in the hope of a codicil ?   Everywhere there are villainous people and villainous things. »

There is no record of a diagnosis of the Duchess' illness.   Ludwig Frankl met Dr. Raiser in Athens after the Duchess' death and was told by him an autopsy had been performed on her body, but Frankl quoted the Doctor only as saying the *pons Varolii* was almost disintegrated. Since the *pons* is a body of tissue merely serving to connect one section of the brain with the other, what the doctor said was not a diagnosis. An obituary in an Athenian newspaper mentioned « a disease of thirty years » without naming it. Writing of her visit to Athens in 1850, the Princess Belgiojoso said the Duchess had contracted « a chronic disease » but, again, she gave it no name. No one before 1850 ever spoke of the Duchess as being seriously ill — not even the gossips who could be relied upon to make the most of any detail that concerned her. Had the ailment been of long duration, it could not have been a grave handicap because the Duchess rode horseback until a few years before her death. Even when her body weakened and she became frail, her mind remained clear. Stamina and will power kept her going when, as the Princess Belgiojoso added, « ninetenths of the most energetic men would have had to take to their beds ». The deterioration of the heart muscle is the most probable diagnosis; and it is known Dr. Raiser treated her for dropsy.

After 1850, her condition worsened rapidly, but she continued to direct her affairs. In October of 1853 she prepared an endowment of 60,000 francs in Eliza's memory for the Consistory of Metz, the annual income of which was to be devoted (and was until it disappeared in the War of 1940) to the education of poor Jewish children of that city especially in the « Profitable and honest vocations of the land. » In appreciation of this gift, the Chief Rabbi of the Consistory decreed that on the first of November of every year a memorial service was to be celebrated in memory of the late Mademoiselle Eliza Lebrun de Plaisance, and on the Day of Atonement in both the Temple and in the Oratory of the Jewish hospice in Metz prayers were to be offered for the Benediction of Heaven upon Madame la Duchesse de Plaisance.

She now had the nephew of Demetraki as her secretary and through him she transferred her orders. George Skouzès collected the interest on her loans and wrote out the receipts, but the Duchess signed them for Degles, Podoski, Soutzos, Levidis... For a quarter of a century the signature did not vary, S. de Marbois, Duchesse de

Plaisance; only on the last receipt, signed eight days before she died, did it waver — slightly.

In the spring of 1854 she grew very weak.   Until 1850 she had ridden horseback, now she could not often endure the jolting of her carriage and rarely so far as Pendeli.   She insisted, however, that the work on Rhododaphne go on and kept Dr. Raiser busy carrying messages there and returning to Ilissia with reports.   She no longer read; and the faithful Elena Skouzès spent hours reading to her which the Duchess rewarded by reciting to her poetry she had learned as a child.   By April it was difficult for her to walk.   She leaned on servants to reach a window or to take a few steps under the colonnade above the Ilissus.   No records tell what her thoughts were.   Had she forgotten Buchy and Noyers ?   The Empire ? The War of Independence ?   Had she a thought for Charles or only a longing for Eliza ? The light lay as heavy as always on Hymettus.   Above and beyond the young trees in the Queen's new garden, it changed the ruins on the Acropolis from gray to maize.   In her courtyard the pigeons and dogs were white.   Where they all too familiar or too dear for comment ?

On the first of May Dr. Raiser spent the night at Ilissia.   The servants stood in the hall outside the Duchess' bedroom.   Inside two dogs lay on the floor with their heads on their paws.   Maria stood by the bed fanning the air above the Duchess' head.   Her breathing was labored but she lingered.   For two weeks, the physician, Elena, and the servants stood helplessly by her.   At nine o'clock on the morning of the fourteenth she died.

George Skouzès took charge of the funeral.   After the Orthodox custom, the casket was uncovered.   It was borne on the shoulders of the Duchess' servants at the head of a cortège which passed under the arch of Ilissia, turned right, and crossing the Attic plain, wound up the slopes toward Pendeli.   As the funeral entered the square in Kalandri, the villagers met it and forced it to halt so that they might pay a final reverence to a trusted friend and neighbor.   Then they, too, fell in line and the procession climbed the road the Duchess had built among olives and pines, cedars and mulberries, by hollies and through spreads of daisies and wild aenemone and hyacinth to the knoll above the Maisonette. There the monks from the monastery led by their Abbott formed a line behind the grave and chanted prayers for the soul of the dead.

Later, what were thought to have been Eliza' ashes were buried with her mother's body. Still later George Skouzès erected a monument over the grave. On a stone base, a marble stylobate supports a miniature Doric temple — just large enough to cover the coffin of a little woman.

At the base of the tomb's eastern facade looking toward Rhododaphne, is carved in Greek, « Erected through the care of George Skouzes », and above this in French,

Sophie Barbé de Marbois
Duchess of Plaisance
A French Woman
Born in Philadelphia
1785
Died in Athens May 14, 1854

VII

TO BE A PHILHELLENE

Et le plus beau, le plus difficile à mériter
de tous ces titres : Ionien, Philhellène.

Mémoires d'Hadrien,
Marguerite Yourcenar.

Three days after the Duchess' death the Athenian newspaper, *Elpis*, announced, « The Duchess of Plaisance, who has lived among us for twenty-five years and who gave great assistance to the Greek Community, died last week. » She departed, the paper said, with the wishes and blessings of the many she had helped. Her eccentricities had been the results of a disease she had had for thirty years and had harmed no one. They had not impaired, the paper concluded, people's respect for her and she was considered a virtuous and charitable woman.

The French Minister to Athens, who was still Thouvenel, did not consider the Duchess' death worth reporting to the Ministry of Foreign Affairs in Paris — a petty retaliation for the Duchess having disagreed with him years before about Colettis.

Letters from Athens carried the news to Paris; and in its issue of July 3, the *Journal des Débats* printed a formal obituary which extolled her charity and attributed it to her religious beliefs.

Upon hearing of her death, the Duchess de Dino recalled the Duchess as a witty, rather strange woman who had been kind to her at a difficult time in her life. But the Duchess' most earnest mourners were the Consistory of Metz, some brigands, and Elena Kapsali. On June 16, at six in the evening, a service was celebrated in the synagogue of Metz for the repose of her soul. The Chief Rabbi delivered a eulogy and recited a Kadesch; and in reporting the service, the *Archives Israélites* remarked, « Thus it is that tolerance provokes tolerance and tears of gratitude fall in a Jewish temple for the death of a Christian benefactress. »

Some years after her death, Charles' nephew, the son of the Baron de Plancy, being in Athens, went to Pendeli to pay his respect to the Duchess' grave. Just before he reached the site, he was surrounded by some heavily armed bandits who asked what he was doing on their territory. Upon being told, the Chief replied, « If you are the nephew of our benefactor, I give you a quarter of an hour for meditation; after that I won't answer for my men. »

There was a hush in Athens following the Duchess' death not from the shock that the « Old Duchess », as her mockers called her, had died, but because she had died intestate. The description she gave About of the clause in her will pertaining to her tomb, remained a figment of her imagination. In letters to her great-niece, Jeanne, she promised to leave Ilissia to her without doing any more about it. She expressed desires that her favorite dogs should be buried with her and that her pigeons should be cared for after her death, but she put nothing in writing. Barbé, in his letter of 1836 to the family lawyer asking him to urge the Duchess to make a will, said she disliked talking of such matters; and after Eliza's death, while she often spoke of her own death, she never overcame her dislike for doing anything with the finality of a will.

The result was, that as that of a French citizen, the Duchess' estate was divided, according to French law, equally between her nearest relations, two second cousins on her father's side, a son of a daughter of her Uncle and Aunt Kellermann, the Viscount Léry, and their other grandson, François-Christophe-Edmond Kellermann, third Duc de Valmy. The Chancellor of the French Legation in Athens drew up an inventory of the assets the Duchess left in Greece : houses, and lands to the value of 2,600,000 francs which, with close to a similar value in farms and woods in France, brought the total of her estate to over 5,000,000 francs. Two and a half months after her death the legal division between her heirs was made.

But in that same month of settlement, September, 1854, there was living in Paris an American woman, Mrs. Mary Ridgway, who received a letter from her father, Richard Willing of Philadelphia, pointing out that as the Duchess had died intestate, half of her 5,000,000 legally belonged to her nearest relatives on her mother's side. Richard Willing was correct. He had married the Duchess' cousin, the daughter of her mother's brother, Thomas Lloyd Moore. Thus, his children were also second cousins; and Mrs. Ridgway immediately took the matter to the French courts.

There then ensued a lawsuit which surpassed in absurdity any the Duchess had ever instigated. With a statutory brainwave, the lawyers for Kellermann and Léry, announced that the parents of the Duchess' mother, William and Sarah Lloyd Moore, had never been legally married and hence the American cousins had no claim upon the Duchess' estate. One argument they used, without substantiation, was that Madame de Marbois had gone insane the day she learned that she was an illegitimate child. The main argument for the defense was that the union of the Duchess' grandparents was illegal because it had never been officially registered in Philadelphia, the only proof of it being in Family Bibles!

At this announcement, Charles, now in his seventy-ninth year, put a pen, that wabbled as much from indignation as from age, to paper and addressed a letter to the lawyer for the American cousins,

Paris, February 1, 1855.

Monsieur,

    Despite my decision to remain completely detached from the disputes which have arisen between the contestants for the estate of Madame la Duchesse de Plaisance,

I cannot remain silent after having read in the Tribunal
Gazette *for January 30 the incredible assertions put forward
in the interests of* M. DE VALMY *and* M. DE LERY.

*No one has the right to make such statements in the
face of justice*

*that suspicions have never ceased to hover around
M. Barbé de Marbois about the legitimacy of his wife's
birth which had been sworn to by witnesses*

*'to prove that the Marquis de Marbois was out of his
mind during the last years of his life.'*

*It is sad to think that for the sake of money people
wish lying fables to be accredited and have no scruple to
attain this end to upset families by defiling the memory
of the most honorable people.*

*Knowing Monsieur that you have the right as the attor-
ney for the other parties in this lawsuit to answer these
indignities I authorize you to reject them in my name
in the most explicit manner since I believe I can declare
in all truth that never did M. le Marquis de Marbois my
father-in-law have the least doubt about the regularity of
his wife's civil status, as the legitimate daughter of the
marriage of William Moore and Sarah Lloyd, and that
no suspicion has ever hovered around him about the legitimacy of that relationship. As for M. le Marquis de Marbois, whose old age was so honorable and so worthy of
being, there is not one of his former friends of whom
many still exist who cannot testify that to the last day of
his life, and by a rare exception, he retained the greatest
lucidity of mind to the point that he was still able to do
useful work and to take part in the discussions of the
Chamber of Peers although he was almost blind.*

*Conscious Monsieur of your entire loyalty and of your
distinguished talent, I do not doubt that you will know
how to reduce to their proper value the odious calomnies*

and I authorize you to put my letter to what ever use it suits you.

Believe, I pray, Monsieur
(unsigned)

After the lawyer for the plaintiffs pointed out to the French Court that in the American Colonies at the time of the marriage of the Duchess' grandparents, no official registry of marriage existed and that Family Bibles were the usual and legal sources and proofs of marriages, the American cousins were granted their half of the Duchess' estate.

The property in Greece was put up for sale. The Greek Government bought Ilissia and unfinished Rhododaphne. After George Skouzès called the attention of all the Duchess' heirs to the devoted and unrewarded companionship of his wife to the Duchess, Elena Kapsali Skouzès was given the Maisonette in return for the care of the Duchess' tomb.

That Elena was embarrassed by her husband's insistence upon some material recognition of her loyalty, is shown in a letter of thanks she wrote in 1857 to the Administrator of the Duchess' estate in Paris. Elena asked him to express to the Duchess' relations how touched she was that they knew how to appreciate the true feelings which had dictated her conduct toward the Duchess, since never, despite the intimacy between them, had any idea of reward or profit entered her mind. The Duchess had found this attitude so rare that she had said to many people and above all to French people, that Elena was sincerely attached to her and that she had never even indirectly asked for anything. The Duchess' eminent qualities had always inspired Elena's respect and in return for the care the Duchess had taken, despite age, rank and health, in perfecting her education, in developing her ideas and forming her judgment, Elena had done all in her power to prove her gratitude. A number of people had often advised her to get the Duchess to make a will, but delicacy had kept Elena from speaking of a subject she knew was painful to the Duchess and in any case, Elena was happy enough to have the Duchess express pleasure at what she did for her. What had now been given her, Elena accepted

as « a sacred souvenir » especially the care of the tomb since the
Duchess had often expressed to her the desire to be buried on Pendeli
and for Elena to be entrusted with the care of her grave and that
of her beloved daughter. (Over a century and a half later, the grand-
daughters of that Little Friend still care for the Duchess' tomb.)

A figure of fun, a poseur, a bore, a silly, a mean, an obstinate
woman, Sophie de Marbois has been called each of these names and
none alone wholly describes her. Even together they suggest only a
part of her character since with equal truth she can be said to have
been sensible, generous, courageous, intelligent, witty, loyal, and idealis-
tic. Contrariness was so of her essence that to generalize about her is
certain to be inexact and unfair; and the larger complex of all her
contradictions is what makes her life the lively footnote it is to the
history of her native land, to the First Empire, and to modern Greece.
Her most obvious quality, rebellion, was unpredictable, asserting
itself when she was thirty-nine seemingly by a whim, the whim to be
independent. Neither then nor later was there evidence of ulterior
motives of principles dictating her act so it was and remained a personal
revolt. Charles bored her, not marriage. The laws governing separation were strict and inequable, but she did not denounce the laws or
think of working to change them; she breached them. The question
of rights for women never entered her head and had she known the
word, Feminism, she would have laughed at its meaning. One of
Charles' descendants still has a pistol which belonged to her and a
descendant of one of her American heirs recently gave to the Ethnological Museum in Athens, her sewing box — symbols of a woman who
wished only to be free to take care of herself. Being neither theorist
nor reformer, what she rebelled against was not so important as what
she gained and created from her success. To judge by these, dissent
was the well-spring of her nature, so evident About called it, « an
invincible inclination toward all that was not commonplace », and so
deep as to suggest had she been born poor or slave, she would still
have been fractious.
Her eccentricities even lacked the usual coquetry of such displays.

Caring nothing for what people thought of her, she indulged her fancies because they were pleasing to her and being both tasteful and bold, she gave a flair to whatever she did. She dressed perversely, yet with far more sense and comfort for a hot country than had she worn the velvets and crinolines of the Paris fashions of her day. She followed her own dietary rules while skimping her guests and tempting Charles with the choicest of foods. She build her houses; she preserved Eliza's body not to call attention to herself nor to enlarge her public image but by preference. In Ilissia and in Rhododaphne she erected frames of elegance around her simple tastes which set off a style as individual as the motives that prompted her choice.

She always had courage whether of her convictions or of her foibles, a courage that first showed in the way she signed her name during the Revolution in Metz and which developed after her separation from her husband into an egotistical self-confidence. Right and wrong, derided and lonely, she was never afraid. Terror and war were too familiar to cause her to consider any dangers she might encounter in Greece in 1829. Her hesitation following her hold-up was short-lived and she soon started to cross and recross the lonely Attic plain with only her dogs as guards. Neither Eliza's death nor her own illness and old age curbed her will to face whatever else there was to life. From experience she learned a portion of the discipline neither Barbé nor Charles had been able to force upon her. She learned it the hard way, from necessity, keeping busy in adversity to keep her sanity, indignantly taking to court Pacifico and Mavromichalis, and others she believed to have wronged her until she acknowledged such actions not as unbecoming and unworthy but futile, for her valor never lacked bravado.

Her peculiar blend of idealism and scepticism often played her tricks producing the inconsequence of her misjudgment of Marie-Louise and the serious results of her marriage. She supported the Maniots, heroes that they were but without administrative experience, against Capodistrias, and later, for equally emotional reasons, Colettis against Mavrocordato.

Enthusiastic and prudent, she made a fool of herself in defending

Pacifico and in becoming an Indian giver to Photini. Sentiment blurred her estimate of the work of Delille and Robert, a feeling that was absent from her clear headed encouragement of Cleanthes and David d'Angers. An obsession turned her sorrows for Eliza into a macabre fetish. Susceptible to flattery, she yet chose her flatterers — no bores; and if among the people who surrounded her in her old age there were hangers-on, she was too intelligent not to know them for what they were. Nothing clouded her judgment in practical matters. She was never known to have made a poor investment in loans or in lands. Shrewd and witty, she told many a salty story among the anecdotes she liked to repeat. Her tongue stung Charles and Otho for their dullness, and Phanariots and Bavarians for their pretentions. Typical of her contradictions was her lack of rancor, and About never succeeded in making her condemn anyone who had really wronged her, Bibisi or miscreants who destroyed one of the bridges she had built. The most confused and surprising aspect of this attitude was her cavalier taking for granted Charles' later friendship — despite his faults and her antics. Reasonableness, which she believed herself to possess, she expected to find in others.

The most mercurial of her traits, the one that modified all others including her rebelliousness, was her generosity. A generosity without self-interest. Her chief mockers could never say that her contributions and gifts were motivated by personal ambition for, while she often demanded agreement, she never asked more for herself. After the King, she was the richest person in Greece and at her death one of the richest women in Europe, yet it would be misleading to say that because of her wealth and rank there was nothing she might not have tried to buy for herself since she had the wisdom to know what she coveted most was not for sale, love — a husband for Eliza, ideals — the purity of motive she sought among the saviors of Greece. She enjoyed her title and her riches as a gardener admires the blooms he has cultivated, for pleasure not exploitation. Her subsidies were the satisfactions she took in nurturing her dreams; her silly relapses into pettiness were the risks of her opulence.

Long before she was attracted by larger human plights, the misery of the Duchesse de Dino had stirred her benevolence. Whatever other reasons there were for her charity to Jews, one was her offended sense of waste, a lost potential, which is, as she herself pointed out, very different from philanthropy. She educated young girls and assisted bankrupt families in Greece not from humanitarian pity or a sense of the injustice of poverty but from a respect for their resources, because they were the potentials of Greece.

Her generosity to Greece began with heroic fancies and ended in their sober corrections. Yet she remained loyal to her ideals. She never lost faith. She believed in the promise of Greece despite the incompetency of politicans and the intrigues of foreign powers, and while she never compared this hope with her private exigencies, she found in Greece her self-fulfilment. The question, why, after Eliza's death, why, when she had the means to move anywhere else in the world, she chose to stay in Athens, is not answered altogether by, « she liked it ». Despite disillusions, despite grief burdened memories, why she liked it is more pertinent.

In the early Nineteenth Century two other parts of the world caught the imaginations of oppressed and romantic Europeans. The discontented also moved far East and far West. Victor Hugo called the decade after Waterloo, « the flight of the eagles » to describe those officers of La Grande Armée who, unlike Charles and the Kellermans, were too restless to adapt themselves to retirement and took off to try their wings elsewhere. Of them only Fabvier volunteered to go to Greece. Allard and Ventura sought their fortunes in India; Lallemand founded a Champ d'Asile, an Utopia, in Texas. But on this unquiet wave the Duchess' imagination stopped short of the exotic. Even before her visit to the Near East, she was not tempted by bedizened sheiks or coon-skin caps. The East was too alien; America still too undefined.

Commonsense cut her romanticism as alcohol cuts the sweetness of syrup. Greece meant to her civilization : mankind's instincts, aspirations, and curiosity directed by reason; and she went there to help to liberate the descendants of those who by their miracle of two thousand years before had liberated the human mind. Her illusions were quickly corrected, but she stayed on to savor the joys of victory and the uses of freedom.   Above all, she stayed because she could not leave.

Throughout the centuries Greece has become for most Philhellenes what their associations with it have meant to them.   To some it has been a nostalgia, the Golden Age; to some an ideal, the Golden Mean.   To others it has been a state of being, an euphoria, or even a love affair, a feeling forever anchored by a private transference. For a few who go there a more subtle spell, which has nothing to do with historical or personal associations, lays hold upon them.   A concord between the place, between the stark grandeur of its land and seascapes and its islands, and the immutable clarity of a light that casts no shadows and permits no gradations, transfixes them.   It is a timeless alchemy which may even have worked upon the ready minds of the men there two thousand years ago to produce their miracle. Today, despite Time's changes, an exposure to this union can be a revelation, and it can be a revelation as much of one's self as of its nature.   What is denied, or perceived darkly, or unknown is laid bare without compromise : the painful or blissful exposure of one's self. To the few to whom this happens, the question of life transcends, To be or not to be, and becomes, What is it to be ? When the greatest of Philhellenes, the Emperor Hadrian, had this experience, he acknowledged its grace and cost by saying that the most beautiful, the most difficult to merit of all his titles, was to be an Ionian, a Philhellene. In the early Nineteenth Century, that most extravagant of Philhellenes, Sophie de Marbois, also learned in Greece the expense of individuality.   Greece owed her much, and there without fear of defeat, she risked willingly and not without amusement, its definition of her stature : a stray, staunch figure of defiance.

REFERENCES

Unpublished Letters.

Forty-three letters in the Lebrun Family Papers, Paris, from the Duchesse
de Plaisance to the Duc de Plaisance (Excerpts from thirty-two of these
letters appear in *Piquantes Aventures de Grande Dames,* by Louis
Hastier).

One letter in the Albert Gallatin Collection in the New York Historical
Society, New York, from the Duchesse de Plaisance to Albert Gallatin.

Two letters in the Albert Gallatin Collection from Barbé-Marbois to Albert
Gallatin.

One letter in the Robert R. Livingston Collection in the New York Historical
Society from Barbé-Marbois to Robert R. Livingston.

Two letters in the Bibliothèque Nationale, Paris, by the Duchesse de Plaisance in reply to M. Eynard.

One letter in the Lebrun Family Papers, Paris, from the Duc de Plaisance
to Monsieur Dufour, Avocat.

Twenty-five letters in the French Consulate, Beirut, from the Duchesse de
Plaisance to Monsieur Henri Guys.

Two letters in the Gennadios Library, Athens, from the Duchesse de Plaisance to the Duc de Plaisance.

One letter in the A. Baltazzi Collection, Athens, from Casimir Delavigne to
the Duchesse de Plaisance.

One letter in the British School of Archeology Library, Athens, from the
Duchesse de Plaisance to George Finlay.

Unpublished Documents.

Application in the Lebrun Familary Papers, Paris, for a separation by Anne-
Charles Lebrun, Duc de Plaisance, from his wife, Marie-Anne-Sophie
de Barbé-Marbois. (Tribunal civil de Première Instance du département
de la Seine.)

Record, in the Lebrun Family Papers, Paris, of the settlement of the estate of the Duchesse de Plaisance. (Cour impériale 1st Chambre Succession Duchesse de Plaisance née Barbé de Marbois.)

Memoranda and receipts written or signed by the Duchesse de Plaisance in the Gripari and Baltazzi Collections, Athens.

Records of the court clothes of the Duchesse de Plaisance and her stipend as Lady-in-Waiting to the Empress Marie-Louise in Archives Nationales. Affaires étrangères, Archives de la Couronne, Cote [2] 1414, and Bibliothèque nationale, Nouvelles Acquisitions françaises 5931, Paris.

Journal of George Finlay in the Library of the British School of Archeology, Athens.

English Translation of Cambouroglou, D. G. By Alexandra Placotari in the possession of the author.

BIBLIOGRAPHY

ABOUT Edmond. *La Grèce contemporaine,* Paris, 1854. *Le Roi des Montagnes,* Paris, 1856.

ABRANTÈS Laure (duchesse d'). *Mémoires,* 3Ts, Paris, 1893. *Histoire des Salons de Paris,* 4Ts, Paris, N. D.

ACTON Harold. *The Bourbons of Naples,* 1734-1825. Metheun. London, 1959.

ADAMS Herbert B. *The Life and Writings of Jared Sparks,* 2 vol., Houghton, Mifflin. Boston & New York, 1893.

ADAMS John. *The Works of John Adams.* Edited by Charles Francis Adam. Vol. VII. Little, Brown, Boston, 1852.

AGOUT Marie C. S. (comtesse d'). *Mes Souvenirs* (1806-1833). Paris, 1877. *Mémoires* (1833-1854). Paris, 1927.

Almanach impérial (puis *Almanach royal*), Paris, 1804-1834.

ANDREWS Wayne. *Architecture, Ambition, and Americans.* Harper Brothers, New York, 1947.

ANTHONY Anne. *Greek Holiday,* Athens, 1957.

Archives israélites. T. XIV, septembre 1853. T. XV, juillet 1854.

AUBERIVE Charles. *Voyage en Grèce,* Paris, 1860.

AUBRY Octave. *Vie privée de Napoléon,* Paris, 1939.

AULARD A. *Paris sous le Premier Empire,* 2 ts., Paris, 1912, 1914.

AVEROFF Michelle. *Sophie de Marbois, duchesse de Plaisance,* Paris, 1961.

BAIRD Henry M. *Modern Greece,* Harper, New York, 1856.

BAINVILLE Jacques. *Napoléon,* Paris, 1931.

BALTZELL E. Digby. *Philadelphia Gentlemen.* Free Grove Press. Glencoe, Illinois, 1958.

BARANTE (baron de). *Souvenirs, 1782-1866,* Paris, 1890-1901.

BARBÉ Jean-Julien. *Les Maisons historiques,* Metz, 1913, 1937.

BARBÉ-MARBOIS François de. *Complot d'Arnold et Sir Henry Clinton,* Paris, 1816. *Journal d'un Déporté non jugé,* Bruxelles et Leipzig, 1835. *Our Revolutionary Forefathers. The Letters of François, marquis de Barbé-Marbois, 1779-1785,* edited by Eugene Parker Chase. Duffield, New York, 1929. *Socrate en délire ou Dialogues de Diogène de Synope,* Dresde, 1772. *Réflexion sur la Colonie de Saint-Domingue,* Paris, 1796.

BARTHÉLEMY François de. *Mémoires 1768-1819,* Paris, 1914.

BAUSSET L.-F.-J. de. *Mémoires anecdotiques sur l'intérieur du palais de Napoléon et sur celui de Marie-Louise,* 4 ts., Paris, 1829.

BEARD Charles A. and Mary R. *The Rise of American Civilization,* Macmillan, New York, 1928.

BELLE Henri. *Trois Années en Grèce,* Paris, 1860.

BÉNÉZIT B. E. *Dictionnaire critique et documentaire des peintres, sculpteurs, dessinateurs et graveurs,* Paris, 1960.

BERTHOUD Dorette. *Lettres de Léopold Robert, d'Aurèle Robert et de leurs parents,* Neuchâtel, 1948. *Vie du peintre Léopold Robert,* Neuchâtel, 1961.

CHURCH E. M. *Sir Richard Church in Italy and Greece,* Blackwood, London, 1895.

CLÉMENT Roger. *La Condition des Juifs de Metz dans l'Ancien Régime,* Paris, 1903.

CLINCHAMPS Ph. du Puy de. *La Noblesse,* Paris, 1959.

CLINE Myrtle. *The American Attitude toward the Greek War of Independence 1821-1828,* Atlanta, Georgia, 1930.

COOPER James Fenimore. *Correspondance,* edited by his Grandson James Fenimore Cooper, 2 vol., Yale University Press. New Haven, 1922. *Gleanings in Europe,* 2 vol., Carey, Lea & Blanchard, Philadelphia, 1837.

COUSINS Norman. *'In God We Trust',* Harper, New York, 1958.

CURIAL DE BRÉVANNES F. A. *Charles-François Lebrun, duc de Plaisance,* Aix-en-Provence, 1941.

CUSSY (le chevalier de). *Souvenirs,* Paris, 1909.

DANGERFIELD George. *Chancellor Robert R. Livingston of New York,* Harcourt Brace. New York, 1960.

DELACROIX Eugène. *Journal 1822-1863,* Union générale d'Editions, Paris, 1963.

DELAVIGNE Jean-François Casimir. *Œuvres complètes.* Avec une notice par M. Germain Delavigne, 6 ts., Paris, 1854.

DEMETERACOPOULOU Polybis. *The Duchess of Plaisance* (in Greek), Athens, 1912. *Jenny Theotoki* (in Greek), Athens, 1912.

Dictionary of American Biography, vols. XIII and XX, Scribners, New York, 1934.

Dictionnaire encyclopédique, Paris, 1888.

DINO (duchesse de). *Chroniques de 1831-1862*, 2 ts., Paris, 1909.

DRAGOUMIS N. M. *Souvenirs historiques*, Paris, 1890.

DRIAULT E. *Histoire diplomatique de la Grèce à nos jours*, t. IV, Paris, 1925-1926.

ELIE Louis E. *Histoire d'Haïti*, 2 ts., Port-au-Prince, Haïti, 1945.

FAUCHIER-DELAVIGNE. *Casimir Delavigne intime*, Paris.

FELTON C. C. *Greece Ancient and Modern*, Osgood, Boston, 1877. *Familiar Letters*, Estes and Lauriat, Boston, 1878.

FERMOR Patrick Leigh. *Mani*, John Murray, London, 1958.

FERRAND A. F. C. (comte de). *Mémoires*, Paris, 1897.

FERRIMAN Z. Duckett. *Some English Philhellenes*, 8 vol., Anglo-Hellenic League, London, 1917-1920.

FINLAY George. *History of the Greek Revolution*, 2 vol., William Blackwood & Son, Edinburgh & London, 1861.

FORSTER John. *The Works and Life of Walter Savage Landor*, Chapman & Hall, London, 1876.

FRANKL Ludwig Aug. *Nach Jerusalem!* Leipzig, 1858.

FRAZER J. C. *Pausanias and Other Sketches*, Macmillan, London, 1900.

FRENILLY (baron de). *Souvenirs*, Paris, 1908.

FROTHINGHAM Paul Revere. *Edward Everett*, Hougton, Mifflin, Boston, 1925.

GANDAR E. *Lettres et Souvenirs*, 2 ts., Paris, 1869.

GAUTIER Théophile. *Histoire du Romantisme*, Paris, 1874.

GIOPHYLLIS Photos. *History of Modern Greek Art* (in Greek), Athens, 1962.

GONCOURT Edmond et Jules de. *Histoire de la Société française pendant le Directoire*, Paris, 1879.

GRÉGOIRE (abbé). *Requête à Nosseigneurs les Etats généraux en faveur des Juifs*, N. D.

GREENOUGH Horatio. *Letters of Horatio Greenough to His Brother*, edited by Frances Boott Greenough, Ticknor, Boston, 1887.

GRENIER P.-A. *La Grèce en 1863*, Paris, 1863.

GRISWOLD Rufus Wilmont. *The Republican Court or American Society in the Days of Washington*, Appleton, New York, 1855.

GROSDIDIER DE MATONS, Marcel. *Guide de Metz*, Metz, 1947.

GUIZOT F. P. C. *Memoirs To Illustrate The History of My Times*, 4 vol., London, 1858-1861.

GUYS Henri. *Beyrouth et le Liban*, 2 ts., Paris, 1850.

HAMEL Frank. *Lady Hester Lucy Stanhope*, Cassell, London, 1913.

HASTIER Louis. *Piquantes Aventures de grandes Dames*, Paris, 1959.

HEIM Maurice. *Le Nestor des Armées françaises, Kellermann, duc de Valmy*, Paris, 1949.

HEROLD J. Christopher. *Mistress to an Age*, Bobbs-Merrill, Indianapolis, 1958.

HOWARTH T. E. B. *Citizen King*, Eyre & Spottiswoode, London, 1961.

HORTENSE. *The Memoirs of Queen Hortense*, edited by Jean Hanoteau, trans. by Arthur K. Griggs, 2 vol. Cosmopolitan Book Corporation, New York, 1927.

HOWE Julia Ward. *From the Oak to the Olive*, Lee & Sheppard, Boston, 1868. *Is Polite Society Polite?* Houghton, Mifflin, Boston, 1900.

HOWE Samuel Gridley. *Letters and Journals*, 2 vol., edited by His Daughter Laura E. Richards, Estes, Boston, 1909.

HUGO Victor. *Choses vues*, 2 ts., Paris, 1913.

IDEVILLE Henry d'. *Journal d'un diplomate en Allemagne et en Grèce*, Paris, 1875.

Intermédiaire des Chercheurs et Curieux, t. LXXXIX.

ISTRIA Dora d'. *Excursions en Roumélie et en Morée*, t. II, Paris, 1863.

JENKINS Romilly. *The Dilessi Murders*, Longmans, London, 1961.

JOUIN Henry. *David d'Angers*, t. II, Paris, 1878.

Journal des Débats, 3 juillet 1854.

LACHOUQUE Cdt. Henry. *Napoléon et la Garde Impériale*, Paris, 1957.

LA FORCE (duc de). *Histoire et Portraits*, Paris, 1939.

LANCASTER Osbert. *Classical Landscape with Figures*, John Murray, London, 1954.

LANE-POOLE Stanley. *Life of Stratford Canning*, 2 vol., Longmans, London, 1888.

LANSDOWNE, the Earl of Kerry. 6th Marquis of. *The First Napoleon, Some Unpublished Documents from the Bowood Papers*, Constable, London, 1925.

Larousse du XXe siècle, 6 ts., Paris, 1929.

LARRABEE Stephen A. *Hellas Observed*, New York University Press, 1957.

LENORMANT Charles. *Beaux-Arts et Voyage*, t. II, Paris, 1861.

LEVIDIS C. N. *Quelques mots sur la Grèce,* Bruxelles, 1863. *The Greek Chronicle* (in Greek), Athens, 1840.

LIDDELL Robert. *The Morea,* Cape, London, 1958.

LONGFELLOW Samuel. *The Life of Henry Wadsworth Longfellow,* 3 vol., Hougton, Mifflin, Boston, 1891.

LUCAS F. L. et PRUDENCE. *From Olympus to the Styx,* Pocket Library Edition. Cassell, London, 1949.

LYON E. WILSON. *The Man Who Sold Louisiana,* University of Oklahoma Press, 1942.

MADISON James. *The Writings of James Madison,* vols. 5 et 6, Putnam, New York, 1904.

MALHERBE Raoul de. *L'Orient 1718-1845,* t. I, Paris, 1846.

MASSON Frédéric. *Cavaliers de Napoléon,* Paris, 1895. *Du Consulat à l'Empire,* Revue des Deux Mondes, 1ᵉʳ novembre 1917. *L'Impératrice Marie-Louise,* Paris, 1911. *Napoléon et les Femmes,* Paris, 1894.

MASUYER Valérie. *Mémoires,* Paris, 1937.

Mémoire particulier pour la Communauté des Juifs établis à Metz. Rédigé par Isaac Ber-Bing. N. D.

MAVROCORDATO John. *Modern Greece, Macmillan,* London, 1931.

MÉRIMÉE Prosper. *Lettres à la comtesse de Montijo,* 2 ts. (Privately Printed), Paris, 1930.

MESNIL Marie de. *Mémoires sur le Prince Le Brun,* Paris, 1828.

MEZIÈRES A. *Au Temps Passé,* Paris, 1906.

MICHELET Jules. *Histoire de la Révolution Française,* 2 ts., Bibliothèque de la Pléiade, Paris, 1952.

MOREMBERT H. TRIBOUT de. *Barbé et Barbé de Marbois,* Metz, 1958.

MORSE Samuel F. B. *His Life and Journals,* Edited by Edward Lind Morse, 2 vols., Houghton, Mifflin, Boston, 1914.

MURE OF CALDWELL William. *Journal of a Tour in Greece,* Edinburgh, 1842.

Murray's Handbook for Travellers in Greece, Turkey, Asia Minor, and Constantinople, London, 1840.

MUSSET A. de. *Correspondance,* Paris, 1907.

My Odyssey. By a Creole of Saint-Domingue. Translated and Edited by Althéa de Puech Parham. Louisiana State University Press, 1959.

National Cyclopedia of American Biography, vol. 2.

Le National, 14 septembre 1850.

NETTER Nathan. *Vingt siècles d'Histoire d'une Communauté juive,* Paris, 1938.

Newsweek, Atlantic Edition, pp. 23 f. May 5, 1961.

NICHOLSON Harold. *Byron. The Last Journey.* Houghton, Mifflin. Boston, 1924.

NORDENPFLYCHT Julie von. *Briefe einer Hofdame in Athen,* Leipzig, 1845.

Nouvelle Biographie universelle, Paris, 1852-1866.

ODDIE E. M. *Portrait of Ianthe,* Cape, London, 1935.

ORS Vedad Zeki. *Jacques Delille,* Zurich, 1936.

Oxford Companion to the Theatre, Phyllis Hartnoll, Ed. Oxford University Press, 1951.

PARQUIN Madame. (Mademoiselle Louise Cochelet.) *Mémoires sur la Reine Hortense et la Famille impériale,* 2 ts., Bruxelles, 1837.

PASQUIER Etienne-Denis. *Mémoires du chancelier Pasquier,* 6 ts., Paris, 1893.

PAQUET René. *Bibliographie analytique de l'Histoire de Metz pendant la Révolution,* 2 ts, Paris, 1926.

PERDICARIS A. M. *The Greece of the Greeks,* 2 vols., New York, 1845.

PHOTIADES Constantin. *La Duchesse de Plaisance,* « Revue de Paris », 1ᵉʳ juillet, 1908.

Plan for Promoting Common School Education in Greece, (A Pamphlet), The Greek School Committee, New York, May, 1828.

PLANCY (Baron de). *Souvenirs et indiscrétions d'un disparu,* Paris, 1892.

POPE-HENNESSY James. *Queen Mary,* Allen & Unwin, London, 1959.

POTOCKA (Comtesse). *Mémoires,* Paris, 1911.

RADET Georges. *Histoire de l'Œuvre de l'Ecole française à Athènes,* Paris, 1901.

RANGABE Alexandre-Rizo. *Mémoires,* Athènes, 1895.

RÉMUSAT Claire-E.-J. de. *Mémoires,* 3 ts, Paris, 1880.

ROBIQUET Jean. *La Vie quotidienne au temps de Napoléon,* Paris, 1945.

ROUX Emmanuel. *Les débuts de l'Ecole française d'Athènes,* Bordeaux, 1898.

SENIOR NASSAU William. *La Turquie contemporaine,* Paris, 1861.

SICILLIANOS Demetrios. *Old and News Athens,* translated by Robert Liddell, Putnam, London, 1960.

SITWELL Sir Osbert. *Left Hand, Right Hand!,* Little Brown, Boston, 1949.

SKOUSÈS Dimitrios. *Bygone Athens* (in Greek), Athens, 1961.

SPARKS Jared. *Life of Gouverneur Morris,* 3 vols., Gray and Bowers, Boston, 1832.

STERN Daniel. *Mes Souvenirs,* Paris, 1880.

STIRLING Monica. *A Pride of Lions,* Collins, London, 1961.

TALLEYRAND Charles-Maurice de. *Mémoires,* 2 ts., Paris, 1957.

TAYLOR I. A. *Queen Hortense and Her Friends,* 2 vols., London, 1907.

Le Temps, 7 novembre 1831.

THIERS M. A. *Histoire de l'Empire,* 4 ts., Paris, 1888.

THOMPSON J. M. *The French Revolution,* Blackwell, Oxford, 1943.

THOUVENEL Edouard. *La Grèce du Roi Othon,* Paris, 1880.

TICKNOR George. *Life, Letters, and Journals,* 2 vols. J. R. Osgood, Boston, 1876.

TOYNBEE Arnold J. *A Study of History,* Abridgement vols I-IV, Oxford University Press, 1946.

TRANT Capt T. ABERCROMBY. *Narrative of a Journey Through Greece* in 1830, Colburn and Bentley, London, 1830.

VALON (vicomte Alexis de). *Une année dans le Levant,* t. 1, Paris, 1846.

VALYNSEELE Joseph. *Les Maréchaux du Premier Empire,* Paris, 1962.

VOSS Richard. *Die Herzogen von Plaisance,* Stuttgart, 1912.

WALTERS Jr. Raymond. *Albert Gallatin,* Macmillan, New York, 1957.

WATSON John F. *Annals of Philadelphia and Pennsylvania,* 2 vols., Philadelphia, 1850.

WELCKER F.-G. *Tagebucheiner griechischen,* 2 Bände, Berlin, 1865.

WILLIS N. P. *Pencillings By The Way,* Carey, Lea and Blanchard, Philadelphia, 1836.

WORDSWORTH D. D. Christopher. *Greece,* London, 1839.

WRIGHT Constance. *Daughter to Napoleon,* Holt, Rinehart and Winston, New York, 1961.

WYSE Sir Thomas. *Impressions of Greece,* London, 1871.

YOURCENAR Marguerite. *Mémoires d'Hadrien,* Plon, Paris, 1951.

ZIEGLER Philip. *The Duchess of Dino,* Collins, London, 1962.

A C H E V É
D'IMPRIMER

S U R   L E S
PRESSES D'AUBIN
LIGUGÉ (VIENNE)